GLOBAL RECESSION – CAUSES, IMPACTS AND REMEDIES SERIES

FINANCIAL MARKETS AND THE GLOBAL RECESSION

GLOBAL RECESSION – CAUSES, IMPACTS AND REMEDIES SERIES

Recessions: Prospects and Developments
Nerea M. Pérez and June A. Ortega (Editors)
2009. ISBN: 978-1-60456-866-0

Financial Crisis in America
Raymund T. Ovanhouser (Editor)
2009. ISBN: 978-1-60692-191-3

Economic Crises as a Result of Distrust
Emilio Gullini (Editor)
2010. ISBN: 978-1-60741-355-4

Financial Regulatory Reform
Stephen E. Moyer (Editor)
2010. ISBN: 978-1-60741-567-1

Economic Stimulus: Plans, Risks and Outlook
Samuel P. Turner (Editor)
2010. ISBN: 978-1-60741-516-9

Financial Markets and the Global Recession
Benjamin Naas and Joachim Lysne (Editors)
2010. ISBN: 978-1-60741-921-1

Assessing Treasury's Strategy - Six Months of TARP
Jarod R. Acosto (Editor)
2010. ISBN: 978-1-60876-139-5

Reassessing TARP: Second Report from the Special Inspector General
George T. Bernhardt (Editor)
2010. ISBN: 978-1-60741-965-5

Reassessing TARP: Second Report from the Special Inspector General
George T. Bernhardt (Editor)
2010. ISBN: 978-1-61668-378-8
(Online Book)

Financial Crisis in the Global Bubble Economy
Akinori Tomohara and Molly Sherlock (Editors)
2010. ISBN: 978-1-61668-339-9

GLOBAL RECESSION – CAUSES, IMPACTS AND REMEDIES SERIES

FINANCIAL MARKETS AND THE GLOBAL RECESSION

BENJAMIN NAAS
AND
JOACHIM LYSNE
EDITORS

Nova Science Publishers, Inc.
New York

LIBRARY OF CONGRESS CATALOGING-IN-PUBLICATION DATA

Financial markets and the global recession / editors, Benjamin Naas and Joachim Lysne.
p. cm.
Includes indexes.
ISBN 978-1-60741-921-1 (hardcover)
1. International finance. 2. Capital market. 3. Recessions. I. Naas, Benjamin. II. Lysne, Joachim.
HG3881.F524 2009
332'.042--dc22

2009037458

Published by Nova Science Publishers, Inc. ✣ New York

CONTENTS

PREFACE

The recent credit crunch of 2008 ignited in 2009 one of the most severe economic slowdowns since World War II. In many countries, such as the United States and the United Kingdom, the intensity of the recession is such that comparisons are made with the Great Depression of 1929. This book will shed some light on the causes of the recession and its effects on the balance of international powers. Furthermore, many regions of the world, and developed countries in particular, are currently in the midst of significant population aging caused by falling fertility rates and increased life expectancy. This may cause a worldwide capital shortage in the long run. This book addresses this issue, as well as the extent to which policy reforms play a significant role in the international capital movement and the impact the worldwide short-term fiscal expansion has made on the global economy. Also examined is the impact of some possible options (US fiscal stimulus, monetary easing in the US, and foreign official purchases of US treasury securities) on the economies of the US and the rest of the world, and the US current account deficits by using structural vector autoregression (SVAR) model. This book also examines the depths and necessary measures for countries in the Eurozone, and the monetary union in particular, to control and counteract the global recession. Other chapters discuss the different methods of modeling volatility of stock prices and exchange rates, the correlation between individual investments, investor preferences and the relative size of risk weights and the effects of regulation, and the future of capital asset pricing models (CAPM0), one of the central areas of research in finance.

The recent credit crunch of 2008 ignited in 2009 one of the most severe economic slowdowns since the World War II. In many countries, such as the United States and the United Kingdom, the intensity of the recession is such that comparisons are made with the Great Depression of 1929. Once again, the

Western economies are in the center of the recession with their financial systems collapsing and their economies strangling to minimize losses. The emerging markets on the other hand, such as China and India, although they also “feel” the burden of a global recession, they are expected to grow significantly even at lower than previous years rates.

Even though there is a consensus that we have entered a serious global economic recession that will probably change the balance of power between emerging countries and Western economies, there are still many unanswered questions. What triggered the recession and what is its true nature? What are the similarities between the current recession and the Great Depression? Has the long-term growth trend of the global economy been compromised or is this recession a cyclical phenomenon? At what extent will it affect the balance of international powers? And the most important question of all: is it a random or a systematic phenomenon that we could have predicted? If so, what can we do now to minimize losses?

In Chapter 1, the authors will try to shed some light on these questions based mainly on a recent study concerning the future of the global economy, published just a few days prior to the collapse of Lehman Brothers in September 2008 that signaled the beginning of the credit crisis. Furthermore, by combining data from this study and other sources, the authors will provide the reader with both qualitative and quantitative insights about the current recession.

The authors have developed a computable multi-country general equilibrium model with overlapping generations of agents to focus investigation on the impacts of worldwide fiscal stimulus measures taken to deal with the global recession in the global economy, especially the US, Japan, EU, China, and Rest of the World, via international capital flows. This global recession decreases the movement of international capital in the short run. Moreover, many regions of the world, and developed countries in particular, are currently in the midst of significant population aging caused by falling fertility rates and increased life expectancy. This may cause a worldwide capital shortage in the long run. In Chapter 2 the authors address three main issues: (i) how does the differential aging process across countries affect international capital flow in the long run, (ii) to what extent do the policy reforms play a significant role in the international capital movement, and (iii) how does the worldwide short-term fiscal expansion make impact on a global economy. Our analysis indicates that the differential aging process promotes international capital flow from aging countries to population-growth countries. Also, by raising the rate of return on capital, international capital flow could improve the economic welfare of the generations in the aging countries. Moreover, the countries with aging populations improve their economic welfare by implementing policy reforms that raise the savings rate with or without policy changes within labor-abundant countries. Finally, the US economic package implemented to manage the global financial crisis actually worsens its fiscal condition, and causes the international capital flow to become more active.

In Chapter 3 I argue that as a response to the introduction of capital requirements in the form of risk weights investors might potentially choose riskier portfolios than before the regulation – this is, presumably, not what the regulation intends to achieve. That is, while regulation most likely diverts investors from their optimum decision it does not guarantee that the new optimum has a lower risk. The effect of the regulation depends on several things, most importantly the correlation between individual investments, investor preferences and the relative size of risk weights.

The outlook for the world economy has deteriorated dramatically since the second half of 2008. One of the underlying forces that put downward pressure on the world economy is the price correction in the U.S. housing market. The sharp decline in U.S. house prices will depress the economies of both the U.S. and the rest of the world, resulting in the unwinding of global imbalances.

To reduce the negative pressure of this synchronized global downturn, more effective policy initiatives are needed. However, there is a fear that the massive fiscal policy of the U.S. may further the global imbalances. It is desirable that we help the world economy recover and at the same time, ensure that the U.S. current account deficit is made more sustainable.

Chapter 4 aims to examine the impact of some possible options (U.S. fiscal stimulus, monetary easing in the U.S., and foreign official purchases of U.S. treasury securities) on the economies of the U.S. and the rest of the world, and the U.S. current account deficits by using the structural vector autoregression (SVAR) model.

The empirical results show that an increase in the foreign official purchases of U.S. treasury securities can expand the GDP of both the U.S. and the rest of the world, and decrease the U.S. current account deficit by improving the U.S. fiscal balance. The stated course of action will help in the recovery of the world economy without expanding the U.S. current account deficit.

Chapter 5 overviews different methods of modeling volatility of stock prices and exchange rates, focusing on their ability to reproduce the empirical properties in the corresponding time series. The properties of price fluctuations vary across the time scales of observation. The adequacy of different models for describing price dynamics at several time horizons simultaneously is the central topic of this study. The authors propose a detailed survey of recent volatility models, accounting for multiple horizons. These models are based on different and sometimes competing theoretical concepts. They belong either to GARCH or stochastic volatility model families and often borrow methodological tools from statistical physics. The authors compare their properties and comment on their practical usefulness and perspectives.

In Chapter 6, the author performs a multivariate time series analysis of 11 world market indexes in order to measure their relationships and to detect the presence of leader market indexes, defined as those indexes whose trend is followed by other indexes. By using the Johansen cointegration test, the author shows that international financial markets are strongly cointegrated, meaning that a long-term relationship does exist. This evidence confutes the theory which supports portfolio strategies based on the international diversification, since in the presence of cointegrated markets the portfolio risk cannot be reduced without sacrificing the expected return. Furthermore, by performing the Granger causality test, the causality realtionships among world indexes is assessed, demonstrating how NIKKEI 225 can be considered as a leader market index.

The CBOE VIX index has been viewed as a gauge to measure investors' fear of market crash. The recent market turmoil has produced historically high volatility levels, in some cases around four times higher than their previous average levels. In Chapter 7, the authors take a new look at the continuous-time dynamics of VIX by including the recent market turmoil into the data. Two methodologies are utilized: the maximum likelihood estimation, and a parametric specification test. For data before year 2008, maximum likelihood estimation shows the need of stipulating a nonlinear drift function, similar to previous studies. However, inclusion of more recent data makes such a nonlinear drift less important. The parametric specification test nonetheless suggest that it is important to take into account both nonlinearity in the drift function and constant elasticity in the diffusion function when modeling the continuous-time dynamics of VIX. The results call for caution when adopting a particular parametric model for the continuoustime dynamics of the VIX index.

It is a common wisdom that individual stocks' returns are difficult to predict, though inmany situations it is important to have such estimates at our disposal. In particular, they are needed to determine the cost of capital. Market equilibrium models posit that expected returns are proportional to the sensitivities to systematic risk factors. Fama and French (1993) three-factor model explains the stock returns premium as a sum of three components due to different risk factors: the traditional CAPM market beta, and the betas to the returns on two portfolios, Small Minus Big (the differential in the returns on stocks of small and big companies) and High Minus Low (the differential in returns on the of companies with high and low price-to-book ratio). In Expert Commentary A, the authors argue that this model is sufficient to capture the impact on returns of companies' accounting fundamentals, such as earnings-to-price, cash flow-to-price, past sales growth, long term and short-term past earnings. Using a panel of stock returns and accounting data from 1979 to the end of 2008 for the companies listed on NYSE, the authors show that this is not the case, at least at individual stocks' level. According to our findings, fundamental characteristics of companies' performance are of higher importance to predict future expected returns than sensitivities to the risk factors. The authors explain this finding within the rational pricing paradigm: contemporaneous accounting fundamentals may be better proxies for future sensitivity to risk factors, than sensitivities, estimated from historical data.

In Expert Commentary B, capital asset pricing models (CAPM) remain of the central areas of research in finance for almost half a century. This is partly due to the practical importance of the subject for explaining stock returns *premia*, but also to the insufficiency of the existing models and ambiguity of the empirical results. The theoretical elegance of the intertemporal consumption CAPM, where representative agents repeatedly rebalance their portfolios and optimize the utility of consumption, contrasts with its poor performance in explaining returns' variations in a cross-section.

In: Financial Markets and the Global Recession ISBN: 978-1-60741-921-1
Editors: B. Naas and J. Lysne

Chapter 1

GLOBAL RECESSION: JUST A GLITCH OR IS IT HERE TO STAY?

George P. Boretos*
Athens, Greece

Abstract

The recent credit crunch of 2008 ignited in 2009 one of the most severe economic slowdowns since the World War II. In many countries, such as the United States and the United Kingdom, the intensity of the recession is such that comparisons are made with the Great Depression of 1929. Once again, the Western economies are in the center of the recession with their financial systems collapsing and their economies strangling to minimize losses. The emerging markets on the other hand, such as China and India, although they also "feel" the burden of a global recession, they are expected to grow significantly even at lower than previous years rates.

Even though there is a consensus that we have entered a serious global economic recession that will probably change the balance of power between emerging countries and Western economies, there are still many unanswered questions. What triggered the recession and what is its true nature? What are the similarities between the current recession and the Great Depression? Has the long-term growth trend of the global economy been compromised or is this recession a cyclical phenomenon? At what extent will it affect the balance of international powers? And the most important question of all: is it a random or a systematic phenomenon that we could have predicted? If so, what can we do now to minimize losses?

* E-mail address: georgeboretos@yahoo.gr. 47-49 Sevastoupoleos St., 11526 Ampelokipoi, Athens, Greece, Tel.: +30210.77.00.351, Mobile phone : +306936.681.105.

In this chapter, we will try to shed some light on these questions based mainly on a recent study concerning the future of the global economy, published just a few days prior to the collapse of Lehman Brothers in September 2008 that signaled the beginning of the credit crisis. Furthermore, by combining data from this study and other sources, we will provide the reader with both qualitative and quantitative insights about the current recession.

Introduction

After many years of considerable growth, World economy entered in 2009 one of the most severe recessions of modern times. The growth trend of the previous years, mainly based on the robustness of the global economy and the vigor of its financial system, came to a sudden end. Disbelief and insecurity moved in quickly and occupied world economy as a new vicious cycle of contraction emerged. Although money markets and financial institutions were the first to be hit by the new downward trend, it soon became apparent that the real economy was not immune to this new "epidemic". Recent forecasts from the International Monetary Fund (IMF) expect the global economy to contract during 2009, at a rate between -1% to -0.5%, for the first time after 60 years thus making this recession probably the most profound of the post World War II era.

Although there is a consensus that we have entered a serious global economic recession that will probably change the balance of power between emerging countries and Western economies, there are still many unanswered questions:

1. What are the key factors that triggered the recession?
2. Is there any similarity to previous economic crises and what are the lessons from history learned?
3. Has the overall growth trend of many centuries or even the after World War II era been compromised or is this recession a cyclical phenomenon?
4. At what extent is this going to affect the relative power of different countries and regions?
5. Is the current recession a random or a systematic phenomenon that we could have predicted based on some early warnings?
6. Now that it is here, how can we deal with the recession and minimize losses?

On the lack of a single universally accepted macroeconomic model or theory that fully explains World economy [1], many of these questions will probably be debated for many years among politicians and economists without a clear winner.

In this chapter, we will try to shed some light on these questions based mainly on a recent study [2] concerning the future of the global economy, published just a few days prior to the collapse of Lehman Brothers in September 2008 that signaled the beginning of the credit crisis. Furthermore, by combining data from this study and other sources we will provide the reader with both qualitative and quantitative insights about the current recession.

The Current Economic Crisis

Throughout the period from 2004 to 2007, the global economy expanded considerably with an average rate of nearly 5% in terms of real GDP growth, the highest rate since the 1970s [3]. During that time, financial institutions capitalised strongly on the belief of continuous growth and future profits to develop new risky but also very profitable financial products. The continuous increase of value of these new products coupled with a substantial rise of real assets value in the housing sector created more wealth, for both the investors and the issuing financial institutions, that infused the market with an increased supply of money and raised corporate and consumer lending through increased leveraging [4], [5]. That resulted in a considerable boost in both investments and consumption that even further stimulated the economy. This self-accelerating process was based on a sensitive balance of trust and optimism concerning the future of the global economy. But the risk that the economy endured for such a prolonged period of time proved to be too high.

The first signs of slowdown made their appearance even as early as 2007 when the housing market collapsed in the United States. Residential real estate values fell by 9% during 2007 [6] thus triggering the subprime mortgage crisis that quickly spread around the globe [3]. What everybody thought (or hoped) to be an isolated event in the overwhelming growth story of the global economy proved to be just the first symptom of a global "decease" emerging in the surface. The first major collapse in the financial sector was a shock. Lehman Brothers one of the oldest and biggest investment banks in the United States filed for bankruptcy in September 2008 [3]. Soon after, many other financial institutions suffered severe losses. Merrill Lynch, Goldman Sachs, Morgan Stanley, Citigroup, and the large insurer American International Group (AIG), were just a few of the victims of the new "epidemic" that started to spread rapidly around the World [7].

The virtuous cycle of the previous years, mainly based on the robustness of the global economy and the vigor of its financial system, came to a sudden end. Disbelief and insecurity moved in quickly and occupied world economy as a new vicious cycle of contraction emerged [3]. Stock exchanges around the World responded immediately to this new "threat" marking significant losses in the following months. Dow Jones alone fell by 24% between September and December of 2008 and another 20% during the first two months of 2009 [8]. According to the IMF the credit crisis of 2008 is probably the most severe financial shock since the Great Depression, at least for the United States [3].

Although money markets and financial institutions were the first to be hit by the new downward trend, it soon became apparent that the real economy was not immune to this new "epidemic". The prolonged financial stress and deleveraging, ignited in 2009 one of the most severe economic slowdowns of modern times for many countries around the World and especially for the most advanced economies [9]. During 2008 real global GDP increased by only 3.4%, significantly lower than the 5.2% performance of 2007. The Western economies are in the center of the recession with their financial systems collapsing and their economies strangling to minimize losses. Real GDP for advanced economies such as the United States and the United Kingdom increased only by 1.1% and 0.7% respectively during 2008. Emerging markets on the other hand, such as China and India, although they also "feel" the burden of the global recession, they continued to grow significantly during 2008 even at lower than previous years rates. China's real GDP expanded by 9% in 2008 down from 13% in 2007. India's real GDP expanded by 7% down from 9% in 2007 [10]. Recent forecasts from the IMF expect the global economy to contract during 2009, at a rate between -1% to -0.5%, for the first time after 60 years thus making this recession probably the most profound of the post World War II era [9]. The significant drop from the earliest estimates of the IMF issued in October 2008 [3] and January 2009 [10], projecting respectively a 3% and a 0.5% increase for global GDP in 2009, is yet another sign of the increased level of uncertainty that currently occupies the market.

Although they were not proactive, world leaders and policymakers responded quickly to the credit crisis of 2008 and the forthcoming recession with a series of measures in order to stimulate the economy. Successive meetings of the G20 countries [4], the World Economic Forum at Davos [11], and the European Union [12] exhibited a more or less similar attitude towards the crisis, which is summarized in the following: simultaneous use of expansionary fiscal and monetary policy combined with a more effective financial regulation in order to support both the financial system and the real economy and regain trust. Stimulus plans with increased Government expenditure have been commissioned by several countries around the World. These plans are usually coupled with low interest rates and extensive support programs to financial institutions in order to increase money supply, improve confidence in the market, and mobilize the economy. But even with all these measures and worldwide coordination we still expect the economy just to increase at the modest rate of 1.5% to 2.5% during 2010 [9].

During the G20 London Summit in April 2009, the leaders of the most advanced economies in the World, reaching a cornerstone decision, committed to an additional $1.1 trillion stimulus package in order to ensure global recovery [13]. Although this is an important decision towards the right direction, signaling a new era of partnership and collaboration among international powers, it is too soon to say at what extent this will change the negative trend unveiled in the recent IMF's projections.

The "Mechanics" of the Recession

It is evident that we are currently facing a worldwide crisis with significant repercussions for the economy and the society. It is the combined result of increased insecurity and a much smaller capacity to spend in both the demand and the supply side. Figures 1 and 2 illustrate the "mechanics" of the new vicious economic cycle that was initiated after the rapid deterioration of the economic climate, which started in 2007 and took "explosive" proportions during 2008.

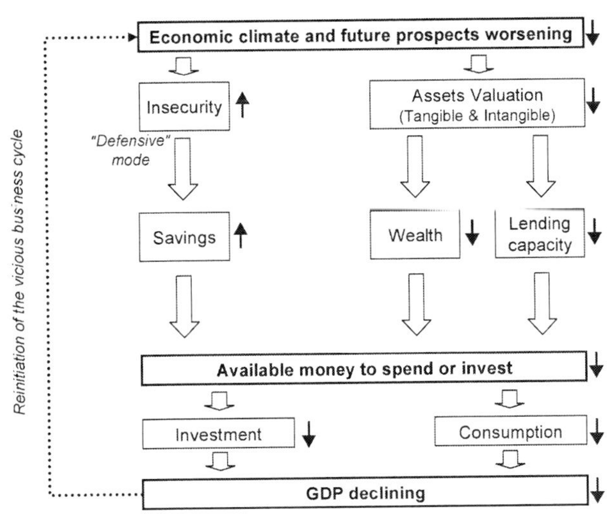

The upward (↑) and downward (↓) arrows indicate an increasing or a decreasing trend respectively.

Figure 1. The vicious business cycle: enterprises and consumers.

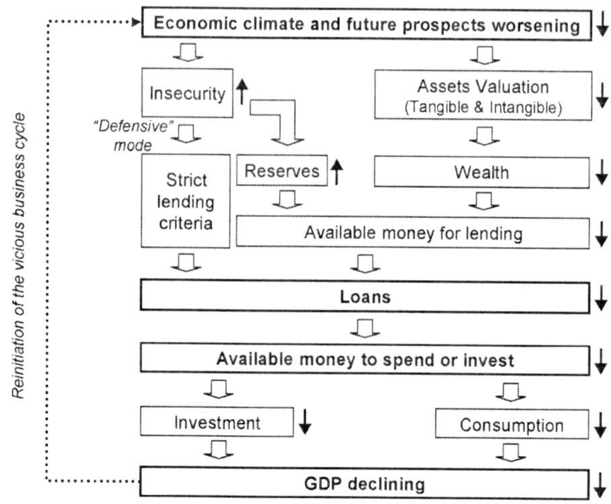

The upward (↑) and downward (↓) arrows indicate an increasing or a decreasing trend respectively.

Figure 2. The vicious business cycle: Banks.

According to Figure 1 as global economic conditions and future prospects aggravate, insecurity moves in quickly and puts everyone in a "defensive" mode. Both consumers and enterprises are now reluctant to invest and to purchase goods. Instead they "save" more money preparing themselves for "rainy" days. Furthermore, assets devaluation, both tangible and intangible, diminishes their wealth and leads to a lesser capacity to receive loans but also to spend or to invest. Banks on the other hand, according to Figure 2, reduce lending as a result of the devaluation of their wealth and also the fear of lenders inability to pay.

All these "shocks" happening simultaneously result in a continuous decline of available money to spend or to invest, which in turn leads to a further decrease of global GDP and a worsening of the economic climate thus reinitiating the vicious cycle of the economy.

As we will see in the following paragraph a similar, although not identical, pattern of negative reaction was also in place during the Great Depression of 1929.

Lessons from History Learned: The Great Depression of 1929

Although the Great Depression was a worldwide recession, it primarily started from the Unites States. At the beginning there was a residential housing bubble in the US during the 1920s, just before the Great Depression. Then there was the crash of the stock market at 1929 [14]. In the following years, from 1930 to 1933, more than 9.000 banks suspended operations. The combination of all these "shocks" resulted in an increasing feeling of insecurity, which drastically changed the behavior of both bankers and depositors into a more conservative one. Depositors started withdrawing their money from banks, afraid of more collapses, thus exhausting the available bank reserves for making loans. Currency to deposit ratio rose from 17% in August 1929 to 41% in March 1933 reflecting exactly that. At the same time banks increased the reserve to deposit ratio from 14% to 21%, in an attempt to secure their liquidity against bad debts and possible losses. In other words, the failure of the banking system in the early 1930s triggered a feeling of mistrust at all levels of the economy, which in turn shrunk money supply from the market and started a vicious circle that resulted in the Great Depression. Between August 1929 and March 1933, the money supply (currency and demand deposits) fell by 28% although the monetary base (currency and bank reserves) increased by 18% during the same period [14]. Unfortunately, this negative trend was further cemented by a contractionary fiscal policy combining increased taxes and lower government spending that even more reduced aggregate demand and deepened the effects of the Great Depression [14]. It wasn't until after 1933 when President Roosevelt launched the "New Deal" that the US economy started to recover gradually from the recession [15].

The similarities with the current crisis are rather obvious. It also started from the US, a housing bubble also preceded the recession, and the financial system collapsed as well. As a result, an increased feeling of insecurity coupled with a reduced capacity to spend or to invest developed in the economy.

But there are also significant differences. 80 years have passed since the Great Depression and we have learned more about the economy and how it works, in a national and worldwide level. Today, as a response to the current recession, most countries have initiated stimulus programs combining a mix of expansionary monetary and fiscal policy, in order to keep the money supply at acceptable levels and mobilize the real economy. All that can be achieved through a more sophisticated coordination of government policies exploiting the increased "bonds" of the globalized economy.

Furthermore, during the last 80 years many new and more sophisticated techniques have come to our aid in our effort to model and forecast effectively the dynamics of the global economy. Such a technique, based on s-curve modeling, we will explore in the following paragraphs where we will demonstrate that the recent recession was not initiated by random causes but rather it was a systematic phenomenon that we could have predicted and anticipated from many years.

A Simple Model of the Global Economy

In a recent study [2] concerning the future of the global economy, s-curves were used in order to model and forecast the global economy as measured by the real global GDP expressed at purchasing power parities (PPP).

The s-curve model (also known as the model of natural growth or the logistic growth model) is described [16] by the following equation:

$$N(t) = \frac{K}{1 + \exp[-\frac{\ln(81)}{\Delta t}(t - t_m)]} \quad (1)$$

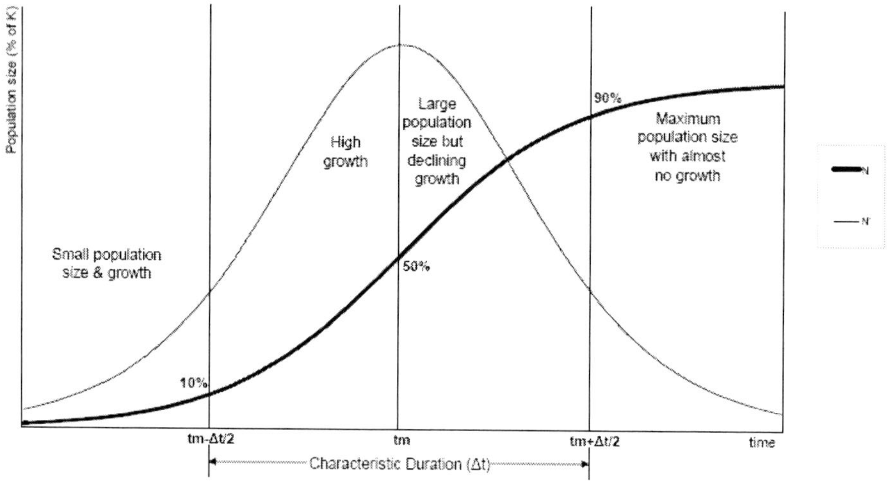

Figure 3. S-curve and successive periods of growth, saturation, and decline.

The curve's name comes from its S-like shape as can be seen in Figure 3. N(t) represents the total number of members of the population over time. N'(t), the first derivative of N, depicts the growth of the population over time. K, the *capacity* of the population, indicates how large the population N will become. Δt, the *characteristic duration* of the curve, shows how quickly the population will approach its maximum capacity. More specifically, Δt is defined as the time needed for N to grow from 10% to 90% of K. Finally, t_m is the *midpoint* of the curve i.e. the point of time where the population will reach 50% of K.

In other words, the three parameters K, Δt, and tm depict how big the population will become, how quickly the growth process will evolve and when exactly in time it will take place.

This is exactly where the core benefit of using logistic fits in forecasting lies. With no detailed knowledge of a certain population, we can make projections about its growth potential based on just three parameters. Moreover, s-curve models, give us the opportunity to distinguish among different periods of time with varying attributes concerning the size and evolution patterns of the population. For instance, the behavior of the logistic growth changes completely around the midpoint tm. After a continuous increase until this point, growth reaches its maximum level and starts to decline afterwards as the population gradually saturates. This kind of observations helps us determine underlying trends about the population and foresee changing behavior throughout the growth process.

Every s-curve described by equation (1) tends to zero when t tends to -∞. Since there may be accumulated levels of growth at the beginning of the curve at t=0, an initial displacement may be added from which the s-curve begins its growth trajectory.

Now let's consider the concept of seasons in s-curves as can be seen in Figure 4. We consider as the full life cycle of an s-curve the time period twice its characteristic duration Δt.

During that time, the s-curve evolves gradually from nearly 1% to 99% of its capacity K. We then divide this period equally into 5 successive seasons, namely Winter, Spring, Summer, Fall, and again Winter. Each season lasts 40% of Δt and represents a different period in terms of growth, acceleration of growth, and population size. Winter is the most difficult season since both population size and growth are negligible. On the other hand, this is also the most creative season where new ideas and innovations struggle to survive and to predominate.

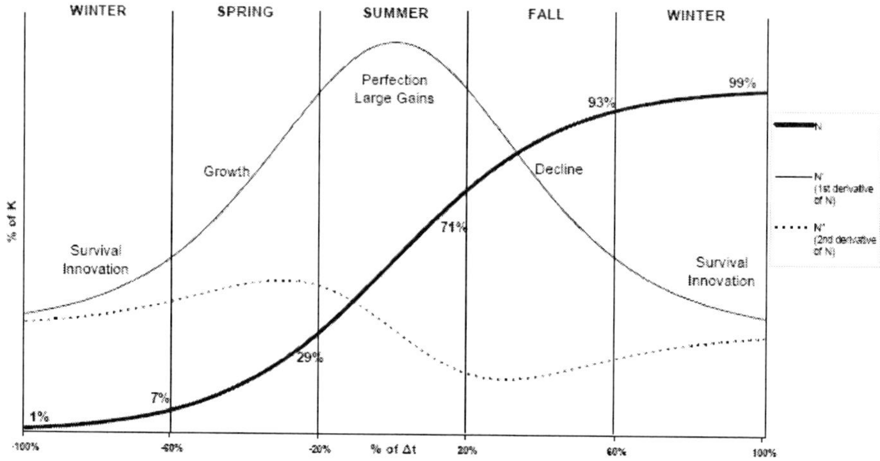

Figure 4[1]. Successive Seasons of growth, saturation, and decline in an s-curve.

If a process succeeds the "test" of Winter, then it proceeds into a full logistic growth starting from Spring, a season of development and accelerating growth. Summer, the next period, although characterized by perfection and increased profitability it is also a critical turning point where the process reaches its highest point of growth. With the emerging of Fall, growth starts to decline rapidly as the process moves towards saturation. Finally, the process reaches yet another Winter, where the population achieves its maximum size but with almost no growth at all, thus signaling the completion of the process. This approach, proposed in the recent study concerning the future of the global economy [2], is actually a slight variation of the original seasons metaphor that was introduced by Modis in the book "Conquering Uncertainty" [17]. The essence and special attributes of seasons are exactly the same but the start and end points, calculated as fractions of the characteristic duration Δt, are slightly different from those proposed by Modis. In his book, Modis also mentions that during natural growth, a second s-curve may be generated, usually in Fall, which if it survives an overlapping Winter with the first s-curve then it proceeds in completing a full logistic curve from Winter to Winter again. In other words, Winter acts as a "nursery" of creative thoughts and new ideas, which are responsible for the growth potential of the years to come following the saturation of the first s-curve.

As a general rule, s-curves work better when applied to populations with natural barriers, which will eventually decelerate their growth as they move closer

[1] Reprinted from Technological Forecasting and Social Change, 76 (3), G.P. Boretos, The future of the global economy, 316-326, Copyright (2009), with permission from Elsevier [2]

to their upper limit. Since we live in a world full of barriers this is true for most of the natural processes regardless of their particular nature thus explaining the successful application of s-curves models in so many diverse fields such as economy, business, stock exchange, energy, and the diffusion of new technologies. In the case of global economy there are indeed barriers such as the number of people in the World, energy resources, and available money for consumption and investment. Therefore, we can use s-curves for modeling that process.

In the recent study [2], published in 2008, s-curve modeling was applied to actual real global GDP expressed at purchasing power parities (PPP) for years up to 2005 [18], in order to produce forecasts concerning the future of the global economy. This study also unveiled a 38 years cyclical deviation of actual World GDP against the estimated from the logistic fit that further increases or weakens global economy's growth potential.

As a measure of relative economic power, in the same study, we took the ratio of a certain region's GDP to global GDP expressed at purchasing power parities. The Logistic Substitution (LS) method [19-20] was used in order to model the continuous rivalry among different regions around the World. According to the LS method, at any point of time all of the competing populations either gain market share following a logistic curve with 100% capacity or decline following a reversed logistic curve towards 0% capacity. There is only one exception, usually the dominant population, that is in a substitution stage and its market share is the remainder after all other populations' market shares are taken off from 100%. The LS method has been successfully used in many different application areas concerning energy, transportation media, and technology substitution just to name a few [20-23].

In the following paragraphs we will use the results of this study in an attempt to better understand and explain the real nature of the current (2009) economic crisis and especially if this consists a cyclical phenomenon or if it has a more permanent nature. Based on this analysis, we will identify early warnings for major shifts in economic activity and the appropriate course of action in order to avoid them or at least minimize losses when they happen.

Forecasting the Global Economy

By using s-curve modeling in the 2008 study [2], as described in the previous paragraph, we were able to build a simple model of real World GDP. This way we identified both long-term and cyclical trends in the global economy. Furthermore, by using the Logistic Substitution method we created a model of the relative power of Western economies against the emerging economy of China. The following paragraphs include tables, figures, and extracts (with minor alterations) from the above mentioned paper[2]. These paragraphs present the most important findings of this study.

Globalization: A Two Century Growth Wave

Figure 5 and Table 1 show the results of the logistic fit for World GDP using actual data for the years 1950–2005.

According to the logistic fit, global economy follows a growth curve with a full life cycle of approximately two centuries, towards a considerably higher level of more than 2 times the recent (2005) GDP level.

As we approach 2015, the midpoint of the process, growth begins to decelerate.

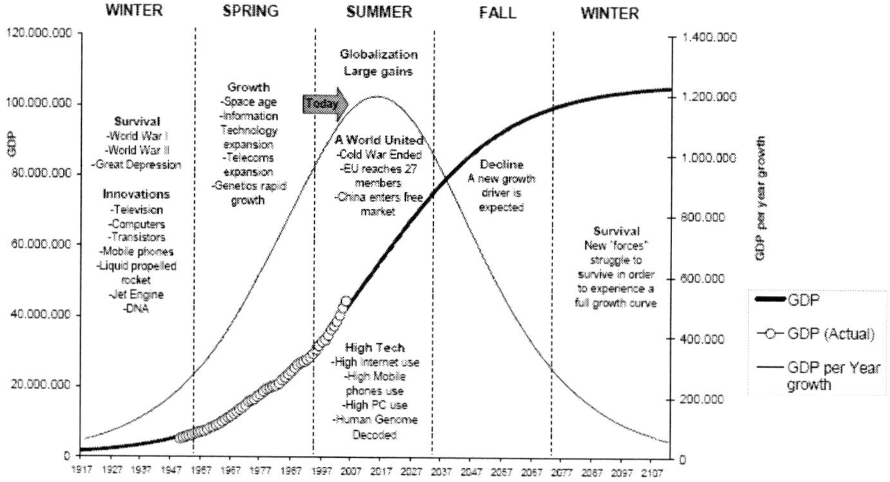

Figure 5[2]. World real GDP (million 1990 International Geary-Khamis dollars).

---

[2] Reprinted from Technological Forecasting and Social Change, 76 (3), G.P. Boretos, The future of the global economy, 316-326, Copyright (2009), with permission from Elsevier [2]

Source of actual real GDP figures, converted to US$ at 1990 PPPs (Geary-Khamis): TCB and GGDC series [18]

Table 1[3]. Estimated parameters and accuracy of the logistic fit

		World GDP (millions 1990 US dollars at Geary-Khamis PPPs)	
		Value[a]	Error[b]
S-Curve Parameters	K	105.888.837	13,0%
	Δt	97,2	2,9%
	2xΔt[c]	194,4	2,9%
	t_m	2015	0,0%
	I[d]	500.000	

a. Value: Parameter Value as estimated from the logistic fit.
b. Error estimated from Debecker and Modis method [24] at 90% confidence level.
c. Full life cycle of the growth process from apprx. 1% to 99% of K
d. Initial displacement i.e. a pedestal from which the s-curve emerges.

Table 2[4]. Actual and forecasted data of World GDP

	World GDP[a]		
	Value	% growth	CAGR[b]
1950 (actual data)	5.249.685		
1975 (actual data)	16.384.276	212%	4,7%
2000 (actual data)	36.197.993	121%	3,2%
2025 (forecasted data)	65.746.190	82%	2,4%
2050 (forecasted data)	88.654.810	35%	1,2%

a. Millions 1990 US dollars at Geary-Khamis PPPs.
b. CAGR: Compound annual growth rate.

This can be seen more clearly in Table 2 where characteristic values are presented from 1950-2050 over 25-years intervals. GDP more than tripled during the years 1950-1975, but only doubled during the next 25 years. During the first half of the 21st century, growth is expected to proceed in a slower pace as world economy approaches saturation. GDP will probably increase in considerably

[3] Reprinted from Technological Forecasting and Social Change, 76 (3), G.P. Boretos, The future of the global economy, 316-326, Copyright (2009), with permission from Elsevier [2]
Source of actual real GDP figures, converted to US$ at 1990 PPPs (Geary-Khamis): TCB and GGDC series [18]
[4] Reprinted from Technological Forecasting and Social Change, 76 (3), G.P. Boretos, The future of the global economy, 316-326, Copyright (2009), with permission from Elsevier [2]
Source of actual real GDP figures, converted to US$ at 1990 PPPs (Geary-Khamis): TCB and GGDC series [18]

smaller growth rates than those experienced in the previous century, 82% during the period 2000-2025, and by 35% until 2050.

One may ask what this 200 years growth curve really stands for. In order to answer that we have to go back in time. One of the greatest inventions of all times is undoubtedly the Steam Engine that was developed by James Watt at 1765 [25].

Table 3[5]. Seasons of World GDP

End	Begin	(t-tm)/Δt	%K	Year
Previous S-Curve Fall	1st Winter	-100%	1,2%	1917
1st Winter	Spring	-60%	6,7%	1956
Spring	Summer	-20%	29,3%	1995
Summer	Fall	20%	70,7%	2034
Fall	2nd Winter	60%	93,3%	2073
2nd Winter	Next S-Curve Spring	100%	98,8%	2112

This important invention initiated the Industrial Revolution that lasted till 1929 [26], and urged global economy to increase rapidly and in rates unmet in the past. World GDP rose by 5.3 times during the 18th and 19th Century as opposed to just 3.5 times from year 1 to 1700 [27]. During the period 1870-1914 technological advancements following the Industrial Revolution led to an increased use of new means of communication and transport such as the telephone, steam engine ships, and trains that gradually united global economy [28]. Automobiles and airplanes were gradually introduced at the end of this period signaling the beginning of globalization i.e. the creation of a unified world economy where interaction among nations in terms of trade, money, arts or scientific matters is easier and more intense than ever. This period, referred to by Robertson [29] as the "Take off phase" of globalization, prepared us for the most overwhelming growth of all times, as World GDP increased by 18.3 times during the 20th Century [18, 27]. The following two periods of globalization, according to Robertson, "Struggle for hegemony phase" (1920s to 1960) and the "Uncertainty Phase" (1960s to 1990s) resemble in many ways, Winter and Spring seasons that we will examine later on in our analysis. The successive seasons of growth for global economy can be seen in Figure 5. Each season spans over approximately 40 years starting from 1917, all the way through the conclusion of the process at

[5] Reprinted from Technological Forecasting and Social Change, 76 (3), G.P. Boretos, The future of the global economy, 316-326, Copyright (2009), with permission from Elsevier [2]
Source of actual real GDP figures, converted to US$ at 1990 PPPs (Geary-Khamis): TCB and GGDC series [18]

year 2112 as can be seen at Table 3. In the next paragraphs we will link our analysis with real historical events in order to demonstrate the metaphor's ability to model successive periods of growth in an s-curve, and bring to light underlying trends of different seasons.

Globalization from 1917-1995: Past Seasons of Global Growth

Winter (1917-1956) is expected to be a difficult season of low growth where different powers struggle to survive and prevail. And that is exactly what this period was. It includes the end of the First World War, the Great Depression, and the Second World War [30]. Clearly, these are the most troubled times of our recent history with lasting repercussions even in our days. As we will see later on, this period weakened the power of established western countries and served as a vessel for the West's substitution by USSR and Japan in the following years.

As expected from the metaphor, Winter is also a period of novelty. Indeed, this period includes many great inventions and technological advancements unprecedented in previous years.

The first Television set appeared at 1927 [31], changing our day to day life in numerous ways. After the Wright Brothers first flight, aviation takes off with the invention of the liquid-propelled rocket at 1926 [32] and the first jet engine at 1930 [33]. The first large-scale, electronic, digital computer, ENIAC at 1946 [34], as well as the Transistor at 1947 [35], appeared during Winter thus building the foundations of the modern Computer Industry. Even Cellular technology for Mobile Phones was first introduced in 1947 [36], although it had to wait for many decades until its further development and commercialization during the 90s.

Through troubled times of War and Recession, innovation reached a climax with the discovery of the DNA structure, the basic element of life, at 1953 [37] thus signaling the emergence of Spring, a season expected to show high growth based mainly on the previous season's novelty.

Indeed, as post war recovery stimulated economic activity, World GDP increased considerably during Spring (1956-1995) by an amount of approximately 22% of its capacity K. As expected, this is considerably higher compared to a just 5% increase during Winter.

Following the invention of liquid-propelled rocket, space age began. First communication satellite Sputnik I was launched at 1957, and Neil Armstrong became the first man on the Moon at 1969 [32].

After the invention of transistor, the Information Technology and Telecommunications industry expanded rapidly. IBM introduced the first Personal

Computer at 1981 [38], and the World Wide Web was launched at 1990 [39]. The first Cellular Phones were introduced during the 1970s, and finally the GSM system was launched for commercial use at 1991 unleashing the true power of mobility [40].

Once again, DNA studies became more and more popular especially after the launch of the Human Genome Project at 1990 [37]. The decoding of Human Genome at 2000, signals the emergence of Summer, a season expected to have steady growth and prosperity where humanity harvest the fruits of previous years' innovations and investments.

Globalization from 1995-2112: Current Status and Future Prospects of Global Growth

We are currently at the beginning of Summer (1995-2034), that will probably extend global GDP by 42% of its capacity K.

The Cold War that started during the Winter has ended and we are now into the age of globalization. USSR dismantled to the countries that originally formed it at 1991 and Germany is united again. Gradually, all countries that were previously related to the Soviet Union engaged into global economy and developed emerging markets around the World [41].

The European Union introduced the Euro and embraced many former Eastern Block countries such as Romania and Bulgaria, reaching 27 member states [42].

China following many reforms emerges as a new superpower following more and more free market rules of engagement.

Internet and Mobile penetration in the population of the more developed western countries is near its peak. 68% of the population in the US and 45% in Europe already use Internet [43]. Around the world, more than 1.5 billion people use mobile phones. Almost every European, apart from the very young or very old, has already a mobile phone and many even have different subscriptions for professional and home use [44].

Biotechnology, a science that emerged during Spring, initiated a new era of scientific development and practical applications after the decoding of the Human Genome at 2000 [37].

The first half of the 21st Century looks promising as it is evident that we have entered a new season of prosperity and development where global community is more than ever integrated in a unified whole. Technological advancements of the previous season lead world economy to a steady growth but after passing 2015, the midpoint of the growth process, we will begin to gradually experience the first mild symptoms of saturation, just before the emerging of Fall (2034–2073).

As mentioned before, logistic growth often proceeds in successive s-curves with overlapping Winters. The second growth curve is launched during the Fall of the first growth curve and if it survives Winter, it proceeds uninterrupted through a complete logistic growth.

That means that as we reach the 2nd half of the 21st Century, a new growth driver is expected in order to compensate for maturity and deceleration of growth during Fall. As it happened before with globalization, this new growth wave is expected to be introduced during the Fall, emerge during the 2nd Winter (2073-2112), and bring global economy to a new upward trend with the emergence of a new Spring after 2112.

Cyclic Patterns in Global Economy

As can be seen from Figure 6 there is a 38 years cyclical deviation of actual World GDP compared to the estimated from the logistic fit. This deviation has a magnitude of approximately 6%.

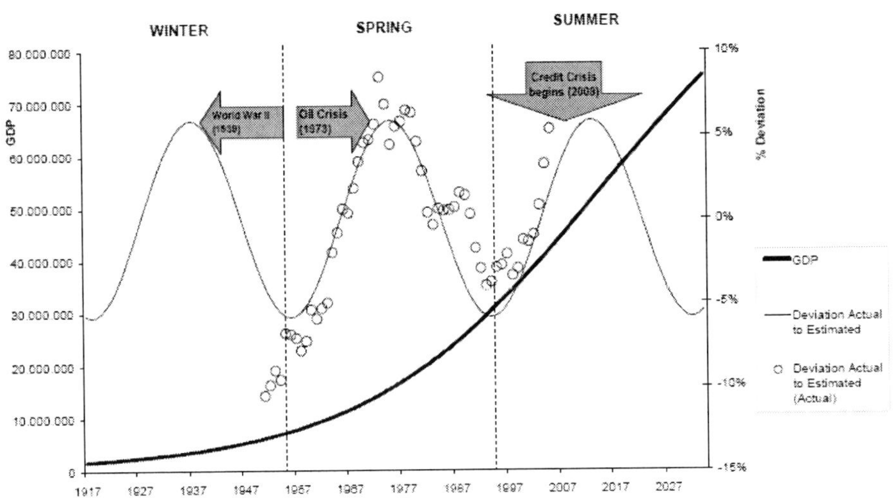

Figure 6[6]. World real GDP (million 1990 International Geary-Khamis dollars) and Cyclical deviation from logistic estimate.

[6] Reprinted from Technological Forecasting and Social Change, 76 (3), G.P. Boretos, The future of the global economy, 316-326, Copyright (2009), with permission from Elsevier [2]
Source of actual real GDP figures, converted to US$ at 1990 PPPs (Geary-Khamis): TCB and GGDC series [18]

That means that although the World undergoes a continuous logistic growth, it also has a cyclic pattern that undermines or further enhances its growth potential.

This is not the first time that such a cyclic pattern is brought forward to the scientific community. In various studies [23, 45, 46] concerning energy consumption, transportation or other areas, a cyclical deviation has been noted that usually varies from 50 to 60 years.

A full cyclic period spans over almost a full season with a peak point at approximately the middle of it signaling the forthcoming cyclical slow down. During Winter this peak point is at year 1937 just two years prior to the outbreak of the Second World War.

During Spring on the other hand, the peak is at 1975, immediately after the Oil Crisis of 1973.

The next cyclic peak will probably occur at 2013, very close to the midpoint of the two-century growth of globalization.

The Emergence of International Powers in a World of Continuous Growth

Figure 7 shows the Logistic Substitution fit against actual GDP contribution for Western Countries, China, and the rest of the World. All data are expressed via the Fisher-Price transformation that converts an s-curve to a straight line [47]. For ease of use the vertical axes of Figure 7 presents the corresponding percentage GDP contribution of the transformation.

Table 4 shows the percentage contribution of West, China, and the rest of the World to global GDP for years 1700-2005. Although recent figures for the three regions are almost identical to those at 1870 when Globalization first appeared, the balance of power continuously and dramatically shifts from one region to another.

As we can see from Figure 7, currently China is at an emerging phase, the West at a decline phase, and the rest of the World is substituting. But it wasn't always like this.

West more than doubled its percentage contribution to global GDP, due to the Industrialization of the 18th and 19th Century, reaching 52% at 1900 from just 22% at 1700. Growth of relative power continued at a slower pace during the 1st half of the 20th Century approaching a ceiling of 57% at 1950.

Table 4[7]. % Contribution of regions to World GDP

Year	China	West	Rest of the World
1700	22%	22%	56%
1820	33%	25%	42%
1870	17%	43%	40%
1900	11%	52%	37%
1950	5%	57%	39%
1975	5%	49%	46%
2000	12%	46%	42%
2005	17%	42%	42%
2025	32%	41%	28%
2050	51%	36%	13%

All data till 2005 are based on actual real GDP figures, converted to US$ at 1990 PPPs (Geary-Khamis), from TCB and GGDC [18], and Maddison series [27].

Data for years 2025 and 2050 are Logistic Substitution Method estimates.

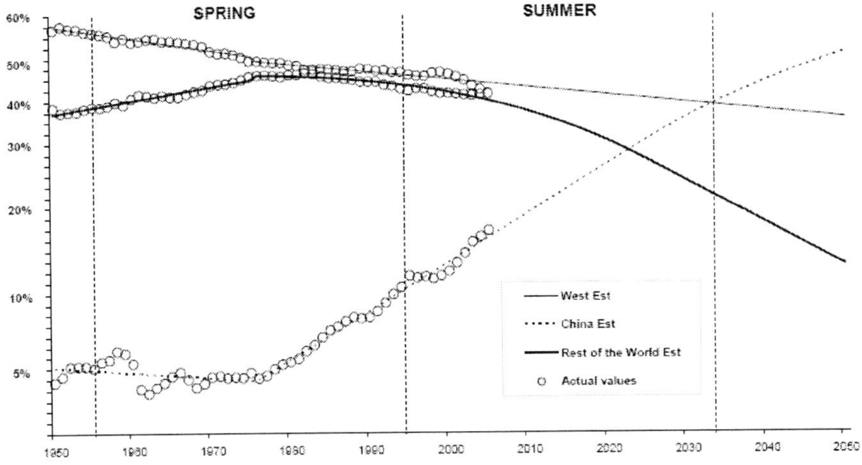

Figure 7[8]. Fisher-Pry transformation of regions % contribution to World real GDP (million 1990 International Geary-Khamis dollars).

[7] Reprinted from Technological Forecasting and Social Change, 76 (3), G.P. Boretos, The future of the global economy, 316-326, Copyright (2009), with permission from Elsevier [2]

Source of actual real GDP figures, converted to US$ at 1990 PPPs (Geary-Khamis): TCB and GGDC series [18] for years from 1950 to 2005 and Maddison series [27] for years from 1700 to 1900

[8] Reprinted from Technological Forecasting and Social Change, 76 (3), G.P. Boretos, The future of the global economy, 316-326, Copyright (2009), with permission from Elsevier [2]

Source of actual real GDP figures, converted to US$ at 1990 PPPs (Geary-Khamis): TCB and GGDC series [18]

During the 2nd half of the 20th Century, Western economies exhausted from the Second World War started to slow down leaving space for growth, for the first time after many years, to other countries such as former USSR, Japan, and more recently China. As substitution from Japan and former USSR commenced, West's relative power fell rapidly to 46% by 2000. West is currently at a decline phase, accounting for 42% of global GDP, considerably less than its maximum contribution at 1950.

The rest of the World, excluding Western Countries and China, is mainly influenced by the "movements" of Japan and former USSR that both challenged USA superiority after the Second World War. During Industrialization the relative power of the region fell considerably from 56% at 1700 to 39% at 1950. Following though rapid development after the Second World War, the percentage contribution to global GDP increased sharply to 46% at 1975. After the gradual collapse of the Soviet Union and the end of the economic miracle of Japan during the last quarter of the 20th Century, the region started to substitute as a new superpower emerged, China. Currently the relative power of the region is at 42%.

After the deterioration of the Chinese Empire that followed the defeat from the British, during the 1st and 2nd Opium Wars [48], China's contribution to global GDP declined intensely from 33% at 1820 to just 5% at 1950. When Mao Zedong assumed power in 1949 thus unifying the country after a century of both internal and external conflicts, an attempt was made to recover and further develop the economy. Although successful at the beginning, the attempt was undermined by the launch of the ineffective programs "The Great Leap Forward" at 1958 and "The Great Proletarian Cultural Revolution" at 1965. That resulted to the "chaotic" fluctuations between 1950 and 1970 (Figure 7) as China unsuccessfully challenges the West's dominance.

It wasn't until 1977, when Deng Xiaoping became the new leader of China, following Mao Zedong's death, that China experienced a shift of economic policy by encouraging foreign trade and investments [30]. The rapid development that followed Deng Xiaoping's economic reforms is pictured in the growth of China's contribution to global GDP that rose from just 5% at 1950 to 17% by 2005, almost the same contribution as 1870.

It is important to mention that by using the Logistic Substitution method one could easily have forecasted China's emergence as a new superpower to the international economical landscape even as way back as 1985. That was at least 10 years before everyone started to talk about the economic miracle of China and its contribution to global GDP was just 7%. More specifically, by applying the LS method to data between 1950 and 1985 we would take almost the same trajectories for the West, China, and the rest of the World as we take when applying the LS method to all available data from 1950-2005. Therefore, if we had made the LS fit back at 1985 instead of now, our forecast for all regions including China, would produce extremely accurate estimates, very close to actual data for all years until 2005.

This unveils the power of the LS method since it delivers good estimates of contribution trajectories, it gives early warnings for major shifts in power, and it is very easy to apply even at the beginning of the substitution process. More important, fits produced by the LS method are in accordance with important historical events that signaled major shifts of relative power among different regions.

But what are the possible trajectories of the three regions' relative power in the future, according to Logistic Substitution method results?

If the current trend continues, the West will follow a slow declining pace reaching 36% at 2050. The rest of the World is expected to fall gradually to 28% at 2025, while entering the decline phase at almost the same time. China is expected to grow even more in the following years reaching 32% contribution at 2025 and 51% at 2050. China's economy is expected to surpass Western countries' combined economies by 2034, and even earlier at 2023 the rest of the World region.

It is evident that in the following years China will probably become the largest economy of the World, surpassing even the leading US economy. By the year 2024 though it will enter the substitution phase, as our world will most likely experience the emergence of a new "superpower" that will take its place, and once more will change the international landscape as we know it today. One of the best candidates to be that superpower is India, which currently accounts for 6% of World GDP and has one of the largest growth rates around the globe (7% CAGR for 2000-2005). If this does happen then our forecast will most likely overestimate China's relative power during 2025-2050 and underestimate the rest of the World and eventually India's contribution for the same period.

Key Findings about the Recent Economic Recession

Based on the key findings of the 2008 study, described in the previous paragraphs, we can give some answers about the recent (2009) economic crisis.

The Double Nature of the Current Recession

A puzzling question about the current recession is if the overall growth trend of many centuries or even the after World War II era has been compromised or if this is a cyclical phenomenon. Based on the analysis presented earlier on, there are both a cyclical and a more permanent long-term trend in place here. According to Figure 5, the global economy has entered the Summer season since 1995, and it is moving rapidly towards the peak of its growth at 2015. As a result, we should expect a gradual slowdown of the two century growth wave that would become more visible after the first half of the process and especially after the global economy enters Fall at 2034. Therefore, the current recession has a more permanent nature as a first symptom of an economy losing momentum and starting to saturate as we approach the midpoint of the long-term growth trend of globalization. However, the symptoms of the current recession are far more intense to be just the result of mild gradual saturation.

Indeed, this is not the only reason for the crisis that we are facing. As we can see in Figure 6, a cyclical downtrend is also in place unveiling at almost the same time with the gradual saturation of the long-term trend. As it did before in 1937 (near World War II) and in 1975 (near the Oil Crisis), at nearly every 40 years and almost at the middle of each s-curve season there is an important event or series of events that signal a significant cyclical slowdown of the economy. The intensity of each cyclic peak seems to be influenced by the season where it occurs. The first cyclic peak inside Winter was one of the darkest days of humankind, World War II. The Oil Crisis on the other hand, the second cyclic peak inside Spring, although severe it had a far less negative effect for both people and economies around the World.

The third cyclic peak is expected at 2013, near the midpoint of the long-term trend and of course near the currently unveiling global recession. Of course we cannot be certain, at the time that this is written, if the current recession is the forecasted cyclical downtrend that came 4 years earlier than predicted (an acceptable 10% error over the 38 year seasonal cycle) or if it is the precursor of the actual peak that will come later on and closer to 2013. After all this has happened before, during Winter when the Great Depression of 1929 was succeeded by another crisis, the World War II in 1939. In any case we expect this cyclic peak to fall between the two previous ones in terms of severity and global impact. It is surely not as intense as a World War but it may be more severe than the Oil Crisis since we are also facing a gradual deceleration of the two centuries growth trend prior to the emergence of Fall.

A Simple "Rule of Thumb"

In order to understand how the cyclical trend influences the actual growth rate of the global economy we will build a simple "rule of thumb". Table 5 presents the actual against the estimated average growth rates (based on s-curve results) for global GDP. As breakpoints for the periods of time where we calculate the growth rate we use the beginning and end points of seasons and also the mid-season cyclical peak points. For the first half of Spring, the period from the beginning of Spring until before the next cyclical peak at 1975, the actual growth rate was 4.7%. Therefore, there was a 16.1% overshoot as compared to the estimated growth rate of 4.0%. For the second half of Spring, the period from the cyclical peak at 1975, until before the beginning of Summer at 1995, the actual growth rate was 3.0%. Therefore, there was a negative overshoot this time by -17.5% compared with the estimated growth rate of 3.6%. Consequently, the results from Spring validate the fact that the part of a season before the mid-season cyclical peak point experiences a higher growth rate than the estimated trend. The exact opposite is true for the remaining of the season. For both parts the overshoot of actual against estimated average growth rate is about 17%. Using the 17% positive or negative overshoot, depending on if we are examining the first or the second part of the season, we can estimate the average growth for future periods of time based on both the long-term trend and the impact of the cyclical trend. We currently are in the first part of Summer that started at 1995. This part extends until before the next cyclic peak at 2013. Based on the "rule of thumb" that we presented before we should expect a 17% positive overshoot compared to the estimated growth rate.

Table 5[9]. Actual against estimated GDP average growth rates

	S-Curve[a]	Actual[b]	Error[e]
1956-1974	4,0%	4,7%[c]	16,1%
1975-1994	3,6%	3,0%[c]	-17,5%
1995-2008	2,9%	4,1%[c]	28,5%
1995-2012	2,8%	3,4%[d]	17,0%

a. GDP average growth rate based on s-curve estimates.
b. GDP average growth rate based on actual data.
c. Actual data until 2005 from [18], data from 2006 to 2008 from [49]
d. "Actual" Data for the 1995-2012 period estimated based on the "rule of thumb".
e. Error of actual against estimated growth rate: (Actual-Estimate)/Actual.

[9] Source of actual real GDP figures, converted to US$ at 1990 PPPs (Geary-Khamis): TCB and GGDC series [18] for years until 2005 and "The Conference Board, Total Economy Database, January 2009" [49] for years from 2006 to 2008

As we can see in Table 5, the estimated average growth rate for the period between 1995 and 2012 is 2.8%. Therefore, the final average growth rate is expected to reach 3.4%. This is lower than the growth rate of the previous years, which for the period between 1995 and 2008 averaged 4.1%. In order to achieve the average rate of 3.4% from 1995 to 2012, given the actual growth rate of 4.1% between 1995 and 2008, we should expect an average growth rate near to 1% in the following four years from 2009 to 2012.

Of course this "rule of thumb" does not stand to scientific scrutiny and should only be used as a mere indication of what lies ahead. Therefore, we cannot say with accuracy when the current recession will end and how severe it is going to be but we can surely say that it will have a lasting impact of more than one year.

The Changing Balance of International Powers

Not all countries are equally affected by the recession. As we have seen before, the more developed Western economies will suffer the most from this economic crisis. From the 2008 study [2], it was indeed anticipated that the relative share of power of Western economies will decline even more, where on the other hand, China will further increase its share in the global economy. The January outlook of the IMF [10] predicts a 6.7% growth for China's economy during 2009 in contrast to a decrease by 2% for advanced economies thus confirming this shift of power towards China.

The Systematic Nature of the Current Recession

Under the light of the new evidence, provided in the previous paragraphs, it becomes apparent that the emergence of the new vicious cycle of the economy and the effect that it has in different regions of the World was not random at all but rather it was a systematic phenomenon exhibiting both a cyclical and a more permanent nature. Based on that, we could have seen the recession coming from many years. The first signs were there all along. The larger than expected average growth rate was a strong early warning that the global economy has been overshooting for some time. As we are approaching 2015, the midpoint of the process, and 2013, the cyclical peak point, we should have expected a deceleration of the economy. Therefore, we could have started preparing many years ago instead of trying desperately to find a "last minute" solution to the crisis.

The Right Strategy for the Recession

According to Modis [17] there are different strategies appropriate for each Season in an s-curve. During Winter, you should "loosen" control and promote creativity in order to identify quickly new growth drivers. You will have to take risks though and experiment with different opportunities. Politicians during the Great Depression failed to do so, at least at the beginning, by applying more strict control through increased taxation and minimized Government spending [14]. This way the Government kept more control on the available spending money in the market thus striping the private sector of desperately needed funding for making investments in new innovative areas. On the other hand, during Summer, the season where we are today, more control is needed in order to increase efficiency and maximize profits. What happened during the previous years was quite the opposite. Financial markets were loosely regulated thus leaving space for the development of very risky "toxic" financial products. We should now expect tighter control as Governments around the World nationalize financial institutions and try to regulate the market [13].

Conclusion

We are currently facing an important economic recession that will probably have a lasting impact of more than just one year. It is the result of both a cyclical downturn and the saturation of the two-century growth trend of globalization. It was initiated after the credit crunch of 2008 by the combined effect of increased insecurity and a much smaller capacity to spend, almost the same reasons that started the Great Depression of 1929. This vicious cycle of the economy was not random at all and it could have been predicted many years ago based on the s-curve model's projections. The recession will affect everyone at every region around the World although the more developed Western economies will suffer the most thus leaving space for developing countries such China and India to further increase their market share, as predicted in the 2008 study.

Although there is a consensus among world leaders and economists regarding the necessary steps against the recession, there are variances in the responses from various countries concerning the appropriate mix of expansionary monetary and fiscal policy. In any case, we expect tighter control and regulation in the market, which is the appropriate course of action according to the seasons' metaphor. Most likely, these measures will relieve the economy, at least in the short run, but at the expense of a larger Budget Deficit for many countries. In the long run, the saturation of the two-century growth trend of the global economy and the mid-season cyclical slowdown will eventually prevail and Governments will find it harder and harder to use the same mix of monetary and fiscal policy to "workaround" the recession again. If we really want to sustain the beneficial effect of the stimulus programs and improve the long-term outlook of the economy it is structural change that will we have to make. In mathematical terms, we need to adjust the "model" of the global economy as well and not just the "input". Governments should revolutionize the regulatory framework of both financial institutions and enterprises, in a coordinated manner, focusing on the transparency, efficiency, and predictability of the worldwide economic system. Additionally, existing modeling techniques have to be further developed and refined to provide more accurate projections and qualitative insights in order to effectively support the decision making process in the macroeconomic level.

In this context, s-curve modeling, in conjunction with practical experience, has proved to be a valuable aid for policy makers and economists by providing us important insights and early warnings, both quantitative and qualitative, about the current recession and also useful guidelines on how to get through it.

References

[1] ECONOMICS,. (2009). The History Channel website. Retrieved 01:09, Apr 4, 2009, from http://www.history.com/encyclopedia.do?articleId=208201.

[2] G.P. Boretos, The future of the global economy, *Technol. Forecast. Soc. Change* **76** (3) (2009) 316-326.

[3] International Monetary Fund, World Economic Outlook, October 2008.

[4] G20, Summit on Financial Markets and the World Economy Declaration, November 2008.

[5] International Monetary Fund, World Economic Outlook, April 2008.

[6] Source: Standard and Poor's, S&P/Case-Shiller Home Price Indices, Composite-20 (SPCS20R), http://www2.standardandpoors.com/spf/pdf/index/CSHomePrice_History_033114.xls.

[7] Highfill, J.: The Economic Crisis as of December 2008: The Global Economy Journal Weighs In, *Global Economy Journal,* **8** (4), Article 4 (2008).

[8] Dow Jones & Company, Dow Jones Industrial Average, April 2009, www.djindexes.com.

[9] International Monetary Fund, "Group of Twenty, Meeting of the Ministers and Central Bank Governors, March 13–14 2009, London, U.K., Global

Economic Policies and Prospects, Note by the Staff of the International Monetary Fund", March 2009, http://www.imf.org/external/np/g20/pdf/031909a.pdf.

[10] International Monetary Fund, World Economic Outlook, January 2009

[11] World Economic Forum, The Global Agenda 2009, www.weforum.org/pdf/globalagenda.pdf.

[12] Commission of the European Communities, Communication for the Spring European Council, Driving European recovery, March 2009, http://ec.europa.eu/commission_barroso/president/pdf/press_20090304_en.pdf.

[13] G20, Global plan for recovery and reform: the Communiqué from the London Summit, April 2009, http://www.londonsummit.gov.uk/en/summit-aims/summit-communique.

[14] Mankiw, N.G.: *Macroeconomics*, 2nd ed., Worth Publishers, New York, 1994, p.276-278, 465-466.

[15] NEW DEAL,. (2009). *The History Channel website.* Retrieved 03:08, Mar 30, 2009, from http://www.history.com/ encyclopedia.do?articleId=217576.

[16] Meyer, P.S., Yung, J.W., and Ausubel, J.H.: A Primer on Logistic Growth and Substitution: The Mathematics of the Loglet Lab Software, *Technol. Forecast. Soc. Change*, **61** (3), 247-271 (1999).

[17] T. Modis, Conquering Uncertainty, McGraw-Hill, New York, NY, 1998.

[18] The Conference Board and Groningen Growth and Development Centre, Total Economy Database, January 2007, http://www.ggdc.net.

[19] Nakicenovic, N.: Software package for the logistic substitution model, *International Institute for Applied Systems Analysis, Laxenburg, Austria,* IIASA Research Report RR-79-12 (1979).

[20] Marchetti, C., and Nakicenovic, N.: The dynamics of energy systems and the logistic substitution model, *International Institute for Applied Systems Analysis, Laxenburg, Austria,* IIASA Research Report RR-79-13 (1979).

[21] Marchetti, C.: Infrastructures for movement, *Technol. Forecast. Soc. Change,* **32** (4), 373-393 (1987).

[22] Modis, T.: Technological substitutions in the computer industry, *Technol. Forecast. Soc. Change,* **43** (2), 157-167 (1993).

[23] Modis, T.: *Predictions-Society's Telltale Signature Reveals the Past and Forecasts the Future*, Simon and Schuster, New York, 1992.

[24] Debecker, A., and Modis, T.: Determination of the uncertainties in s-curve logistic fits, *Technol. Forecast. Soc. Change*, **46** (2), 153-173 (1994).

[25] Barraclough, G. (Editor): *The Times Atlas of World History,* 4rth ed., Times Books, Hammersmith, 1993, p. 197.

[26] Barraclough, G. (Editor): *The Times Atlas of World History,* 4[rth] ed., Times Books, Hammersmith, 1993, p. 196,197,206-209,214-215.

[27] Angus Maddison: Historical Statistics for the World Economy 1-2003 AD, March 2003, http://www.ggdc.net/maddison/Historical_Statistics/horizontal-file_03-2007.xls.

[28] Barraclough, G. (Editor): *The Times Atlas of World History,* 4[rth] ed., Times Books, Hammersmith, 1993, p. 252-253.

[29] Robertson, R: Mapping the Global Condition: Globalization as the Central Concept, *Theory, Culture and Society,* **7,** 15-30 (1990).

[30] Barraclough, G. (Editor): *The Times Atlas of World History,* 4[rth] ed., Times Books, Hammersmith, 1993, p. 248-249,262-263,268-269, 275.

[31] BROADCASTING, RADIO AND TELEVISION,. (2007). *The History Channel website.* Retrieved 06:54, Jul 3, 2007, from http://www.history.com/encyclopedia.do?articleId=203824.

[32] SPACE EXPLORATION,. (2007). *The History Channel website.* Retrieved 07:14, Jul 3, 2007, from http://www.history.com/encyclopedia.do? articleId=222803.

[33] JET PROPULSION,. (2007). The History Channel website. Retrieved 07:17, Jul 3, 2007, from http://www.history.com/encyclopedia.do? articleId=213203.

[34] COMPUTER,. (2007). The History Channel website. Retrieved 07:29, Jul 3, 2007, from http://www.history.com/ encyclopedia.do?articleId=206234.

[35] ELECTRONICS,. (2007). *The History Channel website.* Retrieved 07:31, Jul 3, 2007, from http://www.history.com/encyclopedia.do? articleId=208389.

[36] The origins of mobile, Connected Earth, http://www.connected-earth.com/Galleries/Frombuttonstobytes/Mobilecommunications/Theorigins ofmobile/index.htm.

[37] DNA,. (2007). *The History Channel website.* Retrieved 01:24, Jul 4, 2007, from http://www.history.com/encyclopedia.do?articleId=207706.

[38] PERSONAL COMPUTER,. (2007). *The History Channel website.* Retrieved 01:54, Jul 4, 2007, from http://www.history.com/ encyclopedia.do?articleId=219014.

[39] WORLD WIDE WEB (WWW),. (2007). *The History Channel website.* Retrieved 01:52, Jul 4, 2007, from http://www.history.com/ encyclopedia.do?articleId=226141.

[40] © GSM Association 1999 – 2007, http://www.gsmworld.com/about-us/history.htm.

[41] Barraclough, G. (Editor): *The Times Atlas of World History,* 4[rth] ed., Times Books, Hammersmith, 1993, p. 290-291.

[42] Member States of the European Union: http://europa.eu/abc/european_countries/index_en.htm.
[43] Modis, T.: The end of the Internet rush, *Technol. Forecast. Soc. Change,* **72** (8), 938-943 (2005).
[44] Boretos, G.P.: The future of the mobile phone business, *Technol. Forecast. Soc. Change,* **74** (3), 331-340 (2007).
[45] Marchetti, C.: Fifty-year pulsation in human affairs: Analysis of some physical indicators, *Futures*, **18** (3), 376-388 (1986).
[46] Marchetti, C.: Swings, Cycles and the Global Economy, *New Scientist*, **1454**, 11-15 (1985).
[47] Fisher, J.C., and Pry, R.H.: A simple substitution model of technological change, *Technol. Forecast. Soc. Change*, **3**, 75-88 (1971).
[48] National Geographic: *National Geographic Visual History of the World*, National Geographic Society, Washington D.C., 2005, p. 416-417, 494-495.
[49] "The Conference Board, Total Economy Database, January 2009, http://www.conference-board.org/economics".

In: Financial Markets and the Global Recession ISBN: 978-1-60741-921-1
Editors: B. Naas and J. Lysne

Chapter 2

THE IMPACTS OF GLOBAL RECESSION ON THE WORLD ECONOMY: AN INVESTIGATION WITH A MULTI-COUNTRY OVERLAPPING GENERATIONS SIMULATION MODEL

Manabu Shimasawa* and Kazumasa Oguro
[1]Akita University, Japan
Economic and Social Research Institute, Cabinet Office, Government of Japan
[2]Research Institute of Economy, Trade and Industry, Ministry of Economy, Trade and Industry
Institute for International Policy Studies, Japan

Abstract

We have developed a computable multi-country general equilibrium model with overlapping generations of agents to focus investigation on the impacts of worldwide fiscal stimulus measures taken to deal with the global recession in the global economy, especially the US, Japan, EU, China, and Rest of the World, via international capital flows. This global recession decreases the movement of international capital in the short run. Moreover, many regions of the world, and developed countries in particular, are currently in the midst of significant

* E-mail address: mshimasawa@ed.akita-u.ac.jp Telephone +81-18-889-26575. Facsimile +81-18-889-2657. Corresponding author. 1-1 Tegata Gakuen-machi Akita-city, Akita, 010-8502, Japan.

population aging caused by falling fertility rates and increased life expectancy. This may cause a worldwide capital shortage in the long run. In this paper we address three main issues: (i) how does the differential aging process across countries affect international capital flow in the long run, (ii) to what extent do the policy reforms play a significant role in the international capital movement, and (iii) how does the worldwide short-term fiscal expansion make impact on a global economy. Our analysis indicates that the differential aging process promotes international capital flow from aging countries to population-growth countries. Also, by raising the rate of return on capital, international capital flow could improve the economic welfare of the generations in the aging countries. Moreover, the countries with aging populations improve their economic welfare by implementing policy reforms that raise the savings rate with or without policy changes within labor-abundant countries. Finally, the US economic package implemented to manage the global financial crisis actually worsens its fiscal condition, and causes the international capital flow to become more active.

Keywords: aging; policy reform; international capital flow; overlapping generations, OLG; JEL classification: E27; F21; G15; H55; J11.

1. Introduction

The global economy is now faced with two major challenges that must be managed competently. One is a medium- and long-run issue, i.e. the progress of global population aging, and the other is a short-term issue, i.e. the global recession.

With regard to the former, many regions of the world, and developed countries in particular, are currently in the midst of significant population aging caused by falling fertility rates and by increased life expectancy. Moreover, population aging is forcast to continue throughout this century. While the phenomenon is common to multiple countries, the pace and timing of these population structural changes are not. Thus, all countries are in different stages of demographic transition. However, there are similarities in the most developed countries where the population growth rate is still positive, although at a lower level than previously marked, during this period of population transition. On the other hand, in countries such as Italy, Japan, and Germany, the population growth rate is turning negative. Moreover, though the elderly dependency ratio is projected to remain around 30% in the United States and the United Kingdom, it is projected to reach about 70% in Italy and Japan, according to UN projections.

As is known well, population aging causes a reduction in the savings rate and a decrease in the growth rate of labor supply under the assumption of the lifecycle consumption/saving hypothesis, resulting in various impacts on the macro economy when other conditions are constant. Thus, as the progress of aging causes the savings rate to fall, the current account decreases—if other conditions, especially the investment rate, remain constant. As a result, movement of international capital decreases. Higgins (1998) pointed out empirically by applying a 100-country panel data set that a negative relationship exists between an aging population and international capital flow. Moreover, a change in government budget balance or public pension scheme are other factors that might influence the current account or international capital movement. Specifically, the fiscal deficit and pay-as-you-go pension system caused the current balance deficit because it reallocates resources from future generations to present generations in an intertemporal manner.

Thus, as Japan, China, and Germany—which currently offer capital to the EU and US—begin to experience consequences of aging, a worldwide capital shortage might occur. On the other hand, if the famous Feldstein and Horioka paradox holds, a worldwide capital shortage might be avoided because the bulk of the national investment is financed by national savings. However, as the decline of savings leads to reduced investment, the economic growth rate falls even in that case.

Now we turn to the short-term issue. As the global financial crisis that started with the collapse of the sub-prime loans bubble in the US spread around the world, the global economy has suffered serious damage such as a large drop in the economic growth rate, stock prices, and currency values.

Though signs of recovery of the world economy are beginning to emerge, it is said that 2009 is essentially a lost year in global economic terms. In fact, according to the semi-annual International Monetary Fund (IMF) economic forecast, the current recession will likely be unusually long and severe. A recovery depends on the effects of policies implemented in all countries and regions around the world.

In point of fact, to cope with the serious recession caused by the global financial crisis that began in the third quarter of 2008, the major industrialized countries have taken large economic measures through policies to increase public spending.

In addition, at the G20 meeting held in April 2009 in London, the Group of 20 leaders committed themselves to taking all necessary measures to pull the global economy out of the deepest recession since the Second World War. In that meeting, US President Barack Obama urged the leaders of the G20 nations, which represent about 90% of world economic activity and 80% of trade, to ensure that additional strong and unified actions are taken in the face of what is perceived to be an unprecedented crisis. Both the United States and China have undertaken massive government spending to stimulate domestic demand, and Japan announced plans to create its largest-ever economic stimulus package to achieve a rapid domestic demand-led economic recovery after the G20 meeting.

But EU countries, increasingly suspicious about further fiscal policies, have rejected Mr. Obama's call to spend more because the reckless expansion of public spending creates mountains of new debt that will ultimately require higher tax revenues, which come back to haunt future generations.

Generally speaking, the present global financial recession and the policies implemented to manage it make impacts on a nationwide economy mainly in the following three channels: (i) international capital flow, (ii) international exchange of goods and services, and (iii) rise in the interest rate stemming from the issuance of large amounts of government bonds. As the higher interest rates in turn affect the international capital flow, the current downturn will have a complex feedback effect on both a nation's economy and the world economy.

According to reports by international organizations, the world economy is expected to shrink in 2009 for the first time since World War Two and developing countries may be most severely affected. Most of these countries depend on both international trade and international borrowing for economic growth. But world trade is expected to fall at the fastest rate in the past 80 years.

Some of the developing countries have implemented fiscal stimulus measures, but they are unable to maintain large stimulus packages like those in the industrialized countries. This means that developed countries must support developing economies by turning around their own troubled economies, which will lead to an increase in international trade.

Moreover, rich nations are able to borrow more easily in the global capital market to finance interior spending than are developing countries because capital suppliers usually demand high returns when lending to a developing country due to higher risk. Some countries such as China have sufficient foreign currency reserves, but others don't. So those countries must find new investors to pay their debts.

Those countries that are least developed are in the greatest danger. Part of the reason is that they have limited borrowing power due to higher interest rates in the world capital market, as mentioned above. Moreover, they depend heavily on exports of primary commodities. Recent weakness in many primary commodity markets means that the economy of such countries will deteriorate further. No one will be willing to lend money to those countries.

After all, while the short-term issue of the world economy, i.e. the global financial crisis, causes international capital to flow from the developing countries to the developed countries, the medium- and long-term issue, that of global aging, keeps international capital within countries that are not aging, most of which are developing countries.

In any case, our only tool is quantitative analysis based on certain assumptions to project quantitatively the international capital flow induced by aging and by changes in the world interest rate.

Since it was introduced by pioneers Auerbach and Kotlikoff (1987), the overlapping generations model (OLG) has been used extensively to evaluate the impacts of population aging and the various policy changes including tax policy, pension policy, and public debt policy on national savings and economic welfare and to evaluate policy reforms.

However, most such studies focus on a single, closed economy. More recent contributions, such as Iwata (1991), Sadahiro and Shimasawa (1999), Attanasio and Violante (2000), Kenc and Sayan (2001), Fehr, Jokisch, and Kotlikoff (2004), Bryant (2004) and McKibbin and Nguyen (2004), Börsh-Supan, Ludwig, and Winter (2006), and Aglietta et al. (2007), have begun to study the effects of aging within general equilibrium, open-economy frameworks.[1] This field is comparatively new, and an accumulation of research is expected.

In this paper, we have developed a computable multi-country general equilibrium model with overlapping generations of agents, developed by Sadahiro and Shimasawa (1999) and Shimasawa and Oguro (2009), in order to investigate the impacts of aging and worldwide fiscal stimulus against the global recession on the global economy, especially the US, Japan, the EU, and China, via international capital flows, and calibrated for UN population data to estimate the potential effects of the differential aging processes across countries and policy changes on international capital flow.

To our knowledge, there are only three Auerbach and Kotlikoff type multiple countries OLG simulation models, namely, Fehr et al. (2004), Börsch-Supan et al. (2006), and Aglietta et al. (2007).

Fehr et al. (2004) and Börsch-Supan et al. (2006) incorporate only industrialized countries in their model. Although Aglietta et al. (2007) include both industrialized and developing countries, only 19 generations are contained in their model. Moreover, all three of these models have the same values of deep parameters such as utility and production.

This study, however, models a total of five countries and regions including industrialized and developing countries with multiple agents who live for 65 periods, which makes one period in the model approximately equivalent to one

[1] Iwata (1991) and Kenc and Sayan (2001) used a two-period OLG model. Bryant (2004) and McKibbin and Nguyen (2004) used a multi-country Ramsey model.

year of the real world, and different values of deep parameters depending on their status.

The rest of this paper is organized as follows. Section 2 depicts the model. In Section 3, we present the values of the parameters, the scenarios, and the results of aging simulation with a two countries OLG model. Section 4 shows the findings of the global fiscal expansion against the serious recession caused by the global financial crisis that began in the latter half of 2008 with a multi-country OLG model. Finally, Section 5 concludes the paper.

2. The Model Structure

In this section, we present the model used in this paper. It is a computable multi-country multi-period overlapping generations model with perfect foresight agents developed by Sadahiro and Shimasawa (1999), Sadahiro and Shimasawa (2009), and Shimasawa and Oguro (2009). Each country has a household sector populated by *k*-period living generations, firm sector, government sector, and public pension sector. But before we move on to the main subject, it is necessary to pay attention to some features of the economy from which we abstract. First, our model is entirely real. It has no money, only real debt. Second, uncertainty does not exist, i.e. we consider a non-stochastic world. Finally, we assume an inelastic labor supply. In addition, we do not believe the results gained from the following analysis will be changed greatly by introducing these omitted factors into our model. Below, we briefly review the outline of each sector.[2]

1.) Household Behavior

There is a representative individual for each generation in the household sector. Each individual lives for a fixed number of periods (*k* periods) and maximizes his/her intertemporal utility function with consumption. They are also assumed to be rational, to have perfect foresight. Each generation enters the labor market at age 21 (1st period), retires at age *ret*, is granted a pension at *ret+1*, and dies at age *ie*. In addition, each supplies labor inelastically. His/her utility functions are specified as

[2] Since all countries have the same model structure with the exception of parameters, we omit the subscript that identifies the country.

$$U_i = \frac{1}{1-\gamma}\sum_{j=1}^{ie}\left(\frac{1}{1+\rho}\right)^{j-1} c_{i,j}^{1-\gamma} \tag{1}$$

where i refers to the i th generation, j refers to the j th period of life, ρ is the pure rate of time preference, and γ is the reverse of the elasticity of intertemporal substitution. The arguments of the utility function are the consumption per period ($c_{i,j}$). And we model age-specific labor productivity by assuming a hump-shaped age-earnings profile, i.e., a quadratic form of its age j, so its age-wage profile e_j takes the following form:

$$e_j = \theta_0 + \theta_1 j + \theta_2 j^2 , \quad \theta_0 , \theta_1 \geq 0 \; and \; \theta_2 \leq 0 \tag{2}$$

His/her intertemporal budget equation may be described as follows:

$$\begin{aligned}\sum_{j=1}^{ret} PDV_{i,j}(1-\tau w_t)w_t(1+\lambda)^t e_j + \sum_{j=ret+1}^{ie} PDV_{i,j}p_{i,j} \\ = \sum_{j=1}^{ie} PDV_{i,j}(1+tc_t)c_{i,j} + \sum_{j=1}^{ret} PDV_{i,j}b_{i,j}\end{aligned} \tag{3}$$

where PDV refers to the factor of the present discounted value, w_t is the wage rate at time t, e_j is the wage profile i at age j, τw_t is the labor income tax rate at time t, τp_t is the public pension contribution rate at time t, λ measures the rate of technical progress, τc_t is the consumption tax rate at time t, and $p_{i,j}$ stands for pension benefit of generation i at age j. Each generation maximizes his/her utility function (Equation (1)) under the budget constraint (Equation (3)).

With the maximization procedure, the following Euler equations can be solved, concerning consumption per period.

$$c_{i,j} = \left\{\frac{1+r_t(1-tr_t)}{1+\rho}\right\}^{\frac{1}{\gamma}} \left\{\frac{1+tc_{t-1}}{1+tc_t}\right\}^{\frac{1}{\gamma}} c_{i,j-1} , \quad C_t = \sum_{j=1}^{ie} N_{t,j}c_{i,j} \tag{4}$$

where $N_{t,j}$ measures the number of the people of age j at period t, and C_t is the aggregated consumption at time t.

We can also obtain the following physical wealth accumulation equation with the maximization procedure:

$$a_{i,j} = a_{i,j-1}\{1 + r_t(1 - tr_t)\} + p_{i,j} - b_{i,j} + (1 - tw_t)w_t(1 + \lambda)^t e_j - (1 + tc_t)c_{i,j} \quad (5)$$

$$PA_t = \sum_{j=1}^{ie} N_{t,j} a_{i,j} \quad (6)$$

where $a_{i,j}$ is physical wealth asset of generation i at age j, r_t is the interest rate at time t, τr_t is the tax rate on interest income at time t, $p_{i,j}$ refers to the public pension benefit, $b_{i,j}$ refers to the public pension burden, and PA_t is the aggregated private asset at period t.

2.) Firm Behavior

The input/output structure is represented by the Cobb-Douglas production function with constant return to scale. The firm decides the demand for physical capital (K^D) and effective labor (L^D) to maximize its profit with the given factor prices of wage and rent, which are determined in the perfect competitive markets.

$$Y_t = AK_t^{\alpha} L_{e,t}^{1-\alpha}, \ where\ L_{e,t} = (1+\lambda)^t L_t \quad (7)$$

$$K_t = I_t + (1 - \delta)K_{t-1} \quad (8)$$

$$r_t = \alpha A K_t^{\alpha-1} L_{e,t}^{1-\alpha} - \delta \ , \ w_t = (1-\alpha) A K_t^{\alpha} L_{e,t}^{-\alpha} \quad (9)$$

where Y is output, α stands for capital income share, A is a scale parameter, δ is the depreciation of physical capital, K is the physical capital stock, and L_e is the effective labor.

3.) The Government

The government sector has three types of taxes: wage tax, consumption tax, and capital tax. It also has the public debt issue income as its revenue, and pays the consumption, investment, and interest payments as expenditures.

As the government decides the tax rate according to intertemporal budget constraints, the budget does not have to balance for each period. Here, the wage tax rate is endogenously determined according to the difference of government revenues and government expenditures.

Budget constraint in each period:

$$D_{t+1} - D_t = G_t - T_t + r_t D_t \tag{10}$$

Intertemporal budget constraint:

$$D_t + \sum_{i=0}^{T}(G_{t+i} + GSP_{t+i}) / \prod_{j=0}^{i} R_{t+j} = \sum_{i=0}^{T} T_{t+i} / \prod_{j=0}^{i} R_{t+j} \tag{11}$$

where G_t stands for government expenditure at time t, T_t denotes tax revenue at time t, D_t denotes public debt at time t, and $R \equiv 1/1+r_t$.

4.) Public Pension

The pension sector grants a pension to the retirement generations while pension contributions are collected from the working generations.

$$B_t = \sum_{j=1}^{ret+1} N_{i,j} tp_t w_t (1+\lambda)^t e_j \tag{12}$$

where B stands for the aggregated pension contribution. The aggregated pension at time t is given by the product of the population of retirement age, replacement rate, and wage.

$$P_t = \sum_{j=ret+1}^{ie} N_{i,j} \beta \frac{1}{ret} \sum_{j=1}^{ret} w_t (1+\lambda)^t e_j \tag{13}$$

where p is the pension, β denotes replacement rate, *ret* stands for retirement age, and P is the aggregated pension benefit.

The pension contribution rate is endogenously determined to keep the budget constraint.

5.) World Equilibrium

A part of domestic savings, e.g. capital, can move freely to outside countries according to the difference of rate of return on capital. To satisfy the following constraint, capital is distributed to all over the world through interest rate arbitrage:

$$(1-\tau r_t^m)r_t^m = \tilde{r}_t$$
$$s.t. \sum_{m=1}^{n} PA_t^m = \sum_{m=1}^{n} K_t^m + \sum_{m=1}^{n} D_t^m \tag{14}$$

where m denotes the m th region, and n the total number of regions which is 2 in Section 3 and 5 in Section 4.

This shows that world capital supply equals world capital demand. Moreover, we assume the existing capital stock is removable with no cost, and moves freely.

Current account is shown as a difference of net foreign assets:

$$CA_t = FA_t - FA_{t-1} \tag{15}$$

where CA presents current account, and FA measures net foreign assets.

Consequently, current account converges to zero in the long run. And the total of the current balance of the two countries at time t is zero:

$$\sum_{m=1}^{n} CA_t^m = 0 \tag{15}$$

In addition, trade balance is defined by deducting the net factor income from abroad from the current balance.

$$TB_t = CA_t - r_t FA_t \tag{16}$$

where TB stands for trade balance.

We find that trade balance equal to net factor income in the steady state.

Lastly, to close the model structure, the following condition must hold:

$$Y_t = C_t + I_t + G_t + CA_t - r_t FA_t \tag{17}$$

It requires that the aggregate worldwide supply be equal to total worldwide demand.

3. The Impacts of Global Population Aging

In this section, we describe the choice of demographic, preference, and technology parameters used in the baseline simulations, and present the estimates of the macroeconomic effects of aging as well as the potential impacts on international capital flow, based on the two-country OLG model described in the previous section. First, we present the baseline simulation results on the main economic variables. Second, we compare the results with those of a simulation in which international capital flow is not admitted at all, e.g. a closed economy OLG model. Finally, we provide the results of the two alternative scenarios.

Since our purpose here is to estimate the effects of differences in age structure and the effects of policy changes on international capital flow, the countries we consider (country A and country B) are assumed to be exactly the same in every aspect except for the population growth rate, n, after the transition starts.

First, we present the values of the main parameters of the model in Table 1. In both countries the elasticity of intertemporal substitution γ is set at 4.0. The pure rate of time preference ρ is set to 0.015, as documented in Auerbach and Kotlikoff (1987).

Table 1. Values of Key Parameters and Exogenous Variables

Capital income share	α	0.25
Intertemporal elast. of subst.	$1/\gamma$	4.0
Pure rate of time preference	ρ	0.015
Replacement ratio	β	0.40
Physical capital depreciation	δ	0.05
Wage tax rate	τw	0.10
Interest tax rate	τr	0.20
Rate of technical progress	λ	0.02

The replacement rate β is 40% which equals the value of the Japanese public pension program. The share of capital α is set at 0.25. The technological progress λ is set to 2.0%, which is similar to the value of the long run average annual growth rate in Japan. The depreciation rate of capital δ is set to 5%. The sources of the parameter values are: Auerbach and Kotlikoff (1987) for household preferences and production, and the NIPPA for macroeconomic variables. As both countries have common parameters and model structures, there are no differences between their economic situations before fertility transition starts. Thus country A and country B have the same initial steady states.

Second, we assume that both countries have different population growth rates between generations. Country A has negative growth rate, and country B has positive growth rate. Then we can show the transitional equation of generation growth rate to be:

$$\begin{cases} n_t^A = -0.0001t \;,\; n_t^B = 0.0001t & (1 \le t \le 100) \\ n_t^A = -0.01 \;,\; n_t^B = 0.01 & (100 < t < \infty) \end{cases} \tag{3-1}$$

where $n_t^{A/B}$ indicates the population growth rate between generations at period t in country A/B. Both start from 0% in the original steady state, and converge to –1% (country A) and to +1% (country B) in the new steady state after a 100-period transition. Thus the population decreases (increases), and the elderly dependency ratio increases (decreases) in country A (country B). We plot the population growth rate in Figure 1, and the old-age dependency ratio in Figure 2. Moreover, as we compute forward for 500 periods, we consider a sufficient period for a steady-state to be achieved.

Here we present the results of our baseline simulation. For tractability, we report on the variables of country A. The simulation results describing the macroeconomic impacts of aging are summarized in Figures 3 to 6.

1.) Baseline Simulation

First, we see the baseline simulation results as presented in Figure 3. In our analysis, the demographic shock is generated through changes in the fertility rate. In country A, the birthrate decreases by following the equation (3-1), and converges to a –1.0% growth rate in the steady state.

Thus, aging of the demographic structure will progress in this country. According to Figure 3, aging leads to a decline in savings. As mentioned earlier, the life-cycle theory of savings behavior is a key assumption of the model and one which explains the reduction in the savings rate. According to our results, the national savings rate falls by 4.8 percentage points between the initial steady state and the new one. Moreover, as capital flows from the aging country to the population-growing country for a higher rate of return[K1], the capital labor ratio decreases; this puts upward pressure on the rate of return, and downward pressure on wages. And aging also leads to a rise in the tax and pension contribution rates. As a result, though the lifetime utility exceeds that of the initial steady state generations, the deviation decreases gradually. As capital moves to country B, country A has positive net foreign assets in the long run. Thus, the aging country records a positive rate of return on foreign assets from country B in the long run.

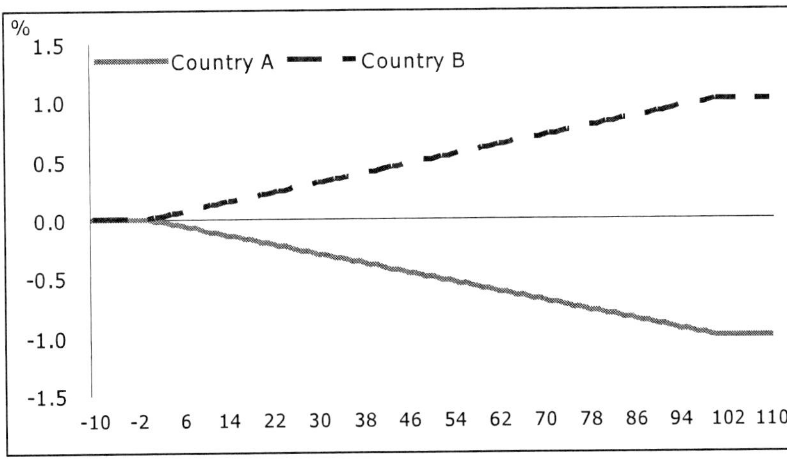

Source: Authors' calculation.

Figure 1. Population Growth Rate in Country A/B.

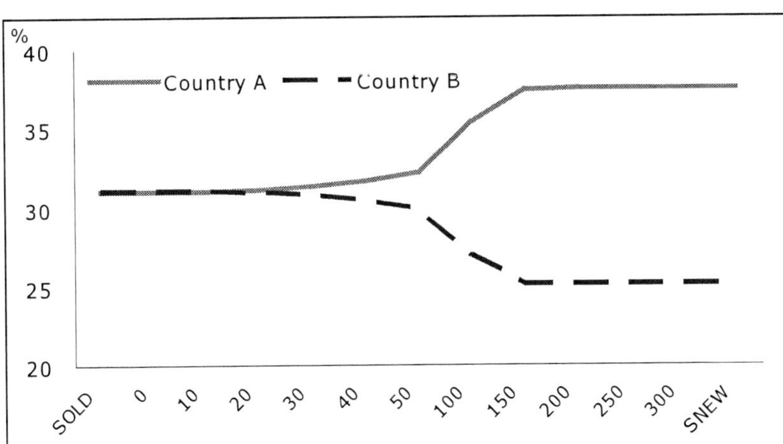

Source: Authors' calculation.

Figure 2. Old-age Dependency Ratio in Country A/B.

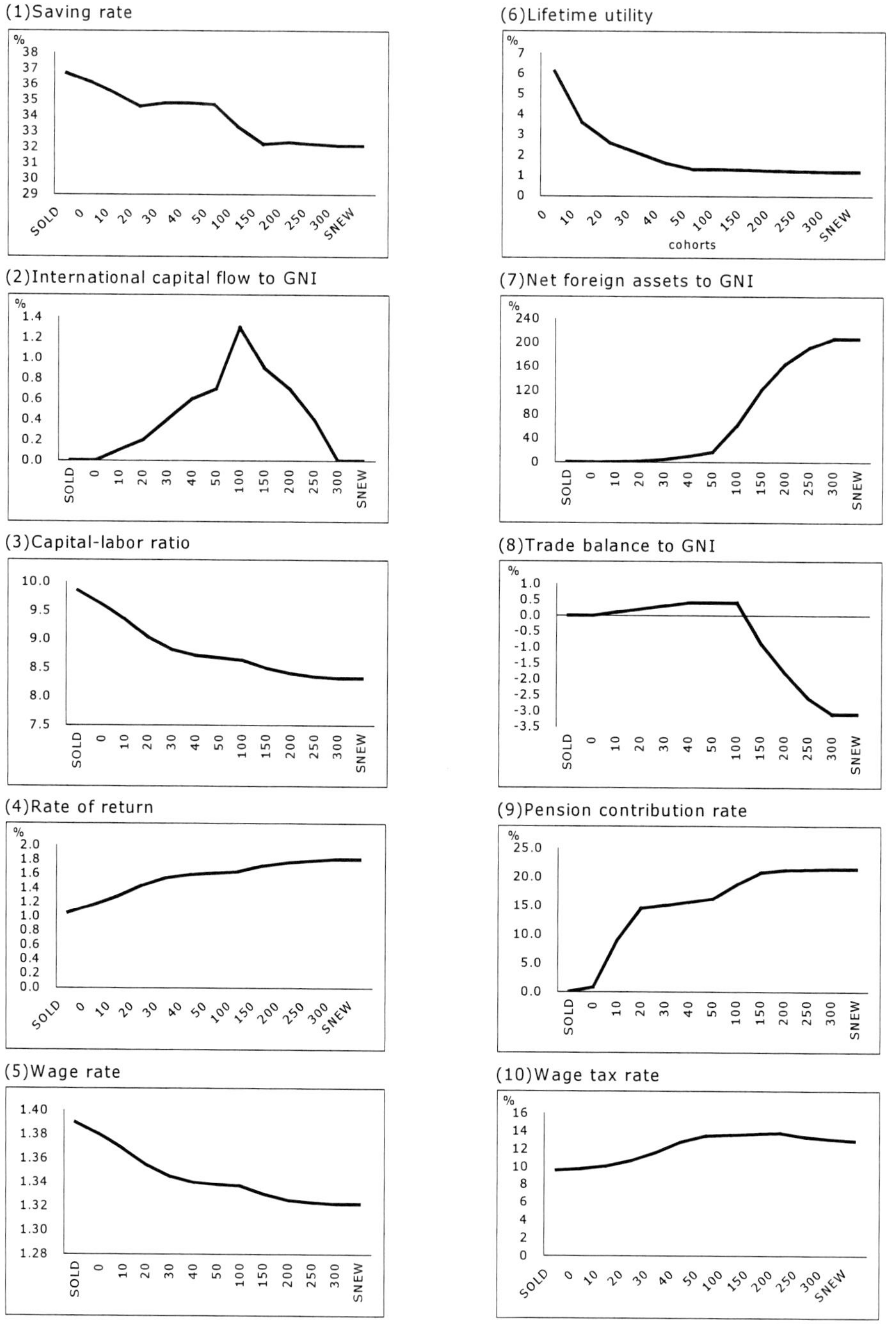

Figure 3. Simulation Results (baseline case).

We next compare the closed economy scenario. Figure 4 shows the results. Aging also leads to a reduction in savings. However, since the labor force is more negatively affected by the demographic shock than is the capital stock, the capital-labor ratio increases; this puts downward pressure on the rate of return on capital, and upward pressure on real wages. As a result, the lifetime utility worsens compared with the open-economy case. Thus we might conclude that these simulation results show the possibility that the effect given to the utility at retirement age by the increase in interest rates overwhelms that of the decrease in wages given to the utility during the working period caused by the international capital movements in the aging country.

2.) Alternative Scenarios

Our figures represent the effect on the savings rate, international capital flow, capital-labor ratio, rate of return, wage rate, lifetime utility, foreign assets, and trade balance in terms of deviations from the baseline simulation results. To evaluate the importance of the policy changes on international capital flow, we examine two alternative scenarios.

In the first alternative scenario, we assume that the public pension system is reformed in one or both countries; Case P_A is the case that a pay-as-you-go pension system is abolished only in country A under perfect international capital mobility. This simulation models a crude transition from a pay-as-you-go pension system to a fully funded private system. Case P_B is the case that pension reform is implemented only in country B. Case P_{AB} is the case that pension reform is conducted in both countries.

The second alternative policy change is a cut in government expenditure. In this scenario, we assume that the government expenditure to output ratio is cut by five percentage points. Case F_A is the case that fiscal reconstruction is executed only in country A in an open economy. Case F_B is the case that the same fiscal reform is implemented only in country B. Case F_{AB} is the case that fiscal consolidation is conducted in both countries. Thus we have two policy change scenarios: public pension reform and government expenditure cuts. We can see the cases in detail in Table 2. The results in Figures 5 and 6 show the deviation from the baseline case.

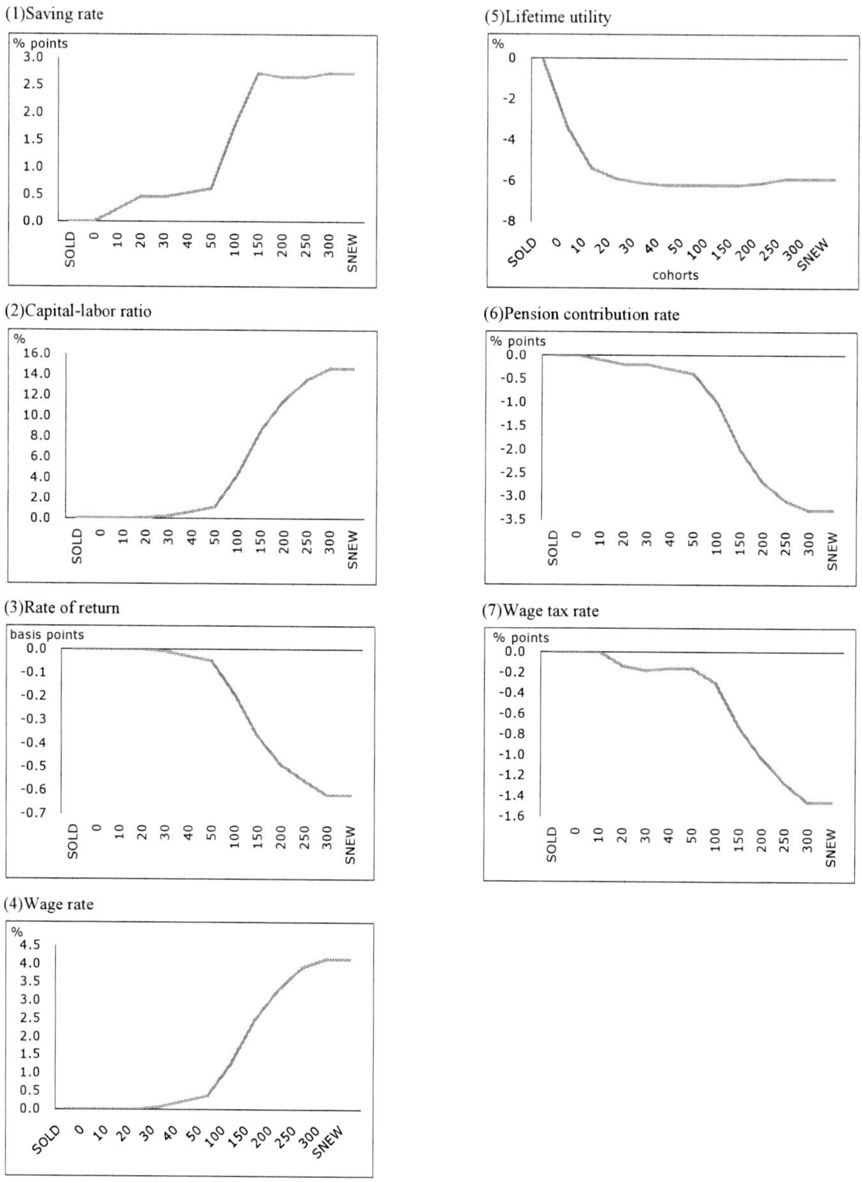

Figure 4. Closed Economy Scenario (deviation from baseline case).

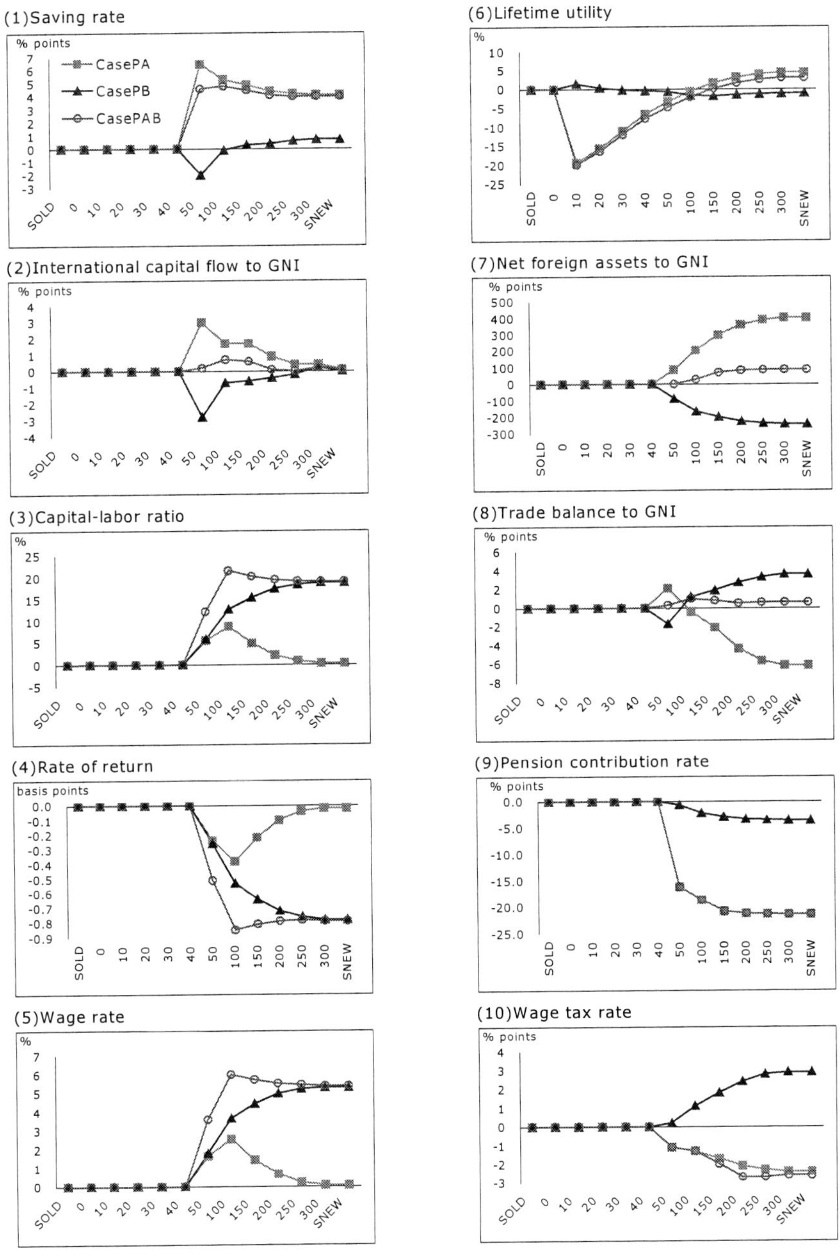

Figure 5. Pension Reform (deviation from baseline case).

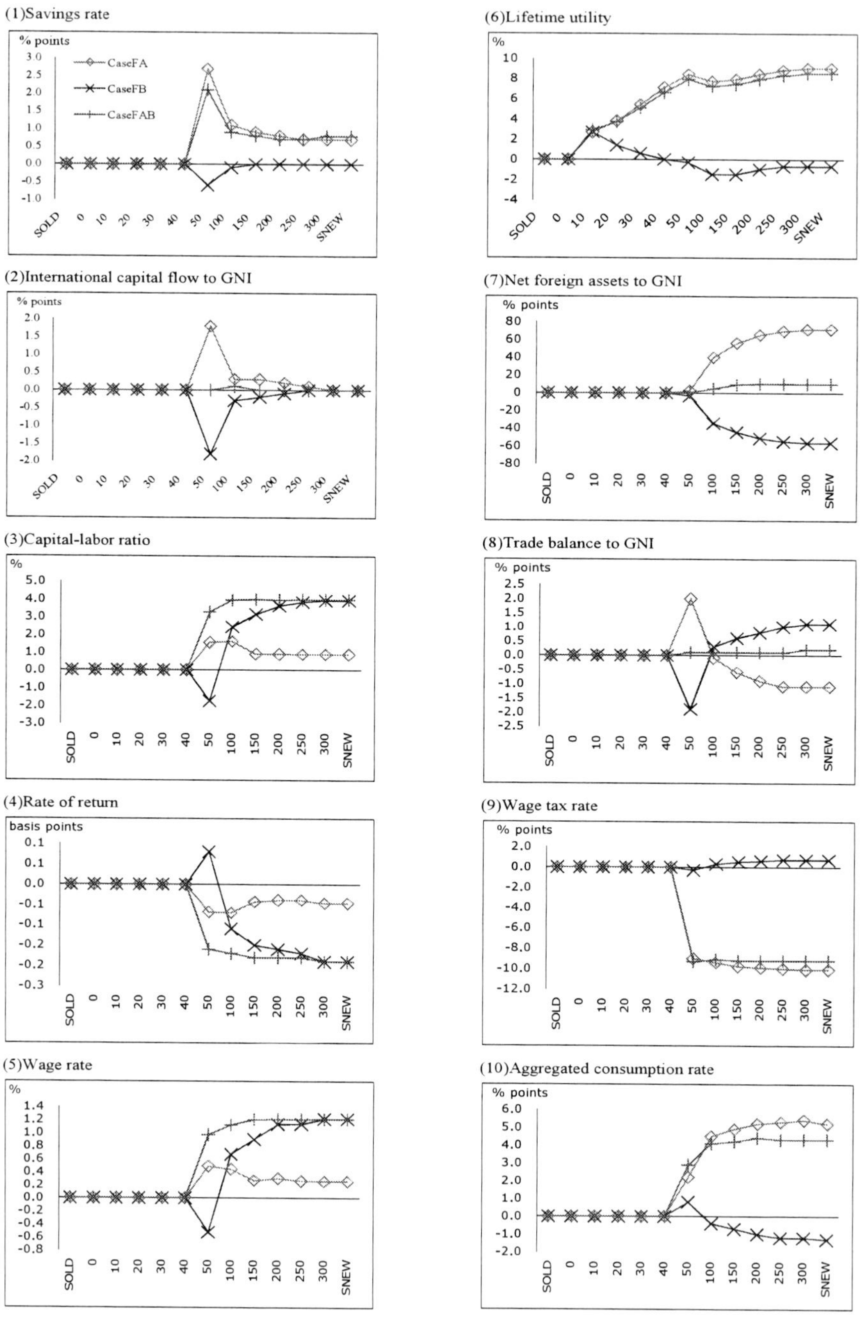

Figure 6. Fiscal Reform (deviation from baseline case).

Table 2. Simulation Cases

	Capital mobility	Pension reform	Fiscal reform
Baseline case	F	×	×
Closed case	N	×	×
Case P_A	F	▲(county A)	×
Case P_B	F	▲(country B)	×
Case P_{AB}	F	●	×
Case F_A	F	×	▲(county A)
Case F_B	F	×	▲(country B)
Case F_{AB}	F	×	●

Notes:
1. F indicates there is perfect capital mobility.
2. N indicates there is no international capital flow.
3. × means no policy reform.
4. ● means policy reform is performed in both countries.
5. ▲(A/B) indicates policy reform is performed in only country A or country B.

Table 3. Values of Key Parameters and Exogenous Variables

	US	JPN	BRICs	EU	ROW
Capital income share	0.25	0.25	0.30	0.25	0.35
Pure rate of time preference	0.02	0.015	0.01	0.02	0.02
Intertemporal elast. of subst.	0.50	0.50	0.50	0.50	0.50
Replacement ratio (%)	30	40	10	75	10
Rate of technical progress (%)	1.5	1.5	2.0	1.5	2.0
Age of retirement	65	65	60	60	60
Age of death	80	85	75	80	70

Table 4. Countries Composing Each Region

Region/Country	Countries
US	United States
JPN	Japan
BRICs	Brazil, Russia, India, China (including Hong Kong, Macao)
EU	European Union, Switzerland, Norway, Iceland, Canada, Australia, New Zealand

Table 4. Continued

Region/Country	Countries
ROW (Rest of the World)	Armenia, Bahrain, Belarus, Bosnia-Herzegovina, Bulgaria, Czech Republic, Cyprus, Estonia, Georgia, Hungary, Korea, People's Republic of Korea, Latvia, Lithuania, Moldova, Poland, Qatar, Romania, Russian Federation, Singapore, Slovak Republic, Thailand, Ukraine, United Arab Emirates, Uruguay, Albania, Argentina, Azerbaijan, Bahamas, Brazil, Brunei, Chile, Colombia, Dominica, Guyana, India, Indonesia, Israel, Jamaica, Kuwait, Lebanon, Malaysia, Mexico, Panama, Peru, Sri Lanka, Suriname, Trinidad and Tobago, Turkey, Vietnam, Afghanistan, Africa, Bangladesh, Bhutan, Bolivia, Cambodia, Costa Rica, Ecuador, El Salvador, Fiji, Guatemala, Haiti, Honduras, Iran, Islamic Rep. of., Iraq, Jordan, Kazakhstan, Kyrgyz Republic, Lao PDR, Melanesia, Micronesia, Mongolia, Myanmar, Nepal, Nicaragua, Oman, Pakistan, Papua New Guinea, Paraguay, Philippines, Polynesia, Samoa, Saudi Arabia, Syrian Arab Republic, Tajikistan, Turkmenistan, Eastern Timor, Uzbekistan, Vanuatu, Venezuela, West Bank and Gaza, Yemen.

3.) Public Pension Reform

The first effect of pension reform is to raise the savings rate in all simulations except Case P_B. The rise of the savings rate leads to increased international capital flow. However, in Case P_B, where pension reform is performed only in country B, the direction of international capital flow is opposite to the baseline case and other simulation cases. As the capital labor ratio increases in Case P_B and Case P_{AB}, the rate of return decreases and wages increase in the long run. Though it has negative effects on lifetime utility in the transitional path, the public pension reform improves utility in the long run because of the net income increase caused by the reduction of the pension contribution rate and the wage tax rate. In Case P_A and Case P_{AB}, as country A begins to have positive net foreign assets in the long run, it receives a positive income gain from country B. However, the level of income gain falls in Case P_{AB} because of a great reduction in the rate of return. On the contrary, country A is to have net negative foreign assets in the long run in Case

P_B where pension reform isn't implemented in country A. We can see the results in Figure 5.

4.) Fiscal Consolidation

First, government expenditure cuts lead to an increase in savings and the aggregated consumption rate in Case F_A and Case F_{AB}. The increase of the aggregated consumption rate corresponds to the decrease in government spending. Though the rise in savings also increases international capital flow, the capital-labor ratio increases compared to the baseline scenario. The increase of the capital-labor ratio causes the rate of return to fall and the wage rate to rise. And since the cut in government expenditures substantially reduces the tax rate, net income increases. Consequently, lifetime utility increases because of the increase in consumption levels. Also in this case, as long as the aging country implements the policy change regardless of whether the country with a young population changes policy, the aging country might improve its economic situation and economic welfare in the long run. We present the results in Figure 6.

4. The Impacts of Global Fiscal Expansion

We present estimates of the macroeconomic effects of fiscal expansion that has been conducted and will be conducted by some economies, e.g. the US, Japan and China, based on the multi-country overlapping generations model described in Section 2. Concretely, we simulate the following scenario: a case in which the US, Japan. and BRICs (Brazil, Russia, India, and China) make expansive fiscal policy that accounts for 2.0% of GDP.

Since the model is simulated over 500 periods, we consider a sufficiently lengthy interval for a steady state to be achieved. We report our analysis focusing on the period 2007–2050, which corresponds to the demographic projection of the UN.

Usually the calibration of dynamic computable general equilibrium models assumes a steady state for the simulation's first year. However, since many countries including Japan have recently been experiencing intense demographic changes, it is very difficult to approximate the economy in 2007 in a steady state. So we begin simulations from non-steady-state initial conditions, which are based on 2007. Therefore, we assume that the economy in 2007 was not in a steady state, but was on the transition path to a steady state in the long run.

We now turn to describe the results of our simulations reported in Table 5. For tractability, we report on the variables of the US.

Table 5. Simulation Results

	Saving rate	Capital-labor ratio*	World interest rate	Wage rate*	Wage tax rate*
2007	14.17	1.000	4.097	1.000	1.000
2010	11.00	1.022	3.959	1.012	1.207
2015	12.72	1.003	4.075	1.020	1.459
2020	11.45	0.980	4.225	1.014	1.663
2025	10.41	0.963	4.341	1.009	1.835
2030	10.13	0.957	4.380	1.018	1.966
2035	10.75	0.967	4.310	1.049	2.074
2040	11.84	0.982	4.212	1.082	2.208
2045	12.87	0.998	4.108	1.089	2.333
2050	13.34	1.022	3.959	1.077	2.456

	Government debt-GDP ratio*	Current account-GDP ratio	Foreign debt-GDP ratio	World GDP per capita*
2007	1.00	-5.30	-24.50	1.00
2010	1.02	-9.00	-26.13	1.05
2015	1.04	-7.68	-27.11	1.10
2020	1.05	-9.49	-32.42	1.16
2025	1.07	-11.12	-41.06	1.24
2030	1.08	-12.43	-52.93	1.30
2035	1.09	-11.93	-65.59	1.36
2040	1.10	-10.15	-75.32	1.39
2045	1.11	-8.48	-81.09	1.42
2050	1.12	-7.74	-84.55	1.45

Note: * indicates index.

As we adopt the lifecycle hypothesis, the savings rate is fundamentally affected by the changes in the elderly population rate, which is strongly correlated with the demographic trend. In our simulation, the national savings ratio shows a tendency to decrease from 14.17% in 2007 to 10.13% in 2030, and then increase to 13.34% in 2050.

As the US receives capital inflows from developing countries and Japan, capital labor ratio increases; this puts upward pressure on the rate of return, and downward pressure on wages.

Now, we briefly valuate factor prices. In our scenario, due to the capital market equilibrium, the interest rate or wage rate fluctuates within a narrow range.

The results of our simulation show that factor prices are surprisingly almost the same as a consequence.

Generally, large fiscal deficits can be expected to negatively affect the fiscal balance through several channels. An inflow of international capital increases the wage tax base and then decreases the capital income tax revenue. According to our simulation, government debt will increase. Further, aging and fiscal deficits caused by the present expansive fiscal policy also lead to the rise in wage tax rate in order to balance the intertemporal government budget.

Table 6 shows generational welfares. These are the welfares of subsequent cohorts in terms of lifetime utility level measured against the cohort born in 1920. According to this table, their lifetime utilities fall to much lower that of the benchmark generation because of the long-run increase in the wage tax rate caused by Obama's fiscal stimulus policy and the pension premium to wage rate caused by the progress of aging. These factors cause the amount of resources available within their lifetime to decrease. And the long-run increase in the public debt to GDP ratio also reduces private capital stock available and decreases future growth. Therefore, this policy shrinks lifetime resources, thereby triggering a severe welfare loss to current and future generations simultaneously and equally.

According to our simulation results, the US is projected to remain a net capital importer. The international capital inflow which seeks a higher rate of return from Japan and BRICs and the fiscal deficit caused by the stimulus fiscal policy make the twin deficits larger in the United States.

As capital moves from Japan and BRICs to the US, the US has negative net foreign assets in the long run. Thus the US gets a negative rate of return on foreign assets in the long run.

The per capita world GDP grows steadily in both scenarios from 2007 to 2050. This is because capital moves from the developing countries e.g. Rest of World (ROW) where the productivity of capital is lower than that of developed countries.

Although the president of the United States plans that his stimulus package of additional spending and tax cuts will move the US economy from an era of borrow and spend to one in which the US consumes less at home and sends more exports abroad, it is unlikely to work without the cooperation of the other countries. To overcome the world's present economic woes, all nations must work together to solve the challenges facing the world. These are challenges that no single nation can overcome alone.

Table 6. Welfare

Birth year	
1920	1.000
1925	0.950
1930	0.898
1935	0.845
1940	0.825
1945	0.807
1950	0.792
1955	0.781
1960	0.773
1965	0.767
1970	0.763
1975	0.758
1980	0.751
1985	0.746
1990	0.746
1995	0.746
2000	0.745
2005	0.744
2010	0.744
2015	0.744
2020	0.743
2025	0.742
2030	0.742

Conclusion

In this paper, first, we have used a computable two-country multi-period OLG model developed by Sadahiro and Shimasawa (1999) and calibrated for assumed population data to estimate the potential effects of differential aging processes across countries and policy changes regarding the international capital flow. We have thus computed the response of the model to three large shocks: population aging (baseline scenario), switch to a fully funded pension scheme (Scenario 2), and government expenditure cut by five percentage points to output (Scenario 3). Our main conclusions are as follows.

First, we have shown that capital basically flows from the aging country to the population-growth country. Second, the aging country will have foreign assets, and the population-growth country becomes indebted in the long run. Third, our results suggest the possibility that lifetime utility worsens due to the drop in the rate of return on capital if the policy reforms are performed to increase savings in a case in which international capital flow is hindered for whatever reason. As a result, there is a possibility that the effects of policy changes to macroeconomic variables, along with the welfare of generations, are overestimated when we analyze the impacts of aging by using a closed economy OLG model. Fourth, the direction of the international capital movement might reverse if the aging country doesn't adopt policies that raise the savings rate while the country with population increase does. Finally, when a labor-abundant country exists, the country with an aging population can improve its economic welfare by implementing policy reforms that raise the savings rate, regardless of any additional policy changes of the labor-abundant countries.

We have developed a computable multi-country general equilibrium model with overlapping generations of agents to investigate mainly the impacts of US fiscal stimulus against the global recession in the worldwide economy, especially the US, Japan, EU, and China, via international capital flows.

Our analysis indicates that the US economic package implemented to manage the global financial crisis actually worsens its fiscal condition, and causes the international capital flow to become more active.

References

Aglietta, M., Chateau, J., Fayolle, J., Juillard, M., Le Cacheux, J., Le Garrec, G., and Vincent Touzé, (2007), "Macroeconomic consequences of pension reforms in Europe: An investigation with the INGENUE world model," *Economic Modelling*, vol. 24, pp.481–505.

Attanasio, O., and G. Violante, (2000), "The Demographic Transition in Closed and Open Economies: A Tale of Two Regions." *Inter-American Development Bank Working Papers* **412**.

Auerbach, A.J. and L.J. Kotlikoff, *Dynamic Fiscal Policy,* 1987, Cambridge: Cambridge University Press.

Axel Börsch-Supan, Alexander Ludwig and Joachim Winter, (2006), "Aging, pension reform, and capital flows: A multi-country simulation model," *Economica*, vol. 73, pp.625–658.

Bryant, R. C., (2004), "Demographic Pressures on Public pension Systems and Government Budgets in Open Economies" International conference paper presented at the Economic and Social Research Institute, Cabinet Office, Government of Japan, in Tokyo, February 18, 2004.

Cabinet Office, *Annual Report on National Accounts of 2008*, 2008, Economic and Social Research Institute, Cabinet Office, Government of Japan.

Feldstein, M. and C. Horioka, (1980), "Domestic Saving and International Capital Flows," *Economic Journal*, vol. 90, pp. 314–329.

Fehr, Hans, Sabine Jokisch, and Laurence J. Kotlikoff (2004). "The Role of Immigration in Dealing with the Developed World's Demographic Transition." *FinanzArchiv* **60**(3): pp. 296–324.

Fougère, M. and M. Mérette, (1999), "Population Aging and Economic Growth in Seven OECD Countries," *Economic Modelling*, vol. 16, pp. 411–427.

Higgins, M., (1998), "Demography, National Savings, and International Capital Flows," *International Economic Review*, vol. 39, pp. 343–369.

Iwata, K., (1991), "Budgetary Balance, Aging, and External Balance: The Future of the United States-Japan External Imbalance," *Journal of the Japanese and International Economics*, vol. 5 No. 4.

Kenc, T., and S. Sayan, (2001), "Transmission of Demographic Shock Effects from Large to Small Countries: An Overlapping Generations CGE Analysis." *Journal of Policy Modelling*, vol. 23 No. 6. pp. 677–702.

McKibbin, W.J., and J. Nguyen, (2004), "Modelling Global Demographic Change: Results for Japan" International conference paper presented at the Economic and Social Research Institute, Cabinet Office, Government of Japan, in Tokyo, February 18, 2004.

Miles, D., (1999), "Modeling the Impact of Demographic Change Upon the Economy," *Economic Journal*, vol. 109, pp. 1–36.

Sadahiro, A., and M. Shimasawa, (1999), "On Three Issues of the Future Japanese Economy (in Japanese)," *ERI Discussion Paper* No. **85**, Economic Planning Agency.

_________ and __________, (2001), "Fiscal Sustainability and the Primary Surplus: A Simulation Analysis with OLG Model (in Japanese)," *JCER Economic Journal*. No. **43**. pp. 117–132.

_________ and __________, (2009), "The macroeconomic implications of ageing in a global context: Simulation Analyses with the OLG model (in Japanese)," Y. Ishii eds. *The Frontier of Open Microeconomics*. pp. 152–177, Waseda University Press, Tokyo, Japan.

Shimasawa, M., and K. Oguro, (2009), "Impact of Immigration on Japanese Economy: A Multi-Country Simulation Model," *RIETI Discussion Paper Series*, The Research Institute of Economy, Trade and Industry.

In: Financial Markets and the Global Recession
Editors: B. Naas and J. Lysne
ISBN: 978-1-60741-921-1

Chapter 3

WHEN RISK WEIGHTS INCREASE THE RISK: SOME CONCERNS FOR CAPITAL REGULATION

Zoltan Varsanyi*
Citibank, Hungary

Abstract

In this chapter I argue that as a response to the introduction of capital requirements in the form of risk weights investors might potentially choose riskier portfolios than before the regulation – this is, presumably, not what the regulation intends to achieve. That is, while regulation most likely diverts investors from their optimum decision it does not guarantee that the new optimum has a lower risk. The effect of the regulation depends on several things, most importantly the correlation between individual investments, investor preferences and the relative size of risk weights.

I. Introduction

In this paper I examine the question whether introducing capital requirement by the application of risk weights it is true that the new optimal portfolio or investment mix of regulated entities is necessarily of lower risk than before the regulation. I show that it is not the case under all circumstances and that the only affect of the regulation that can be taken as granted is that it imposes a new, worse

* E-mail address: varsanyiz77@yahoo.com

optimum on investors (of course, whenever it is binding). Moreover, I argue that this problem may arise even with risk weights that are derived directly from a loss distribution (rather than being more exogenously determined). Thus, regulation through risk weights is not "absolute" in the sense that its effects and effectiveness have to be monitored in a changing environment.

In the first part of the paper I am mainly talking about risk weights in general; in the second part I also try to be more practical: I will interpret the results with an eye on the Basel II regulation.

There is already a large body of critical literature on Basel II (see, for example, Danielsson et al. (2001)). One can say that the rules are too complex, the model behind the advanced risk measurement approach is too simplistic, the Value-at-Risk approach embedded in the way risk weights are set is inappropriate, the regulation is pro-cyclical, and so on.

Here I won't join the critics in any of these above issues but try to give a fresh perspective of the Basel II risk weighting scheme. A fresh and, in a sense, deeper insight than some of the existing ones: I address the fundamental principle of the regulation, the idea, that simply by imposing risk weights on individual investment assets the system as a whole is necessarily stabilised. The question here to start with is this: 'what can we expect from risk weights?'. While there is a lot of talk about regulation and Basel I/II this simple, fundamental question seems to be forgotten. There are related questions like, for example, 'how do risk weights change institutions' portfolio selection?', or 'how should risk weights be set to achieve the regulatory purpose?'.

The paper is structured as follows. In the second and third parts I show how a simple framework can be applied to the question. It comes from modern portfolio theory and simply consists of a utility maximising investor in the risk-return space. In this part of the paper – since the applied modelling framework is so specific and is not applied too commonly to such problems – I will intentionally omit any reference to any existing regulation. By this I try to avoid the situation that the reader raises scepticism at every sentence of this first part. On the other hand, I will also argue that this framework does not restrict the validity of the findings in more general setups and, eventually, that my findings can be valid for real-life financial institutions, as well. Thus, in the fourth part of the paper I discuss some implications for actual financial regulation. Section five concludes.

II. Portfolio Theory

Our starting point is the mean-variance framework of Markowitz. Here, given the individual investment options along with their expected return and risk (standard deviation) it is possible to draw the efficient frontier in the mean-standard deviation space representing for each level of return the attainable lowest volatility over all portfolios (combinations of the individual investment options). Then, a straight line can be drawn starting from an appropriate point on the y-axis (the risk-free rate) that is tangential to the efficient frontier (and extends beyond this tangential point). Under certain restrictions, each point on this line represents a portfolio that is superior to even portfolios on the efficient frontier in the sense that it yields higher return for a given level of volatility (except for the tangential point where there's equality in returns). This line is called the CML (capital market line). Each point on this line represents an investment in the combination of the risk-free asset and the optimal mix of the risky assets (which is the tangent itself). For portfolios on the CML that are in the section to the left of the tangent exactly 100 percent of the capital is invested and no more (i.e., there is no leverage); to invest in portfolios on the right side of the tangent it is necessary that the investor borrows additional funds (so that it invests over 100 percent where the excess is financed by borrowing). The following figure shows these basics (here and throughout the paper I have three individual assets):

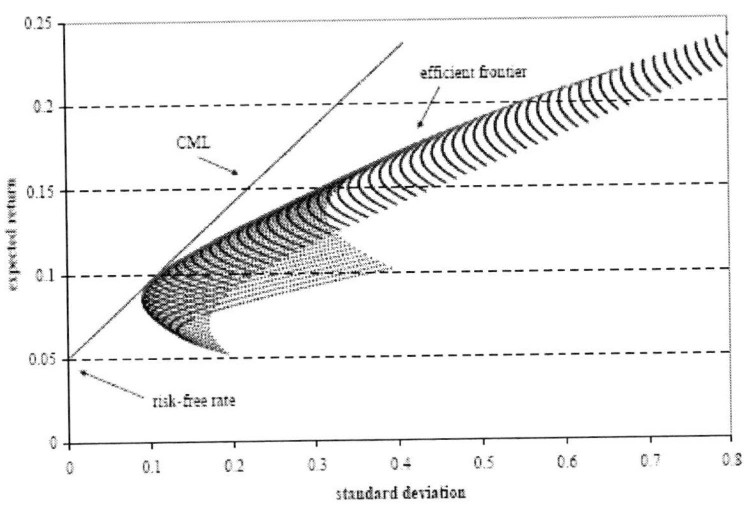

Figure 1.

II.1. Correlations: the Shape of the Efficient Frontier

Correlations have a pronounced effect on the set of investment opportunities: the more correlated the assets the more difficult it is to diversify; with lower correlations, on the other hand, the same level of risk is rewarded by a higher return. A high- and a low-correlation scenario are shown in the figure below:

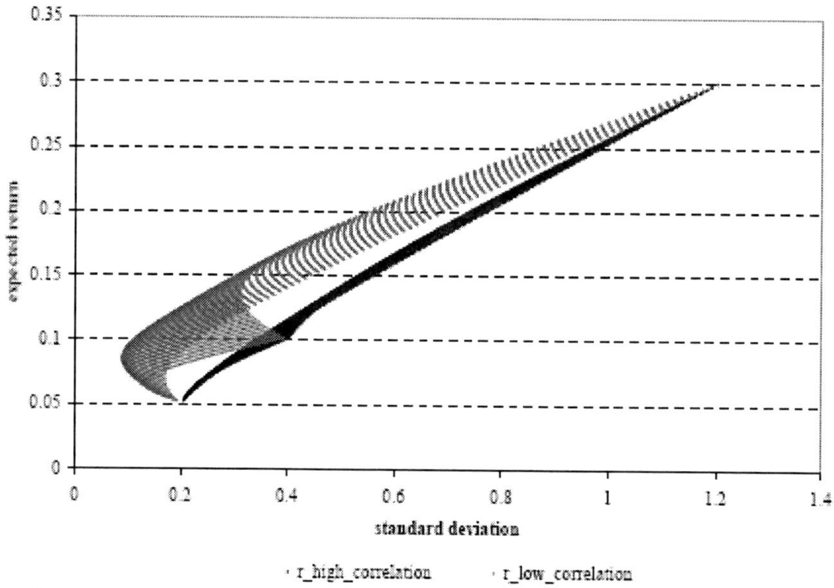

Figure 2.

II.2. Investor Preferences

We know that the optimal investment must lie on the CML (since it "dominates" all the other portfolios). Investors' ultimate choice is determined by their preference in the risk-return space. A more risk averse investor can be expected to chose a portfolio on the CML closer to the risk-free asset, while a less risk averse one will chose a portfolio closer to the optimal risky asset-mix, or even beyond that point.

A common and easy way of modelling investor's preferences is the exponential utility. I will use it, too; the reason for it is that it is easy to work with and, besides, I don't think that other functional forms would change the result meaningfully.

The functional form to be used here is:

$$E(U(x)) = -\exp(-\mu + a\sigma^2), \tag{1}$$

where μ is the expected return on the portfolio and σ is the volatility of the portfolio return. Parameter a represents risk aversion; the higher it is, the more risk averse the investor: for a given level of volatility it requires higher (expected) return to stay at the same level of utility. The following figure shows utility functions with different risk aversions (a) and utility values (u):

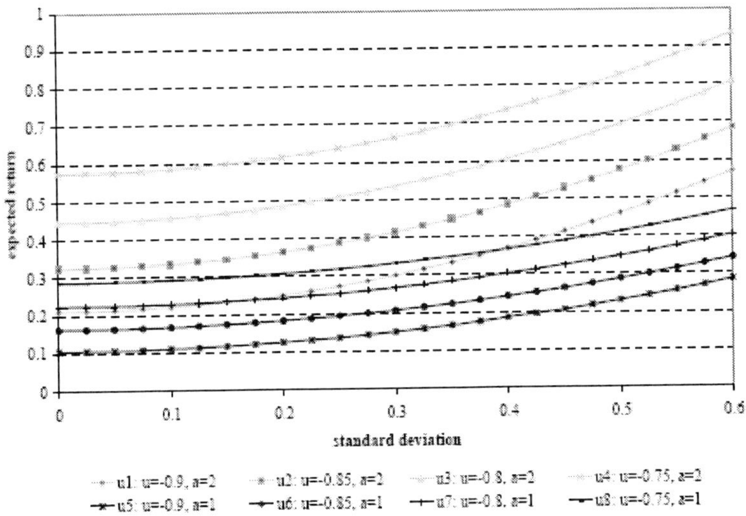

Figure 3.

The first four curves (u1–u4) represent an investor with higher risk aversion than the second four curves (hence these curves are in general above the second four curves). For each level of risk aversion we can see four different, increasing utility levels: with the same aversion parameter and the same level of risk if the investor receives a higher return he feels better. With their lower level of risk aversion investors with utilities u5–u8 can at a given risk level reach the same level of satisfaction with lower return than the ones with higher risk aversion.

II.3. Choosing the Optimal Portfolio

Now we can apply the preference curve over the set of portfolios to find the investment that brings about the highest utility to the investor. This optimal point is shown in the figure below:

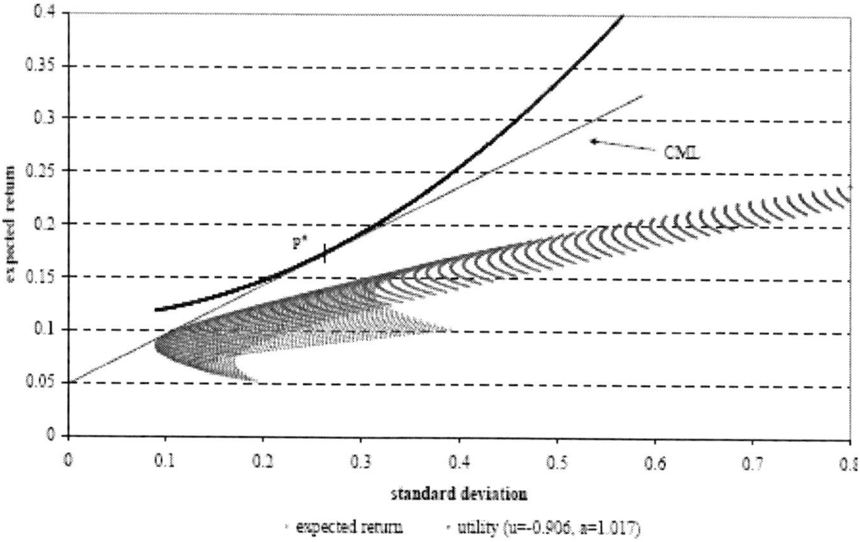

Figure 4.

In this case the investor chooses portfolio p*. As we see this point is beyond the tangent – this means that the investor has to borrow money (in fact, even more than its own share) to realize that investment. By this investment the investor can expect a much higher return than without borrowing and can achieve maximal (unconstrained) utility. Of course, with additional constraints on the optimisation things will change, as we shall see in the next section.

III. Optimal Investments without Borrowing and Other Restrictions

In Markowitz's model the efficient frontier is made up of those portfolios that have the highest return for a given level of risk (standard deviation). Furthermore, in that model it is possible to define the capital market line (CML) which is the straight line starting from the risk free rate and being tangential to the efficient frontier.

There are two reasons, however, why this approach would not be feasible here. First, the CML beyond the tangential point represents investments over 100% of the capital. In our problem it makes no sense to allow this extension since, by definition, we cannot model more than 100% of assets – we assume that an institution wants to optimally invest its total assets and not its total equity with additional borrowing.

The other reason is purely technical: finding first the efficient set, then the CML and, finally, the optimal point on the CML using the utility function would lead to algebraic expressions that would be highly complex and this would make the interpretation of the results hugely (and, in my view, unnecessarily) difficult.

For these reasons I will modify the above representation of the problem by adding the risk free asset to the individual asset pool (thereby making it possible to solve the optimisation in one single step) and assuming that for all feasible portfolios the asset weights are positive (i.e. there is no borrowing). The following figure shows a typical situation under these circumstances with the set of feasible portfolios and a utility function:

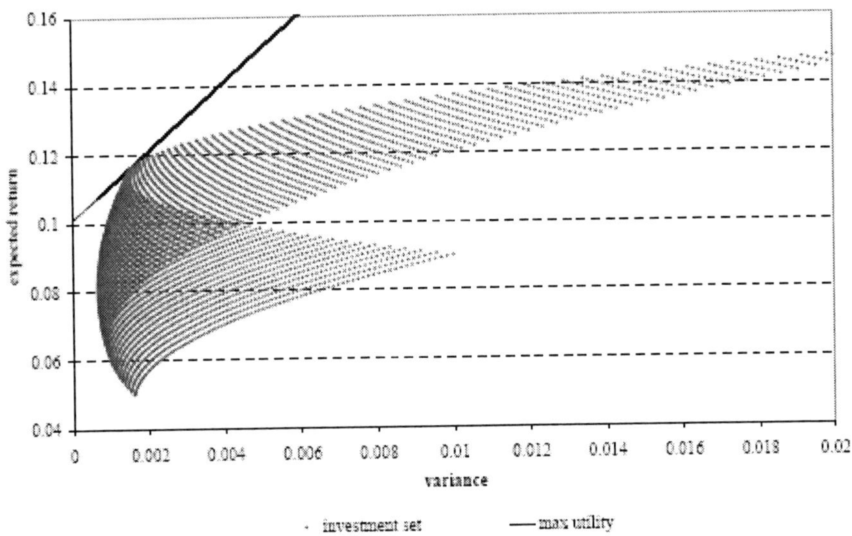

Figure 5.

It also has to be clarified that in graphical presentations from now on I will have the variance of the portfolio on the horizontal axis, instead of the often used standard deviation (that was used even here in previous sections). This has an effect on the shape of the set of investment options and also on the shape of the utility function which is a straight line now.

As I will detail in the Appendix this approach leads to the following formalisation of the problem of finding the optimal portfolio:

$$\begin{aligned} & kxQx^T - cx^T \quad \rightarrow \min \\ & s.t. \quad Ax \le b \end{aligned}, \qquad (2)$$

where k is the investor's risk-aversion parameter (a greater k means greater risk-aversion), x contains the portfolio weights, Q and c are the covariance matrix and the expected return vector of the individual assets, respectively. Vector b represents the constraints and the elements of matrix A show how each individual asset contributes to each constraint.

In our case, without risk weights, A is simply a vector of ones:

$$A = [1 \quad 1 \quad 1],$$

and $b = [\ 1\ ]$.

Formally, the requirement that all the asset weights be positive does not appear here because that would make the analysis again analytically intractable. Instead, I will concentrate on solutions (optimums) in which this constraint is satisfied by itself.

III.1. Introducing Risk Weights

Once we have formulated the problem introducing risk weights is straightforward: the only thing to be done is to modify the appropriate vectors and matrices in (2) by the inclusion of the new constraint: the weighted sum of the risk weights can't be larger than the available capital. This means that now A and b look as follows:

$$A = \begin{bmatrix} 1 & 1 & 1 \\ t_1 & t_2 & t_3 \end{bmatrix},$$

$$b = \begin{bmatrix} 1 \\ T \end{bmatrix},$$

there t_i is the risk weight for asset i and T is the available capital.

Perhaps, however, it is best to look at the effect of risk weights graphically at first. In the following figure it can be seen that risk weights directly change the set of feasible portfolios by cutting off a part of the original set:

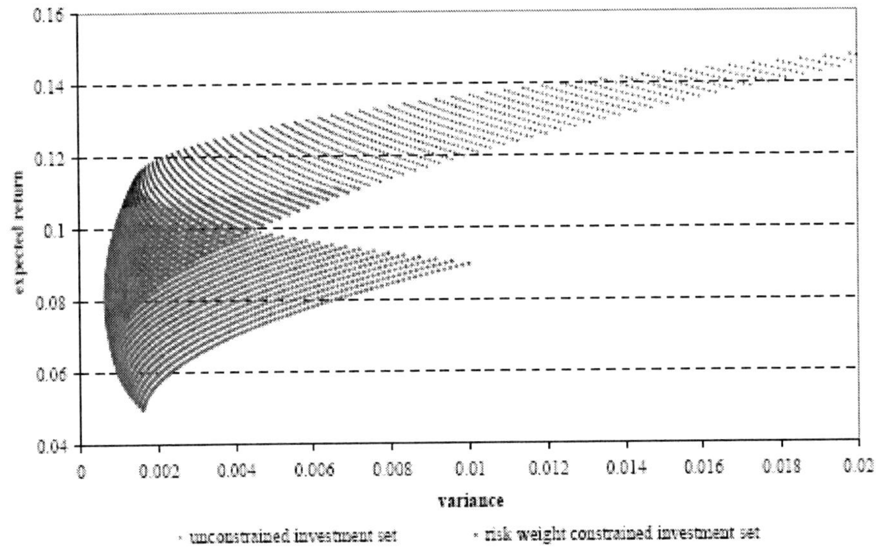

Figure 6.

In the above figure the blue area denotes the feasible set without risk weights and the red one the feasible set with risk weights (the total blue area includes the red area, they are not complementers). As we can see the effect of risk weights is simply that they make a part of the unconstrained feasible set unfeasible.

As we shall see the effect of the risk weights on the optimisation depends on the following factors:

- the absolute and relative size of risk weights
- the investor's preferences
- asset returns and variances/covariances
- the available capital

All of these factors (but preferences) appear in some form in the above figure since they are the determinants of the portion of the originally feasible portfolios that has to be cut off as a result of introducing risk weights. For example, as the available capital decreases, the red area representing the new feasible set shrinks; increasing the risk weights has similar effect.

In the Appendix I derive some formulas to be able to check these effects analytically. There are two reasons, however, why I won't use too much algebra to present the ideas. First, – to my knowledge – the optimisation has an exact analytical solution only if equality-constraints are used. The requirement that the asset weights must all be non-negative implies an inequality constraint given which the problem can only be solved numerically. Second, the analytical solution even with only equality constraints can be rather complex and I would like to place the emphasis on the ideas rather than on mathematics. Thus, my purpose here is to demonstrate scenarios in which "anomalies" can arise rather than carrying out a "full scale" analysis of the issue; in simpler cases I will refer to the formulas, though, and I will also use them to double check some of the intuitive insights. As I show in this section there can be three basic types of situations where introducing risk weights can lead to an optimum with increased variance. These are, schematically, as follows:

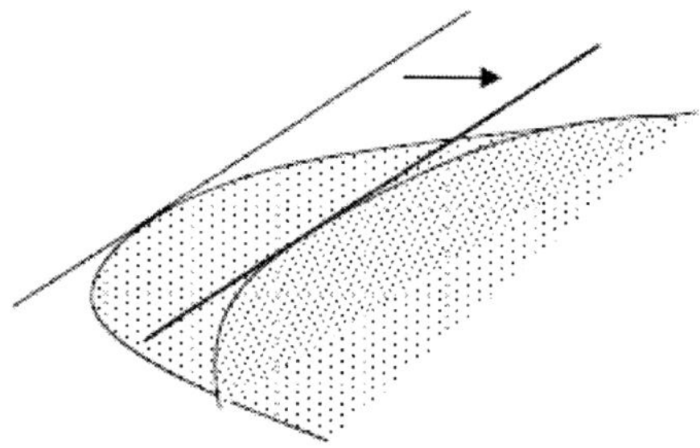

Case 1

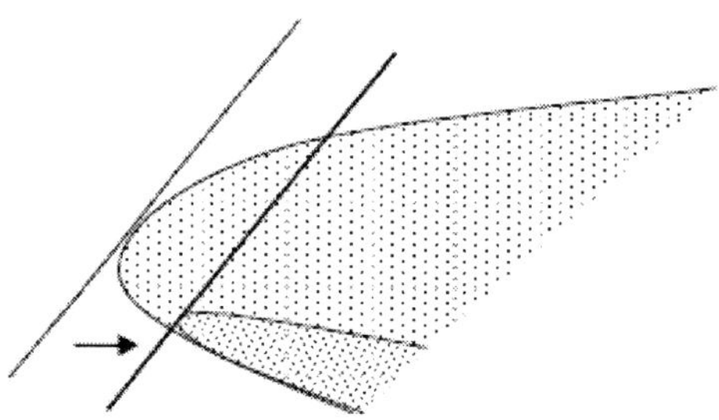

Case 2

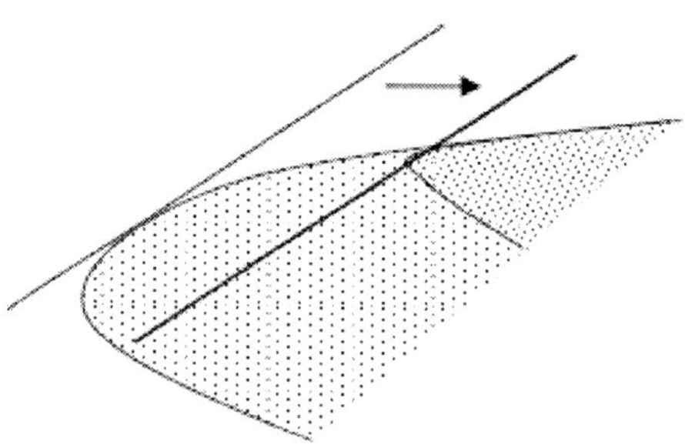

Case 3

Figure 7.

In all of the above figures the blue and the red (more densely dotted) area designate the unconstrained and the constrained investment set, respectively. The thin straight line shows the maximal utility in the unconstrained scenario and the thicker line that in the risk weight constrained scenario.

For further analysis it is useful to separate two broad set of scenarios: in the first we do have a riskless asset (with zero risk weight) and in the second we don't (and all the risk weights are strictly larger than zero).

III.1.1. Optimisation Including Zero-Risk Asset

A riskless asset does not only change the results because its variance is zero, but also because its covariances with the other assets are also zero. This latter fact simplifies the analytical solution so much that in this subsection I will use some of my formulas derived in the Appendix.

The question whether introducing risk weights can lead to an optimal portfolio with a higher variance can be answered by formally examining to what direction a change in the available capital changes the variance. The rationale behind this idea is as follows. We can calculate the portfolio risk weight (which is the same as the required capital) even without formally introducing asset risk weights in the optimisation problem (i.e. the risk weight that *would be* assigned to the unconstrained optimum had risk weights been introduced). If the derivative of the variance of the (unconstrained) optimal portfolio with respect to the available capital is negative then as we start to decrease the available capital from the level implied by this unconstrained optimum after introducing asset risk weights we will see the variance of the optimal portfolio increase. Formally, it can be shown that:

$$\frac{\partial s^{2*}}{\partial b} = b^T\left(AQ^{-1}A^T\right)^{-1} < 0 \Leftrightarrow \frac{a_{21}(q_{33}q_{22} - q_{23}^2) + a_{22}q_{11}(q_{33} - q_{32}) - a_{23}q_{11}(q_{23} - q_{22})}{q_{33}q_{22} - q_{23}^2 + q_{11}q_{33} + q_{11}q_{22} - 2q_{11}q_{32}} > b_2, \quad (3)$$

where a_{2i} denotes the risk weight of the ith asset (the second row of matrix A), q_{ij} contains the ij[th] element of the covariance matrix of the asset returns, Q, and b_2 is the available capital.

One can observe that the expression to the left of the second inequality sign is the weighted average of the risk weights (a_{2i}, where, in fact, a_{21} is zero), where the weights are different expressions including elements of the covariance matrix. The first element in the numerator is zero, since the risk weight of the riskless asset is zero. The other two elements contain the variance of the riskless asset – which, for technical reasons we can't set exactly to zero so we use a very small positive number – so these will be very close to zero. This implies that the quotient is generally very, very low – so low that if we decrease the available capital (b_2) below that level it will enable hardly any risk-taking. This result will be independent of the other parameters of the problem (e.g. the correlation between the risky assets). That means that if we introduce risk weights in this case the volatility of the optimal portfolio will decrease – most probably even if there are "problems" or inconsistencies with the risk weight (see below).

Notice, however, that by making use of the analytical results here, implicitly, we didn't apply the restriction that each asset-weight must be non-negative (we only have analytical results without such a constraint). This restriction should indeed be applied (it naturally follows from the way we approached the problem) and if we do so it has a very remarkable effect on the feasible investment set. To analyse this effect I won't use any algebra but will demonstrate the ideas graphically.

The following figure shows a typical situation in which risk weights restrict the feasible investment set in such a way that the constrained optimum has a higher variance than the unconstrained one:

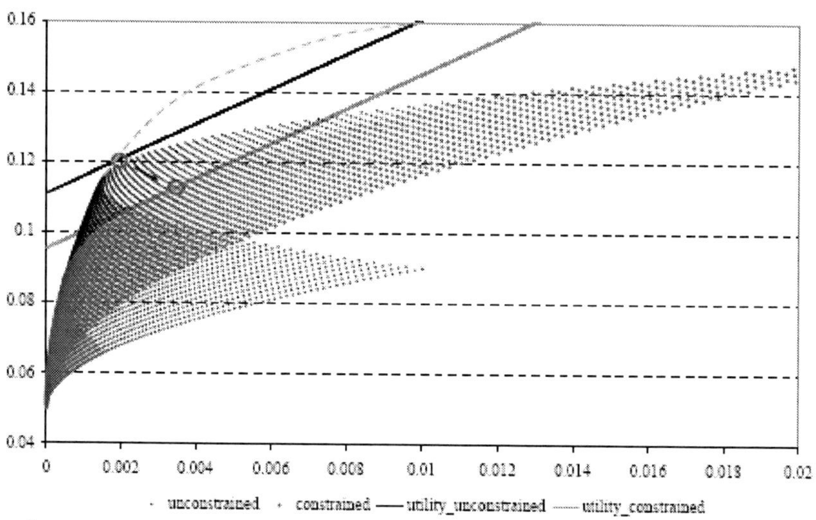

Figure 8.

In the above figure green circles mark the optimums in the constrained and unconstrained cases. We can see that as risk weights are introduced the new optimum has a higher variance and lower expected return (and, of course, utility).

The orange curve is a rough indication of the border of the feasible set when we allow the asset weights to go negative to a certain extent.

Under what circumstances (parameters) can such a situation arise? First, and most importantly, the risk weights have to be set in an inconsistent manner, i.e. the risk weight, for at least two assets, should be inversely related to the risk of the assets (a riskier asset receives lower risk weight than a less risky one). At the same time, an inconsistency is not sufficient to lead to such an adverse effect: this discrepancy has to exceed a 'certain level'. In the example above the risk weight of the second asset was much higher than that of the third asset while it was less risky.

Second, the correlation between the risky assets should be low – the more it is true the higher the increase in the variance can be expected when applying risk weights. A lower (negative) correlation enables lower variance; and the higher the proportion of these risky assets with low correlation in the portfolio the higher the decrease in the variance – thus, in the figure above the area in red will be pulled towards the vertical axis to a lesser extent than the blue area (that contains more of the second and the third assets) above it.

Third, investors can't be 'too' risk-averse: in this case the utility curve would touch the unconstrained feasible set at a point where the border of the unconstrained set is steeper than that of the constrained set which would mean that the variance in the constrained optimum is lower than in the unconstrained one.

III.1.2. Optimisation without Zero-Risk Asset

In our formal derivation of the solution to the portfolio selection problem we couldn't impose the condition that all the asset weights must be non-negative (i.e. there is no borrowing); as a consequence, we have many parameter settings where the optimal solution violates this requirement. More exactly, it is notable that a low level of return on the riskless asset and a moderate level of risk aversion at the most will probably lead to situations where there is a high negative weight on the riskless asset meaning it is in the best interest of the investor to borrow substantially at that low rate. Now, if we don't allow for negative weights the optimal weight of the riskless asset in the above situations can be expected to be zero – this allows the investor to invest in the risky asset mix to the maximum extent. If risk weights are introduced, there will still be optimal solutions with a negative weight for the risk-free asset – with the same reasoning we can leave the non-negativity-constrained optimal weight of this asset at zero. Thus, the investor still invests only in the risky asset-mix, and the introduction of or a change in the risk weights will only result in a realignment of the weights within this mix. This reasoning underpins the idea that we examine the portfolio selection problem without a riskless asset.

When we lock out the existence of a risk-free asset the above results change somewhat. Above I identified three situations in which the introduction of risk weights leads to an optimum with increased variance. We saw an example for Case 1 above in a situation where the zero-risk asset is a possible investment choice. Of course, we can have the same situation when we do not allow investment in the risk-free asset.

Case 2 and Case 3 are specific to situations where there is no risk-free asset. To get into the situation represented by Case 2 it is not necessary that the asset risk weights be adversely related to risk; it is enough that the available capital is very low: in this case only a small part at the 'bottom' of the unconstrained feasible set remains feasible after the introduction of risk weights:

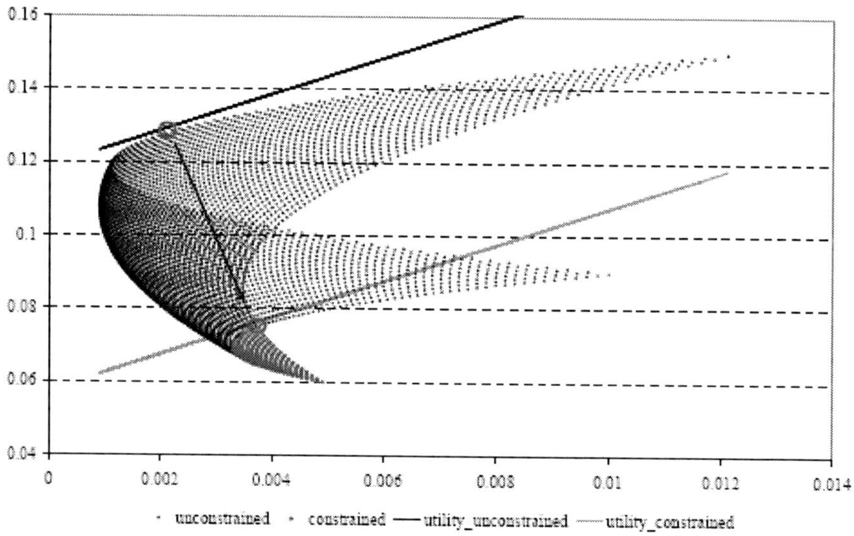

Figure 9.

As we can see from the above figure in this case even if investors' risk aversion varies over a wide range the adverse effect of risk weights can be observed. The problem is related to low correlations again: given these (and without risk weights) investors can find a very good trade-off between risk and return containing high proportions of risky assets. When these assets receive high risk weights (relative to available capital) investors will be forced by the capital constraint to invest increasingly into low-risk assets – the risks of which are higher though than that of an appropriately chosen portfolio of more risky assets without risk weights. In other words, investors cannot benefit from the risk moderating effect of low correlations.

In Case 3 we have a more serious breach of the natural requirement that more risky assets should receive a higher risk weight than in Case 1: now the system of risk weights is turned "upside-down", with riskier assets receiving smaller risk weights.

IV. Some Implications

In this section I will touch on some important practical questions that can be related to the above analysis. I discuss and argue in favour of the model's applicability to credit portfolios; I interpret the findings in light of the Basel II regulation; and I discuss some policy implications.

IV.1. The Application of the Model to Credit Risk Related Portfolios

One might argue that virtually none of the assumptions of the mean-variance model applies to banks' credit portfolios. We can be pretty sure that none of the assets' payoff in which banks invest has a standard normal payoff; none of the banks have a simple exponential utility; banks won't use standard deviation as a risk measure, for example.

Still, such the assets have *some kind* of payoffs and the bank *somehow* ranks these assets based on their return and risk profile; and banks probably have *some kind* of a utility function. Thus, even if preferences, when depicted in the risk-return space, are not as smooth as in the model it doesn't necessarily invalidate our findings – rather, additional aspects in the portfolio selection together with a regulation that is based on risk might create further room for anomalies.

Our finding that risk weights can alter portfolio choice adversely could be translated using more general terms. We could use 'risk' instead of 'variance', 'reward' instead of 'expected return', we could omit the reference to 'utility' and simply refer to the 'choice' of a bank. But let's move to an even more general level instead and summarize our conclusion as follows. *When the introduction of risk weights makes a bank's so far optimal choice unfeasible, under certain conditions, the best feasible choice will have a higher risk.* The above analysis shows that one important (although insufficient) condition is the existence of diversification opportunities which banks might be prevented to benefit from after the introduction of risk weights. Another such condition is the relatively low level of capital in which case banks can't diversify into higher risk assets. This is not to say that each bank always wants to diversify; but the banks that do want to diversify might have such problems.

Another argument against the application of the model to banks is that banks' investment horizon (at least, in credit risk) is much longer than what the model was originally created for. A bank can't change its (credit) risk profile from one day to another thus can't carry out such a fine-tuning of its optimal portfolio as the investor does in the model. Banks have a more straightforward option: they would rather raise their capital level. This might be true, but what if banks find it difficult to do so?[1]

IV.2. Regulation

The current Basel II regime is a successor to Basel I which was the first comprehensive, international initiative for harmonised capital requirement rules (see BCBS (1988)). It applied five categories of fixed risk weights on credit risk related assets – this relative lack of risk sensitivity was one major criticism of the regime; for example most corporate assets would have come under 100 percent risk weight irrespective of the credit quality of the corporate. This simplistic approach led to another problem of the regulation, regulatory arbitrage: institutions had the incentive to circumvent the rules by, for example, securitising low-risk loans (which were 'over-penalised' by receiving the same risk weight as higher-risk loans).[2] This situation, in fact, can be reflected in the above model simply in the form of inappropriately calibrated risk weights (and we saw that such situations can lead to an 'adverse' portfolio selection).

Basel II brought about large changes compared to Basel I. From our point of view one of the most important of these is the introduction of a completely new approach: the "internal ratings-based", or "IRB" method for credit risk and a similar, internal model approach for market risk in which banks can make use of their internally estimated risk parameters in calculating risk weights and capital requirement. Perhaps even more importantly, there is a big shift in the approach itself, in the meaning of risk weights: while in Basel I these were set

[1] On the other hand, if one argues that risk weights are not capable of modifying the portfolio selection of banks than one should question the effectiveness of such efforts in Basel II (e.g. preferential risk weights for SME credit exposures in the form of lower correlations).

[2] It is interesting that while regulation (and especially Basel I) hardly gives any benefit to the yield of the assets, this, in turn, is a crucial component in securitisations!

'exogenously' with the aim of risk differentiation only between the broad risk categories (and without any reference to an actual estimated risk measure of the assets), in the internal model based methods the risk weights equal an (estimated) high percentile of the loss distribution, that is, a percentage loss that can be exceeded with only a low probability. This difference is important from our point of view: the whole logic of the problem changes now since the 'correctness' of the risk weights can't be questioned any more; the risk weight – at least at the individual asset level and assuming that the model behind the approach is more or less accurate – becomes in line with the risk.

Generally speaking, the correlation argument applies here, too, *since we still have individual asset-level risk weights while the investment strategy is implemented on a portfolio basis.*[3]

One could argue that the risk measurement in the IRB approach is not necessarily accurate thus leading to situations where risk weights are not in line with the risk of assets thus having adverse effects on portfolio selection. However, if banks use the same models to calculate risk weights and to decide on their investment strategy (i.e. they accept that risk weights are representative of the true risks) there is no such problem.

The other major approach for credit and market risk – besides the internal model based approach – in Basel II still contains simpler risk weighting schemes. These are now linked to ratings of exposures by rating agencies. Since ratings are updated over time (most importantly, they are updated more often than the frequency by which banks can substantially adjust their balance sheet) we can't expect long-standing discrepancy between risk weights and ratings.

Finally, for most non-rated assets still a single 100% (of 8%) risk weight is applied – which, as we saw earlier, might change portfolio selection in an undesired way.

IV.3. Policy Issues

Throughout the paper the major concern was whether and how the introduction of risk weights can actually lead to riskier (optimal) portfolios, that is, how regulation changes investors' choice. But once we have some ideas as to the effect of (introducing/changing) the risk weights on the optimal portfolio

[3] On the one hand the IRB approach contains a kind of diversification: it assumes that the asset pool is perfectly fine-grained. On the other, to assets in this diversified pool it assigns risk weights based on a specific correlation assumption (one that is derived from the default probability of the asset).

choice we can start to deal with policy questions such as, for example, how investment in certain sectors could be encouraged. This is not to say that capital regulation *should* directly be used to change investors' preferences but we know that it actually does.

One example of such intention can be found in the CRD itself whereby small enterprises receive more favourable risk weights compared to larger companies with comparable risk parameters.

The analysis above is not tailored to answer such questions since it has more to do with the risk of the optimal portfolio globally than with the composition of the optimal portfolio. However, the model can be used to track the changes in the composition of the optimal portfolio resulting from the application of risk weights. As an example, it may sound strange at first hearing that increasing the risk weight of an asset can lead to an increase in the weight of the same asset in the optimal portfolio. But this is the case when the risk weight of the lowest risk asset increases and the capital constraint is binding, since higher risk assets (with higher risk weights) have to be substituted with this asset with the lowest risk weight. This is quite obvious a case; however, depending on the actual parameters, trying to influence portfolio selection by risk weights may not always be successful in more general settings either.

Conclusion

In this chapter we examined some potential effects of capital requirements in the form of risk weights on portfolio selection. The analysis was carried out in the mean-variance framework of modern portfolio theory. Given the specific nature of this model we had to argue that we can use it to our more general problem. Indeed, the model is just a helpful tool for demonstrating the ideas; we can word our conclusions without reference to the model's key notions.

Our most important finding is that when risk weights are introduced investors might – under certain conditions – choose a new optimum that is riskier than the one before the introduction of risk weights. The primary reason for it is that risk weights – that are applied over the individual asset level – are not sensitive to the (risk-reducing) effect of low correlations at the portfolio level.

Reconciling the findings that were based on a simplified model with actual financial market regulation is far beyond the cope of this paper. Thus, throughout a large part of the chapter I tried to avoid direct and strong language regarding actual financial markets or regulations; for example, I didn't examine the reasonability of assuming substantial negative correlations between asset classes –

I simply pointed out that if this is the case, regulation might have undesired effects.[4]

Unintended outcomes can be the results of violations of otherwise correct rules-of-thumb, for example, identical risk weights for a broad range of assets; and can be reinforced by features of the model behind the regulation that are not reflective of the underlying reality (e.g. correlations). In any case, the results lead to an important conclusion regarding regulation: it is not only what regulation wants to achieve, but also what it actually achieves taking into account the possibility of errors. A good regulation not only achieves its purpose effectively and efficiently, but also minimizes the potential for damages stemming from any problems arising after its implementation.

Appendix. A Formal Analysis of the Change in the Optimal Investment

Our intention here is to demonstrate formally how the optimization leads to a different solution as risk weights are introduced. The investor wants to maximise its utility, that is, wants to solve the following quadratic programming problem:

$$\begin{aligned} &kxQx^T - cx^T \quad \rightarrow \min \\ &s.t. \quad Ax \le b \end{aligned}, \tag{A.1}$$

where k is the investor's risk-aversion parameter (a greater k means greater risk-aversion), x contains the portfolio weights, Q and c are the covariance matrix and the expected return vector of the individual assets, respectively. Vector b represents the constraints and the elements of matrix A show how each individual asset contributes to each constraint. In our case there are 3 assets and 1 constraint when there are no risk weights (the portfolio weights sum to unity) and 1 additional constraint when there are risk weights (the portfolio risk weight should be less then or equal to a pre-set level).

It has to be noted that I found three common formalisation of the portfolio selection problem in the literature one of which is what I presented above. It has the advantage that it is directly aimed at finding the optimum, whereas the other

[4] One might note that during stressful periods correlations have a tendency to increase substantially. However, Value at Risk – the current 'best practice' of market risk and credit risk measurement, forming also the basis of a large part of regulation – assumes 'normal' market conditions (see, for example Jorion (2000), preface, page xxii).

two can be only used to find the efficient frontier (either by finding the portfolio with minimum variance for a given level of expected return or the portfolio with the maximum expected return for a given level of variance).

Now, it can be shown that with equality constraints (A.1) has the following solution:

$$\lambda = -k\left(AQ^{-1}A^T\right)^{-1}\left(AQ^{-1}c/k+b\right)$$
$$x = \frac{1}{k}\left(-Q^{-1}A^T\lambda + Q^{-1}c\right) \tag{A.2}$$

Using (A.2) it can further be shown that the variance of the optimum can be expressed as:

$$s^{2*} = x^TQx = \frac{1}{k^2}\left[-c^TQ^{-1}A^T\left(AQ^{-1}A^T\right)^{-1}AQ^{-1}c + c^TQ^{-1}c\right] + b^T\left(AQ^{-1}A^T\right)^{-1}b \tag{A.3}$$

From (A.3) it follows that the effect of the change in the risk weight constraint on the variance of the new optimum is determined by the following expression:

$$\frac{\partial s^{2*}}{\partial b} = 2b^T\left(AQ^{-1}A^T\right)^{-1},$$

or, more precisely, its second element (it's a 2x1 vector). Calculating it is straightforward though requires some complicated algebra. First, the inverse of the covariance matrix is (with three investments assets):

$$Q^{-1} = \frac{1}{\det_Q}\begin{bmatrix} q_{33}q_{22}-2q_{23} & -(q_{33}q_{12}-q_{32}q_{13}) & q_{23}q_{12}-q_{22}q_{13} \\ -(q_{33}q_{12}-q_{32}q_{13}) & q_{33}q_{11}-2q_{13} & -(q_{23}q_{11}-q_{21}q_{13}) \\ q_{23}q_{12}-q_{22}q_{13} & -(q_{23}q_{11}-q_{21}q_{13}) & q_{22}q_{11}-2q_{12} \end{bmatrix},$$

where

$$\det_Q = q_{11}(q_{33}q_{22}-2q_{23}) - q_{21}(q_{33}q_{12}-q_{13}q_{23}) + q_{31}(q_{23}q_{12}-q_{13}q_{22}).$$

Introducing the notation q_{ij}^{-} for the ij-th element of Q^{-1} and a_{ij} for the ij-th element of matrix A and making use of the fact that the first row of A consists of ones we can write $AQ^{-1}A^{T}$ as:

$$\Omega = AQ^{-1}A^{T} = \frac{1}{\det_Q}\begin{bmatrix} \omega_{11} & \omega_{12} \\ \omega_{21} & \omega_{22} \end{bmatrix}, \text{ where}$$

$$\omega_{11} = (q_{11}^{-} - q_{21}^{-} + q_{31}^{-}) + (-q_{12}^{-} + q_{22}^{-} - q_{32}^{-}) + (q_{13}^{-} - q_{23}^{-} + q_{33}^{-})$$
$$\omega_{12} = \omega_{21} = (q_{11}^{-} - q_{21}^{-} + q_{31}^{-})a_{21} + (-q_{12}^{-} + q_{22}^{-} - q_{32}^{-})a_{22} + (q_{13}^{-} - q_{23}^{-} + q_{33}^{-})a_{23}$$
$$\omega_{22} = (a_{21}q_{11}^{-} - a_{22}q_{21}^{-} + a_{23}q_{31}^{-})a_{21} + (-a_{21}q_{12}^{-} + a_{22}q_{22}^{-} - a_{23}q_{32}^{-})a_{22} + (a_{21}q_{13}^{-} - a_{22}q_{23}^{-} + a_{23}q_{33}^{-})a_{23}$$

Finally, inverting Ω we obtain:

$$\Omega^{-1} = \left(AQ^{-1}A^{T}\right)^{-1} = \frac{1}{\det_Q \det_\Omega}\begin{bmatrix} \omega_{22} & -\omega_{12} \\ -\omega_{21} & \omega_{11} \end{bmatrix}, \text{ where}$$

$$\det_\Omega = \omega_{11}\omega_{22} - 2\omega_{12}$$

Now, the change in the variance of the optimal portfolio following a small change in the capital constraint is:

$$\frac{\partial s^{2*}}{\partial b_2} = \frac{2}{\det_Q \det_\Omega}\left(-b_1\omega_{12} + b_2\omega_{11}\right)$$

I wouldn't go into the element-by-element interpretation of this expression; however, we are now in a position to point out the factors on which the effect of changing the risk weights depends and the direction of the relationship. Recall that we are interested in such situations where the above derivative is negative, i.e. increasing the available capital (a lower b_2) leads to an increase in standard deviation. Thus, we are interested in the sign of the above derivative, first of all.

The three groups of factors are: the available capital, the individual asset risk weights and the covariance matrix. The effect of the available capital is straightforward: roughly speaking, as it decreases the derivative also decreases thus getting closer to an 'adverse' situation.

Since b_1 is fixed at 1 (the portfolio weights sum to unity) and ω_{11} does not depend on the risk weights the only item of interest (apart from the determinants) is ω_{12}. It can be shown that the derivative is negative if and only if the following relationship is satisfied:

$$\frac{\partial s^{2*}}{\partial b} = b^T\left(AQ^{-1}A^T\right)^{-1} < 0 \Leftrightarrow \frac{(q_{11}^{-} - q_{21}^{-} + q_{31}^{-})a_{21} + (-q_{12}^{-} + q_{22}^{-} - q_{32}^{-})a_{22} + (q_{13}^{-} - q_{23}^{-} + q_{33}^{-})a_{23}}{(q_{11}^{-} - q_{21}^{-} + q_{31}^{-}) + (-q_{12}^{-} + q_{22}^{-} - q_{32}^{-}) + (q_{13}^{-} - q_{23}^{-} + q_{33}^{-})} > b_2$$

This is a more complicated expression than what I use in the main text for the case where the first asset is risk-free (thus having no correlation with the other assets).

References

BCBS (1988). Basel Committee: International convergence of capital measurement and capital standards. *Basel Committee on Banking Supervision,* July 1988.

Danielsson, J., Embrechts, P., Goodhart, Ch., Keating, C., Muennich, F., Renault, O., and Shin, H.S. (2001). An Academic Response to Basel II. *FMG Special Paper No.* 130, May 2001.

Jorion, Ph. (2000). Value at Risk. *McGraw-Hill Professional*, 2000.

In: Financial Markets and the Global Recession ISBN: 978-1-60741-921-1
Editors: B. Naas et al, pp. 79-102

Chapter 4

THE ROLE OF FOREIGN MONETARY AUTHORITIES IN THE GLOBAL ECONOMIC CRISIS IN TERMS OF REDUCING PRESSURE FROM DECLINING U.S. HOUSE PRICES

Hideki Nishigaki
Hitotsubashi University, Japan

Abstract

The outlook for the world economy has deteriorated dramatically since the second half of 2008. One of the underlying forces that put downward pressure on the world economy is the price correction in the U.S. housing market. The sharp decline in U.S. house prices will depress the economies of both the U.S. and the rest of the world, resulting in the unwinding of global imbalances.

To reduce the negative pressure of this synchronized global downturn, more effective policy initiatives are needed. However, there is a fear that the massive fiscal policy of the U.S. may further the global imbalances. It is desirable that we help the world economy recover and at the same time, ensure that the U.S. current account deficit is made more sustainable.

This paper aims to examine the impact of some possible options (U.S. fiscal stimulus, monetary easing in the U.S., and foreign official purchases of U.S. treasury securities) on the economies of the U.S. and the rest of the world, and the U.S. current account deficits by using the structural vector autoregression (SVAR) model.

The empirical results show that an increase in the foreign official purchases of U.S. treasury securities can expand the GDP of both the U.S. and the rest of the world, and decrease the U.S. current account deficit by improving the U.S. fiscal balance. The stated course of action will help in the recovery of the world economy without expanding the U.S. current account deficit.

1. Introduction

1.1. The Fall in U.S. House Prices and the Unwinding of the U.S. Current Account

The prospects for the global economy have deteriorated dramatically since the second half of 2008. The tensions in global financial markets escalated to a full-blown financial crisis and a global economic crisis after the collapse of Lehman Brothers in September 2008. The world economy is experiencing its most severe downturn since the Second World War.

One of the underlying forces that put downward pressure on the world economy is the price correction in the U.S. housing market. The crisis started in summer 2007, as the losses in the U.S. sub-prime mortgage market triggered the ongoing financial turmoil.

The immediate reason for the start of the crisis was the housing market bubble in the U.S., which began to deflate in 2006. The fall in U.S. house prices accelerated against the backdrop of a rising number of foreclosures and the slowdown in the U.S. economy since 2007.

Unless the U.S. housing sector bottoms out, prospects for the U.S. economy would remain gloomy and the economy of the rest of the world would lose momentum because of the drop in the exports to the U.S..

Some economists say that the current global economic crisis may be related to global imbalances. Before the U.S. housing bubble burst, U.S. house prices increased dramatically owing to the low interest rates that were facilitated by the global saving gluts such as in China and oil-producing countries. A part of these savings was used to purchase U.S. treasury bonds, which pushed the yields on U.S. debt to historical lows. Therefore, in some ways, the global financial and economic crisis may be a product of these global imbalances.

Recently, however, the U.S. house prices have continued falling. The sharp decline in U.S. house prices will depress the economies of the U.S. and the rest of the world, resulting in the unwinding of global imbalances[1].

[1] During economic recessions (or booms), output falls (or rises) and the fiscal balance worsens (or improves). At the same time, the current account will improve when the fall in output leads to a fall in investment that is sharper than the fall in national savings (Kim and Roubini, 2008).

1.2. Policy Responses to the Crisis

To reduce the negative pressure of this synchronized global downturn, more effective policy initiatives are needed. Whether the correction will be smooth or abrupt and painful depends on the actions of policymakers. Many policy options are available. This paper focuses on the effect of three policies on U.S. house prices and the world economy.

The first is the U.S. fiscal expansionary policy, with regard to which there is still considerable debate and little theoretical consensus. For example, when consumers behave in a non-Ricardian fashion, their consumption is a function of their current disposal income. In this case, fiscal expansion may boost the economy. On the other hand, with infinitely-lived Ricardian households, an increase in government spending lowers the present value of after-tax income and declines private consumption (Baxter and King, 1993; Christiano and Eichenbaum, 1992). When individuals work more and earn more labor income while having smooth consumption over an infinite horizon, a transitory reduction in the tax rate on labor income can increase private saving. Fiscal expansion may lead to an increase in the real interest rate, which may crowd out private investment but stimulate private savings.

Empirical work has not settled the theoretical debates. Estimates of fiscal multipliers vary significantly ranging from positive through insignificant to negative (IMF, 2008). As a recent study—Afonso and Sousa (2009)—showed, using a Bayesian SVAR approach, in general, the government spending shocks have a small effect on GDP and do not significantly impact private consumption. The effects on private investment are rather negative, supporting the idea of crowding-out effects in the case of the U.S.. Moreover, Afonso and Sousa revealed that the positive shocks of the U.S. government's revenue have a negative effect on private consumption and are roughly insignificant with regard to private investment.

The second policy pertains to the easing of the U.S. monetary situation. The Fed has responded aggressively to the crisis since it gathered full force in the summer of 2007. The Fed started to ease the monetary policy in September 2007, reducing the target for the federal funds (FF) rate by 4.25% by October 2008. Moreover, the Fed reduced its target further to 0–0.25% in December 2008. While there is little room left to boost the economy by cutting the key rate in the U.S., it is important to estimate the effect of the FF rate cut on the economy and external balance[2].

The third pertains to the official policy of countries across the globe with regard to the purchase of U.S. treasury securities. Although there are few studies about the effect of the foreign policy on the U.S. economy, we think the empirical investigation is important. In the U.S., the low interest rate policy of the early 2000s is said to have helped create the housing market bubble. However, the bubble may have also been helped by the long-term interest rate. Low long-term interest rates led to a very liquid market and increased the asset price. Warnack and Warnack (2006) show that the foreign official purchases of U.S. government bonds have an economically large and statistically significant impact on long-term interest rates such as the 10-year treasury yield and the 30-year fixed mortgage rates by OLS regressions.

Figure 1 shows the foreign share of U.S. treasury securities outstanding is increasing, and has been growing rapidly since the 1970s. In particular, foreign official investors held only about 15 percent of the U.S. government bond market in 1975 but in 2008Q3, they held 34 percent of all outstanding bonds issued by the U.S. government.

Foreign official investments in U.S. treasury securities can influence the U.S. interest rates as well as the dollar exchange rate. The investment policy of foreign monetary authorities can also depend on the financial environment of their own countries. However, more importantly, foreign monetary authorities may signal investment policy intentions and can affect the market expectations of the future price in the U.S. government bond market (signaling channel hypothesis). Therefore, the foreign official investment in U.S. treasury securities may decrease the borrowing costs of the U.S. government and households, and influence house prices and the real economy in the U.S. through the bond market because the 30-year mortgages are closely linked to the price of the treasuries.

The movement of foreign investors could prove to be critical to U.S. government plans to issue mountains of debt to fund stimulus efforts.

---

[2] Although the federal funds rate is now close to zero, the Fed has developed sets of policy tools-lending to financial institutions, providing liquidity directly to key credit markets and buying longer-term securities. The Fed has executed a new monetary policy called the credit easing policy leading to expand the monetary base since 2008. However, this paper focused on the conventional monetary policy changing the target federal funds rate.

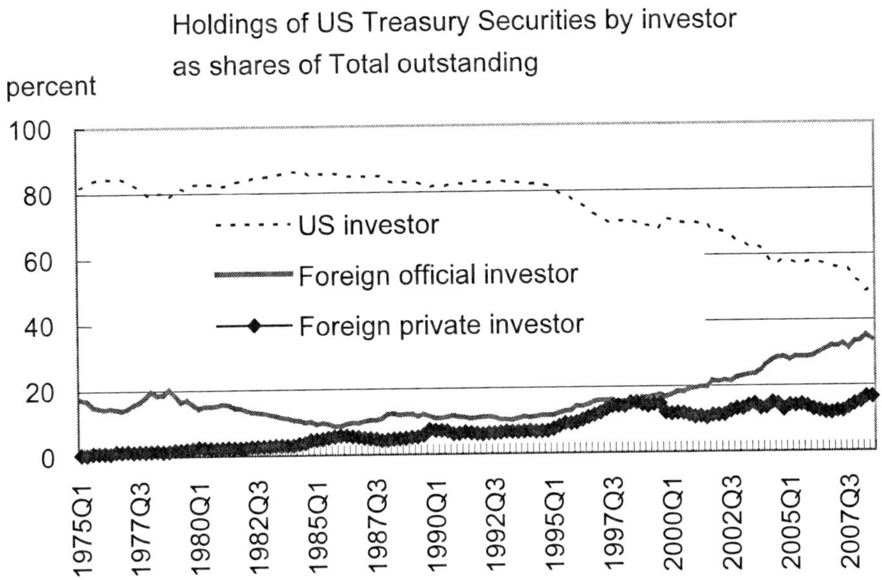

Source: Flow of Funds Accounts of the United States.

Figure 1. The investors in U.S. treasury securities.

In sum, we focus on the U.S. fiscal policy, U.S. monetary policy, and foreign official investment in U.S. treasury securities that can have an important impact on the U.S. economy through the bond or housing market. For example, the U.S. bond yield can rise on the grounds of fears about the growing budget deficit. At the same time, the Fed's rate cut or the continued appetite of foreign investors for U.S. government debt can hold the U.S. interest rates down.

1.3. The Risk of Re-Expanding the U.S. Current Account Deficit

Although global economic recovery is important, the massive policy reaction in the U.S. and the rest of the world may again expand the U.S. current account deficit. Thus, it is desirable that we help the world economy recover and at the same time, ensure that the U.S. current account deficit is made more sustainable.

Although there are a lot of analyses on the relationship between the policy and the U.S. current account, the empirical results are not unique.

For example, the impact of the fiscal balance on the current account depends on the behavior of private sector or private net savings.

Some studies regard the U.S. budget deficits as an important factor in the economy's external imbalances (Cline, 2005; Chinn, 2005; Chinn and Ito, 2005). In other words, it is believed that if the U.S. government reduces fiscal deficits, the external imbalance will unwind.

However, other analyses using simulation models suggest that the budget deficit may not have played a central role (Erceg et al., 2005; Ferguson, 2005). Historically, movements in the general government surplus and the current account balance have scarcely been identical (Bems et al., 2007). Kim and Roubini (2008) discovered that an expansionary fiscal policy shock can improve the current account. Bussiere et al. (2005) performed a cross-country analysis of current account imbalances and government deficits and discovered that a percentage point reduction in government deficits leads to less than a 0.1 percentage point improvement in the current account.

The objective of this paper was to examine the impact of some possible options (US fiscal stimulus, monetary easing in the U.S., and foreign official purchases of U.S. treasury securities) on the economies of the U.S. and the rest of the world, and the U.S. current account deficits by using structural vector autoregression (SVAR) model. We hope that our empirical analyses will produce good suggestions for policymakers.

This paper is structured as follows. Section 2 explains SVAR modeling and the empirical methodology. Section 3 presents the estimation results. Section 4 reports the impacts of the fall in U.S. house price and the various polices. Section 5 concludes.

2. Methodology

2.1. Model

The model is very simple and is as follows:

$$Y = Y^d(\overset{+}{HP}, \overset{-}{i}, \overset{-}{GOV}\ \overset{+}{OY}) + \varepsilon_{IS} \quad \text{US goods demand function} \qquad (1)$$

$$Y = Y^s(\overset{+}{P}) + \varepsilon_{AS} \quad \text{US aggregate supply function} \qquad (2)$$

$$M = M^d(\overset{+}{Y}, \overset{-}{i}, \overset{+}{P}) + \varepsilon_{LM} \quad \text{US money demand function} \qquad (3)$$

$$i = i(\overset{+}{Y}, \overset{+}{P}, \overset{?}{GOV}) + \varepsilon_{MP} \qquad \text{US monetary policy function} \qquad (4)$$

$$GOV = GOV(\overset{+}{HP}, \overset{+}{Y}, \overset{+}{P}) + \varepsilon_{FP} \qquad \text{US fiscal policy function} \qquad (5)$$

$$PRI = PFI(\overset{-}{HP}, \overset{+}{i}, \overset{-}{GOV}, \overset{?}{Y}) + \varepsilon_{PRI} \qquad \text{US private net savings} \qquad (6)$$

$$HP = HP(\overset{-}{i}, \overset{?}{BFO}) + \varepsilon_{HP} \qquad \text{US house price function} \qquad (7)$$

$$BFO = BFO^{d}(\overset{-}{GOV}) + \varepsilon_{BFO} \qquad \text{Foreign official holdings of U.S. bonds} \qquad (8)$$

$$GOV + PRI \equiv CA \qquad \text{US current account} \qquad (9)$$

$$Y + OY \equiv Y^{w} \qquad \text{World GDP} \qquad (10)$$

where Y is the U.S. GDP; HP, U.S. house price; i, U.S. interest rate (policy rate); P, U.S. general price level; OY, overseas GDP; M, U.S. money supply; GOV, U.S. fiscal balance; PRI, U.S. private balance (savings minus investment); BFO, foreign official investment in U.S. treasury securities; Y^{w}, World GDP; and CA, U.S. current account.

(1), (2), and (3) represent the U.S. goods demand function, aggregate supply function, and U.S. money demand function, respectively.

We assume that the U.S. monetary policy function (4) reacts against Y and P; however, we also assume that the monetary policy is affected by the fiscal policy. If the Fed's monetary policy accommodates fiscal expansions, the expected sign is positive.

We consider that the fiscal policy (5) is affected by house price and business cycle. Given the automatic stabilizers on the tax and spending side, the economic and housing boom will lead to an improvement in fiscal balance.

We assume that the U.S. private balance (6) is influenced by the house price, interest rate, fiscal policy, and real income.

We also assume that the U.S. house price (7) is affected not only by the policy rate[3] but also by the demand and supply condition in the government bond market. The government bond market will influence the housing market through the long-term interest rate. The house price will rise if the policy rate decreases. Moreover, if the signaling channel hypothesis holds for the foreign official investment in U.S. treasury securities, the house price will rise by the expansion of the investment.

Further, we assume that the overseas functions of goods demand, aggregate supply, monetary demand, monetary policy, and house price are similar to those in the U.S. model. Overseas GDP (*OY*) is assumed to have no contemporaneous interactions. We use the real GDP data of non-US OECD economies as overseas GDP.

In this paper, we focus on the effect of the policy in terms of reducing the pressure put by the U.S. housing bubble burst on the world GDP (*Y*, *OY*) and the U.S. current account (*GOV*, *PRI*). Here, we assume eight variables—*Y*, *OY*, *GOV*, *PRI*, *i*, *M*, *BFO*, and *HP*—to be endogenous and the others to be exogenous. In this paper, we consider *GOV*, *i*, and *BFO* as policy variables.

2.2. SVAR Model

To estimate the effects of several likely factors on the U.S. economy and the U.S. current account deficit, we use a structural vector autoregression (SVAR) model.

In our SVAR model, we consider the following seven factors[4]: (1) U.S. house price (*HP*), (2) U.S. fiscal balance to GDP ratio (*GOV*), (3) U.S. FF rate (*FFR*), (4) foreign official investment in U.S. treasury securities (*BFO*), (5) U.S. real GDP (*Y*), (6) overseas real GDP (*OY*), and (7) U.S. private net savings (savings minus investment) to GDP ratio (*PRI*).

Our model includes U.S. house price because the correction in U.S. house price is thought to be the source of continuing losses to the financial system, declines in household wealth, and dropping construction activity, resulting in deterioration in U.S. economic activity.

Here, the sum of the U.S. fiscal balance to GDP ratio and the U.S. private net savings to GDP ratio represents the U.S. current account to GDP ratio.

[3] Jarocinski and Smets (2008) show that U.S. house prices are very sensitive to monetary policy shocks.

Our identifying assumptions involve a contemporaneous coefficient matrix and can be summarized in the following equations that link the reduced-form errors to the structural shocks[5].

$$\begin{bmatrix} e_{HP} \\ e_{GOV} \\ e_{FFR} \\ e_{BFO} \\ e_{OY} \\ e_{Y} \\ e_{PRI} \end{bmatrix} = \begin{bmatrix} c(11) & 0 & c(13) & c(14) & 0 & 0 & 0 \\ c(21) & c(22) & 0 & 0 & 0 & c(26) & 0 \\ 0 & c(32) & c(33) & 0 & 0 & c(36) & 0 \\ 0 & c(42) & 0 & c(44) & 0 & 0 & 0 \\ 0 & 0 & 0 & 0 & c(55) & 0 & 0 \\ c(61) & c(62) & c(63) & 0 & c(65) & c(66) & 0 \\ c(71) & c(72) & c(73) & 0 & 0 & c(76) & c(77) \end{bmatrix} \begin{bmatrix} u_{HP} \\ u_{GOV} \\ u_{FFR} \\ u_{BFO} \\ u_{OY} \\ u_{Y} \\ u_{PRI} \end{bmatrix}$$

In the above equations, e_j represent the residuals in the reduced-form VAR equations, and the u_j represent the structural disturbances.

Our SVAR model was estimated with four lags[6]. We used quarterly observations from 1976:2 to 2008:3. The variables *HP*, *BFO*, *Y*, and *OY* were converted into natural logarithms.

Prior to conducting the SVAR analysis, we tested the order of integration for all the time series.

We consider all the variables to be integrated to be of the order one. Our model is estimated in first differences. Data are shown in Figure 2.

The specification is over-identified; however, the LR test for over-identification verifies the validity of our restrictions[7].

---

[4] We excluded the variable of U.S. money supply (*M*) in order to lessen the number of variables in the SVAR model. Although we estimated using eight variables including *M*, our basic results remained the same.

[5] Although we also experimented using only six just-identified SVAR using the Cholesky decomposition, our basic conclusion in this paper remained the same.

[6] The Akaike criterion suggests that such long lags would be optimal. However, the likelihood ratio test (with a correction to improve the small sample prosperities suggested by Sims (1980)) rejected the models with 2 and 3, but not the model with 4 lags at the 1% significance level. Therefore, the model with 4 lags is chosen.

[7] We assume the restrictions c(62) = 0 and c(63) = 0, considering the lag effect of the policy on U.S. GDP.

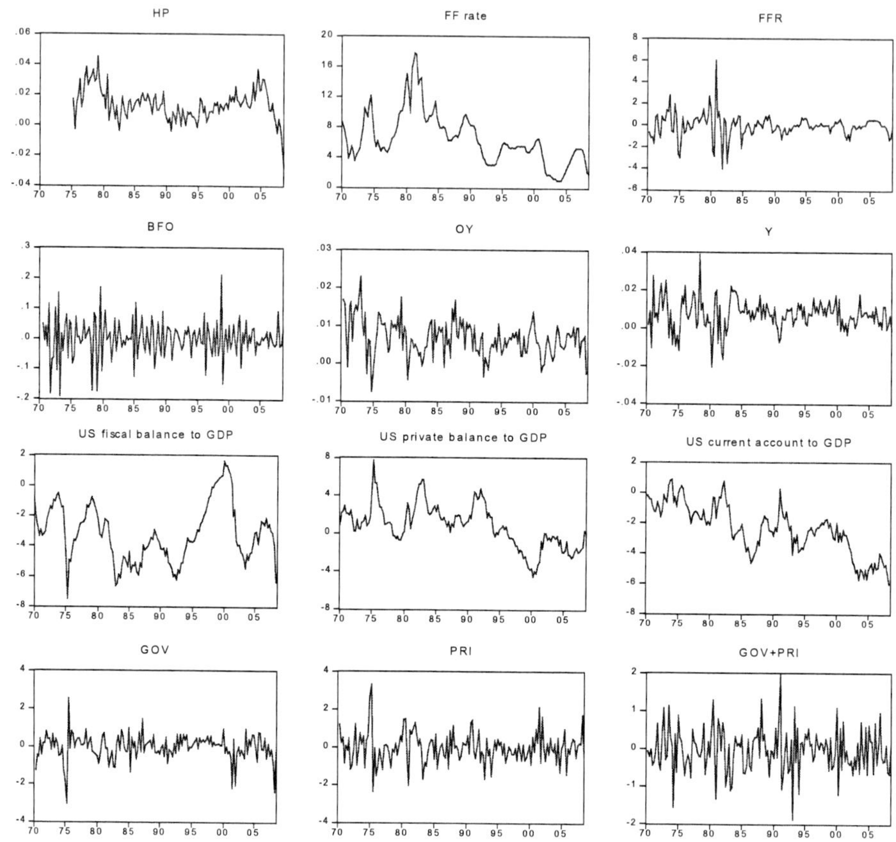

Figure 2. Data (1976Q2-2008Q3).

3. Estimated Results

3.1. Impulse Response

Figure 3 displays the responses of *HP*, *Y*, *OY*, *GOV*, and *PRI* to a one-standard deviation innovation of a particular structural shock to U.S. fiscal policy (shock2), monetary policy (shock 3) and the foreign official investment policy (shock 4) over a twenty-quarter period and also shows the ±2 standard error bands. Here, we will pay attention to the impact in the first 3 years.

First, we assess the impact of U.S. fiscal policy shock (shock 2). In Figure 3, the positive shock to *GOV* shows the U.S. fiscal tightening.

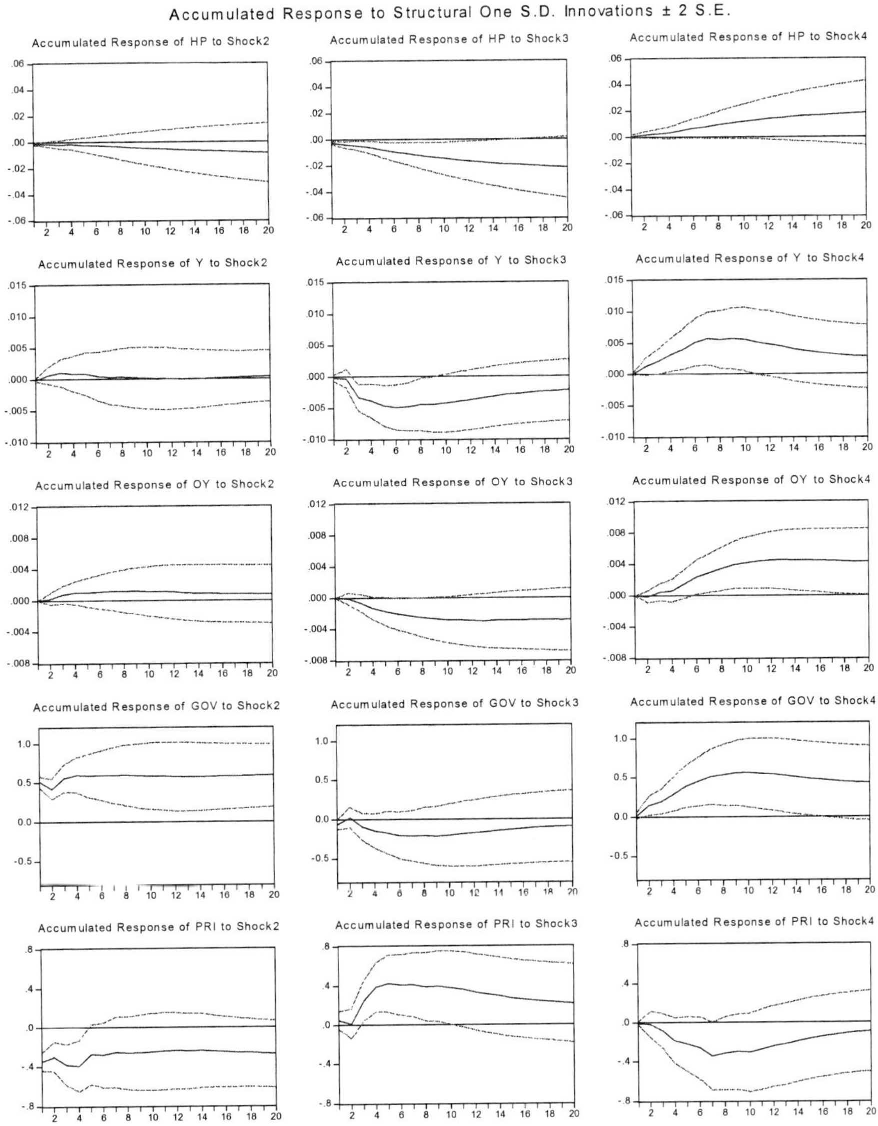

Shock2. U.S. Fiscal Tightening Shock.
Shock3: U.S. Monetary Tightening Shock.
Shock4: Foreign Official Investment Expansion Shock.

Figure 3. Impulse responses of the variables to each policy shock (1976:2-2008:3).

With regard to the impact on the business cycle, we notice that the U.S. fiscal policy shock does not have significant impact on U.S. house price (*HP*), U.S.

GDP (*Y*), and overseas GDP (*OY*)[8]. This is because although fiscal expansion reduces the FF rate, it increases private net savings. The fiscal effect may depend on private sector expectations of the debt implications. The estimated results seem to be supportive of the Ricardian effects. Thus, we cannot expect the U.S. fiscal policy to attain the set goal[9].

On the other hand, with regard to the impact on external balance, we find that a 1% increase in U.S. fiscal deficit will lead to a 1.1% decrease in the U.S. fiscal balance to GDP ratio(*GOV*) and a 0.5% increase in the private balance to GDP ratio (*PRI*) in the first 3 years. This leads to a 0.7% decrease in the U.S. current account to GDP ratio (*CA*).

Following this, we assess the impact of the U.S. monetary policy (shock 3). We find that the policy of easing the U.S. monetary situation can almost significantly increase the U.S. house price (*HP*), U.S. GDP(*Y*), and overseas GDP (*OY*). A 1% decrease in the FF rate will increase the U.S. house price by 2.1%, and expand the U.S. GDP and overseas GDP by 0.5% and 0.4%, respectively in the first 3 years. This results in the expansion of global GDP by 0.4%.

Therefore, we can expect the U.S. monetary policy to attain the set goal. However, the major problem with this policy is that there is little room for cutting the FF rate further. The FF rate is almost zero since December 2008.

On the other hand, with regard to the impact on external balance, a 1% decrease in FF rate will lead to a 0.2% increase in the fiscal balance to GDP ratio (*GOV*) and a 0.4% decrease in the private balance to GDP ratio (*PRI*) in the first 3 years. This results in a 0.2% decrease in the U.S. current account to GDP ratio (*CA*)[10].

Finally, we assess the impact of the foreign official investment policy (shock 4). Under the foreign official policy shock, an expansion in the investment can increase U.S. house price (*HP*), U.S. GDP (*Y*), and overseas GDP (*OY*). The estimated results support signaling channel hypothesis holds for the foreign official investment in U.S. treasury securities. We find that a 10% increase in the

---

[8] According to the estimated results, if *GOV* decrease by 1%, the FF rate will decrease by 1% in the first four quarters. However, as the fiscal expansion leads to an increase in *PRI*, the U.S. GDP will not increase.

[9] We estimated the model by replacing *GOV* and *PRI* with the first differences of the natural logarithms of U.S. real government expenditure (*GOVGE*) or first differences of natural logarithms of U.S. real government revenue (*GOVRE*), and the U.S. current account to GDP ratio (*CA*), respectively. The effect of fiscal variables on the U.S. GDP was as expected but was not significant. However ,as IMF (2008) points out, one concern is that separating out changes in discretionary fiscal policy (policy shock) and from automatic stabilizers and evaluating their effects is too difficult. There is room for further examinations. As for the relationship between fiscal policy and the current account, we found that fiscal tightening significantly improved the current account.

investment in U.S. treasury securities will increase the U.S. house price by 3.3%, expand U.S. GDP by 1.2%, overseas GDP by 1.1%. This results in the growth of world GDP by 1.1%.

On the other hand, with regard to the impact on external balance, a 10% increase in investment will increase the fiscal balance to GDP ratio (*GOV*) by 1.3% point and decrease the private balance to GDP ratio (*PRI*) by 0.7% in the first 3 years. This results in an improvement in the U.S. current account (*CA*) of 0.6%.

We can expect the foreign official policy to attain the goal of recovering the world economy while maintaining a sustainable U.S. current account deficit.

3.2. Variance Decompositions

Next, we focus on the results of the variance decomposition. The relative importance of the contribution of the seven shocks to the variance of each endogenous variable can be deduced by decomposing the forecast error variances. Table 1 provides this information.

With regard to the variance in U.S. house price (*HP*), the monetary policy shock (shock 3) explains around 10 to 17% of the variance in *HP*. On the other hand, the foreign official investment shock (shock4) explains around 12% of the variance of *HP* in the long run.

With regard to the variance in the U.S. GDP (*Y*), the monetary policy shock (shock3) explains the highest percentage of the variance in the U.S. GDP, apart from its own shock. Further, we note that the foreign official investment shock (shock4) accounts for the variance of the U.S. GDP(*Y*) better than U.S. fiscal policy shock (shock 2) in the long run.

Regarding the variance in overseas GDP (*OY*), we find that the largest share of shock to *OY*, apart from its own shock, is the foreign official investment policy (shock 4).

These results suggest that an increase in the foreign official purchases of U.S. treasury securities is important to attain the recovery of the economies of the U.S. and the rest of the world.

With regard to the variance in the U.S. fiscal balance (*GOV*), the contribution of the foreign official investment shock (shock 4) is larger than that of the monetary policy shock (shock 3) in the long run. This suggests that an increase in foreign official investment is also important for improving the U.S. fiscal balance.

---

[10] The result that U.S. monetary easing leads to an expansion of the current account deficit in the mid-term is consistent with Nishigaki (2009), who uses a similar SVAR model including real effective exchange rate.

Table 1. Variance decomposition

shock		HP	GOV	FFR	BFO	OY	Y	PRI
Variance Decomposition of HP:								
Period	S.E.	Shock1	Shock2	Shock3	Shock4	Shock5	Shock6	Shock7
1	0.01	85.60	1.69	10.74	1.01	0.01	0.95	0.00
2	0.01	80.51	1.55	11.97	2.26	0.21	1.24	2.27
4	0.01	78.10	1.47	12.04	3.11	0.23	3.19	1.86
8	0.01	68.76	1.75	15.43	9.29	0.47	2.22	2.08
12	0.01	65.32	2.09	16.25	11.42	0.56	1.90	2.45
20	0.01	63.93	2.51	16.65	11.91	0.59	1.76	2.65
Variance Decomposition of GOV:								
Period	S.E.	Shock1	Shock2	Shock3	Shock4	Shock5	Shock6	Shock7
1	0.56	10.83	82.24	1.36	0.13	0.08	5.36	0.00
2	0.60	9.93	74.91	3.36	4.49	0.70	6.21	0.39
4	0.65	9.31	68.10	6.86	6.51	1.34	7.06	0.82
8	0.67	9.01	64.04	6.85	9.93	1.97	6.95	1.24
12	0.67	9.50	63.26	6.89	9.98	1.96	7.10	1.31
20	0.68	9.81	62.54	7.04	10.24	1.96	7.08	1.33
Variance Decomposition of FFR:								
Period	S.E.	Shock1	Shock2	Shock3	Shock4	Shock5	Shock6	Shock7
1	0.89	1.94	10.45	80.82	0.02	0.10	6.67	0.00
2	0.97	10.57	10.02	67.90	1.11	0.46	9.92	0.03
4	1.06	11.65	10.07	65.20	2.87	0.75	9.28	0.20
8	1.12	14.11	9.16	59.02	6.01	1.16	9.67	0.87
12	1.14	14.58	8.93	57.54	7.01	1.18	9.46	1.30
20	1.15	15.02	8.93	57.04	7.11	1.18	9.36	1.36
Variance Decomposition of BFO:								
Period	S.E.	Shock1	Shock2	Shock3	Shock4	Shock5	Shock6	Shock7
1	0.04	0.15	1.15	0.02	98.60	0.00	0.08	0.00
2	0.04	0.40	1.16	0.02	96.93	0.72	0.25	0.53
4	0.05	0.36	1.18	0.90	88.80	2.34	1.68	4.74
8	0.05	1.00	1.43	1.41	81.73	3.05	6.06	5.32
12	0.05	1.19	1.52	1.69	81.16	3.09	6.05	5.31
20	0.05	1.21	1.53	1.71	81.07	3.09	6.07	5.31
Variance Decomposition of OY:								
Period	S.E.	Shock1	Shock2	Shock3	Shock4	Shock5	Shock6	Shock7
1	0.00	0.00	0.00	0.00	0.00	100.00	0.00	0.00
2	0.00	2.97	0.46	0.04	0.13	94.92	0.50	0.97
4	0.00	6.17	2.08	4.53	2.18	80.45	3.68	0.91
8	0.00	7.49	1.82	5.67	11.45	68.08	4.19	1.30
12	0.00	7.40	1.84	5.76	12.92	66.16	4.28	1.64
20	0.00	7.40	1.90	5.75	12.94	65.91	4.42	1.68
Variance Decomposition of Y:								
Period	S.E.	Shock1	Shock2	Shock3	Shock4	Shock5	Shock6	Shock7
1	0.01	1.37	0.03	0.17	0.02	1.40	97.01	0.00
2	0.01	4.65	1.11	0.16	2.79	2.55	88.58	0.15
4	0.01	4.66	1.18	16.27	5.06	4.04	67.86	0.92
8	0.01	7.07	1.36	15.80	8.12	5.26	61.35	1.03
12	0.01	8.12	1.35	15.63	8.38	5.13	60.19	1.20
20	0.01	8.77	1.37	15.71	9.03	5.06	58.81	1.26
Variance Decomposition of PRI:								
Period	S.E.	Shock1	Shock2	Shock3	Shock4	Shock5	Shock6	Shock7
1	0.64	0.63	28.89	0.59	0.01	0.23	16.05	53.60
2	0.67	4.27	26.93	0.84	0.03	1.12	15.90	50.90
4	0.77	4.73	21.65	13.31	2.55	4.93	12.98	39.84
8	0.81	6.16	22.01	12.40	3.91	6.45	12.44	36.63
12	0.81	6.77	21.61	12.36	4.18	6.35	12.61	36.13
20	0.82	7.21	21.32	12.46	4.61	6.29	12.47	35.64

3.3. Robustness Check

We examined the robustness of the important role of the foreign official purchases of U.S. treasury securities (*BFO*) for recovering the U.S. economy. First we estimated the model with the sample of 1976:2-2000:4 in order to check the impact of the boom and bust in the U.S. housing market around the 2000s. Figure 4 reports the impulse responses.

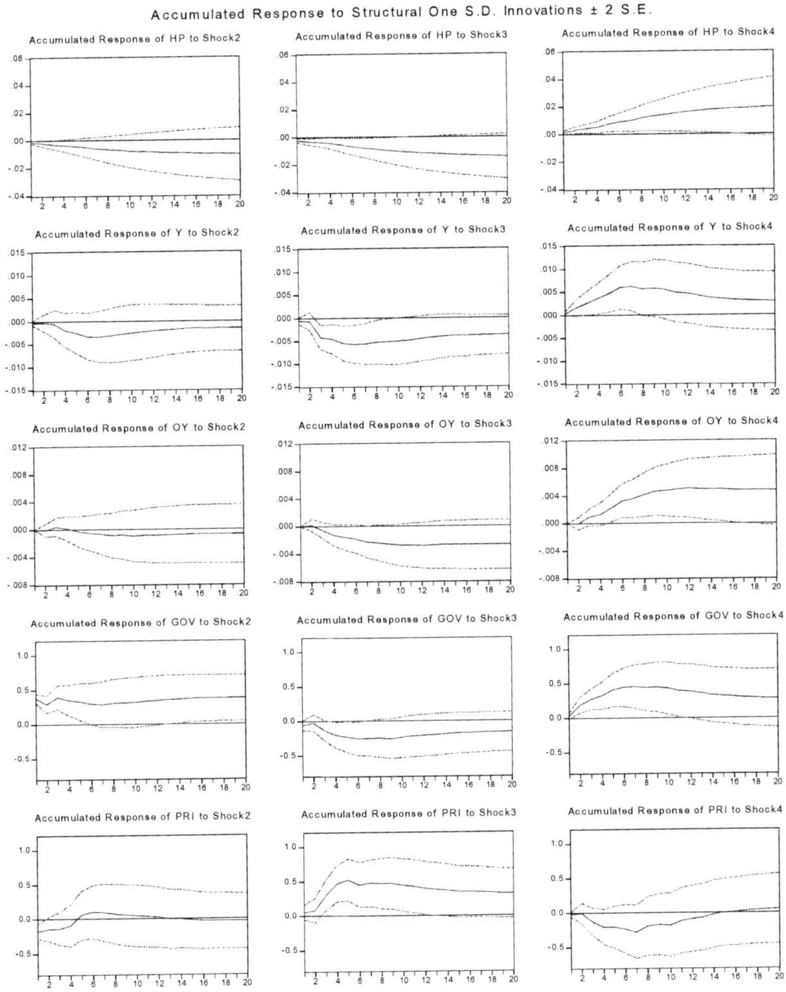

Shock2. U.S. Fiscal Tightening Shock.
Shock3: U.S. Monetary Tightening Shock.
Shock4: Foreign Official Investment Expansion Shock.

Figure 4. Impulse responses of the variables to each policy shock (1976:2-2000:4).

We notice that the main results estimated for the 1976:2-2008:3 period are almost all maintained in this figure.

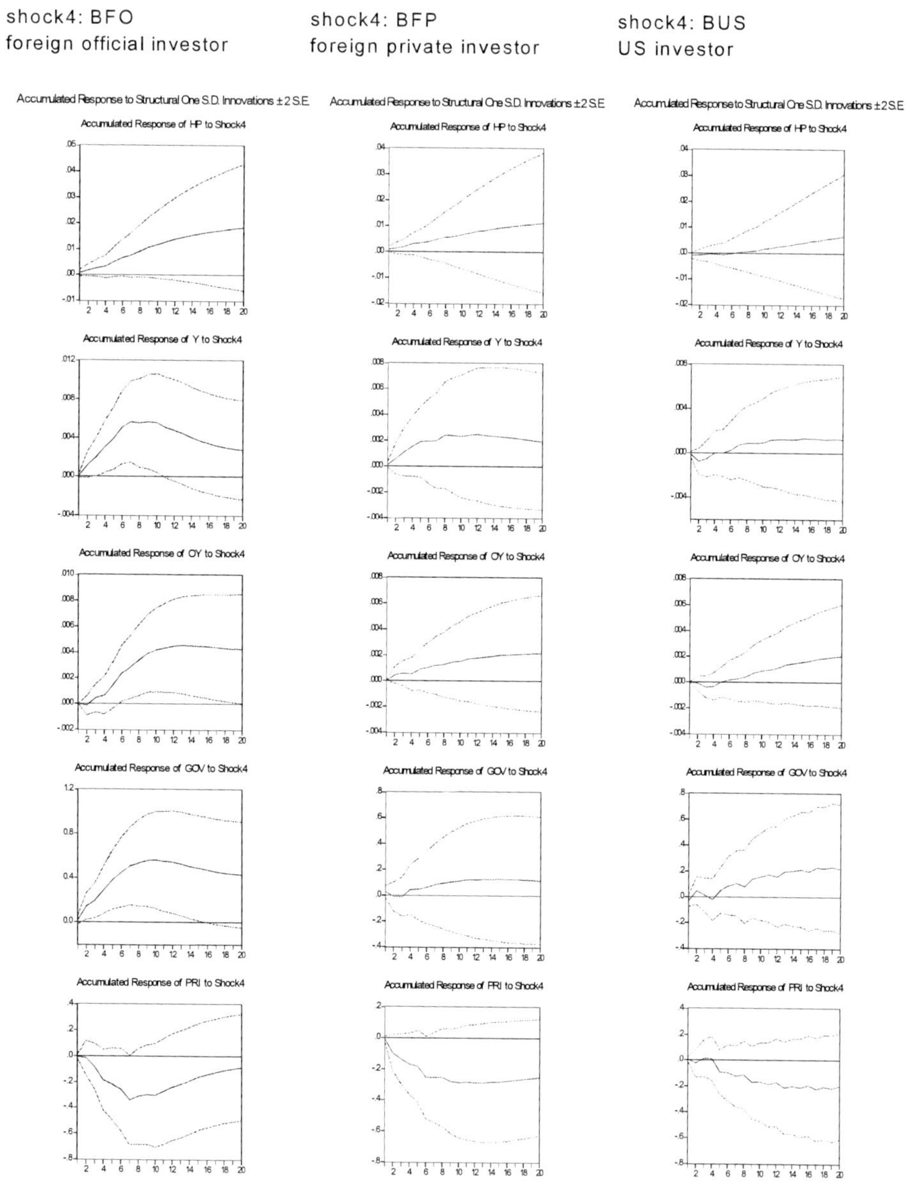

Figure 5. Impulse responses of the variables to positive shock to the investment in the U.S. treasury securities.

Second we estimated the similar models by changing the composition of holders of U.S. treasury securities. Here, we consider as the holders of the U.S. treasury securities, foreign private investor (*BFP*) and the U.S. investors (*BUS*), other than the foreign official investor (*BFO*)[11]. Figure 5 shows the impulse responses to the positive shocks to *BFO*, *BFP* and *BUS*. As the Figure 5 shows, the impacts of a positive shock to *BFO* on *Y*, *OY*, *GOV* and *PRI* differ clearly from those to *BFP* or *BUS* on them. These results may be because the foreign official purchases of U.S. treasury securities can give a signaling effect on the government bond market.

Third, we estimated the six-variable SVAR model including the first difference of U.S. 10-year treasury yield (TS10) with the ordering of {*BFO, TS10, HP, Y, GOV, PRI*} in order to investigate the impact the foreign official purchases of U.S. treasury securities have on U.S. treasury yields[12]. Our basic conclusion remains the same. As shown in Figure 6, the positive shock to *BFO* will significantly decrease the U.S. 10-year treasury yield in the short term, consistent with Warnack and Warnack (2006) and almost significantly increase U.S. house price, U.S. GDP and U.S. fiscal balance to GDP in the medium term. The U.S. current account will improve in the long run.

4. Impacts of the Fall in U.S. House Prices and the Various Policies

Here, we will simulate the effect of three policies on the U.S. GDP, non-US GDP, the U.S. fiscal balance to GDP and the U.S. private balance to GDP based on the result of the impulse response. We can find the movements of the growth rate of world economy and the U.S. current account balance to GDP ratio.

Figure 7 illustrates the future time path of each variable to given shocks as accumulated responses.

Case 1 shows the impacts of the negative shock to U.S. housing price. The size of shock given to the house price is 1 % decline[13].

In this case, the U.S. private savings will increase because of reductions in housing wealth. The U.S. GDP will continue to decline for the first 3 quarters and the non-US GDP will not recover the initial level in the long run.

---

[11] *BFP* and *BUS* are obtained from Flow of Funds of the United States in the Fed. We estimated with the first differences of natural logarithms.

[12] The structural shocks are identified through a Cholesky decomposition of innovations .

[13] The average growth rate of U.S. house price during 2007Q4- 2008Q3 is minus 1%.

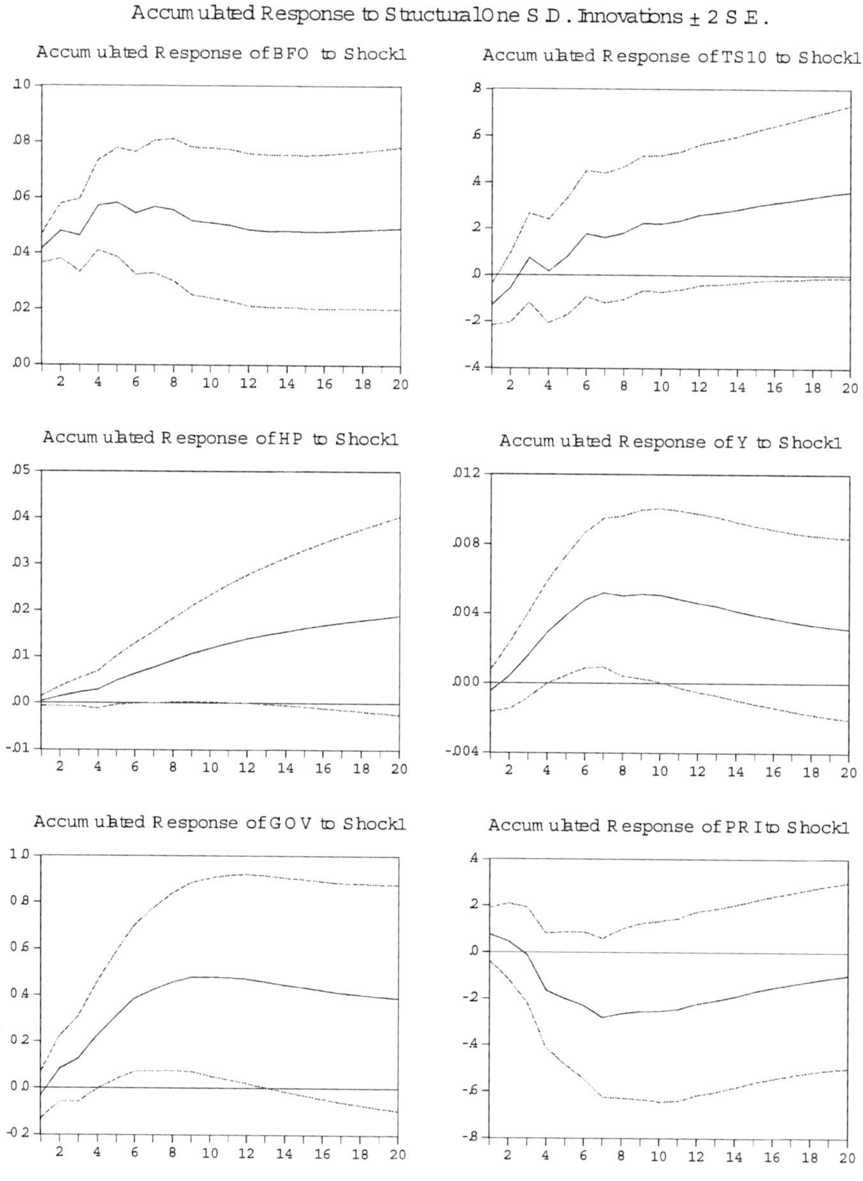

Figure 6. Impulse responses of the variables to positive shock to *BFO*.

The U.S. fiscal balance will deteriorate, resulting in the expansion of U.S. current account deficits in the long run.

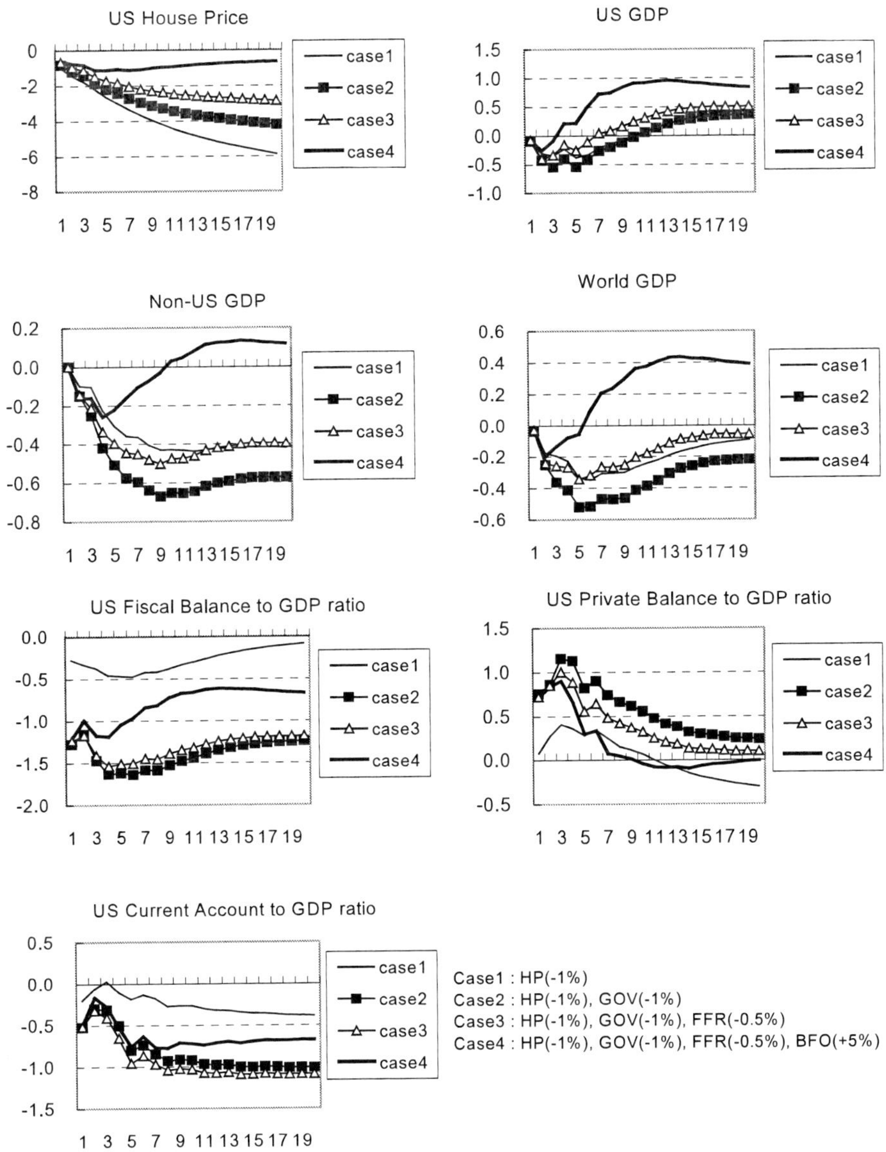

Figure 7. The Scenarios for global economy depending on policy choices.

Case 2 represents the impacts of the negative shocks to the U.S. house price and U.S. fiscal balance. Concretely, the sizes of the given shocks to their variables are a 1% decline in U.S. house price and a 1% point decrease in GOV at the same time.

In this situation, the U.S. private savings will increase more than Case 1 because of Ricardian effect by the fiscal easing shock. And the U.S. GDP will not recover for the first 11 quarters. The non-US GDP will decline more than Case 1. This may be because the federal funds rate cut caused by the fiscal expansions leads to the depreciation of the U.S. dollar, resulting in drop of the export competitiveness of the non-US. In Case 2, the U.S. fiscal balance will deteriorate and expand the U.S. current account deficits more than Case 1.

Case 3 is the combination of the negative shocks to U.S. house price and U.S. fiscal balance and the FF rate. Concretely, the sizes of the given shocks to their variables are a 1% decline in U.S. house price, a 1% point decrease in GOV, and a 0.5% point decrease in the FF rate simultaneously. In this case, the impact of fiscal policy is expected to increase by monetary accommodation, alleviating the crowding-out effect.

In the estimated SVAR model, the FF rate will decrease by 0.2% as the responses to a 1% negative shock to U.S. house price and decrease by 0.8% as the responses to a 1% point negative shock to GOV in the first quarter. Here we consider the rate cut by further 0.5%, in addition to such reaction effect of 1% caused by the changes of HP and GOV. The size of 0.5% rate cut is comparable to the effect that offsets the negative pressure to the U.S. GDP by an increase in the U.S. private savings that the U.S. fiscal expansion causes. In this case, the U.S. GDP will almost recover the initial level without shock in two year.

The movements of the U.S. fiscal balance, private balance and current account will change little from Case 2.

Case 4 is the combination of the negative shocks to U.S. house price, U.S. fiscal balance, the FF rate and the positive shock to foreign official investment in U.S. treasury securities. Concretely, the sizes of the given shocks to their variables are a 1% decline in U.S. house price, a 1% point decrease in GOV, a 0.5% point reduction in the FF rate, and the recent growth rate of 5% increase in foreign official investment in the U.S. treasury securities at the same time[14].

In this condition, U.S. house price will stop dropping in the first 8 quarters and the U.S. and non-US GDP will recover gradually.

While the private balance does not change dramatically from Case 3, the U.S. fiscal balance improves more than Case 2 and Case 3 due to economic recovery. As a result, the U.S. current account will improve more than Case 2 and Case 3.

---

[14] The average growth rate of foreign official investment in U.S. treasury for 2007Q4- 2008Q3 is 5.5%.

Thus, we find the foreign official investment in U.S. treasury securities can contribute to bolster the world economy without expanding the U.S. current account deficits. It is very important to maintain the stable investment in U.S. government bonds from foreign official institutions.

Conclusion

The objective of this paper was to examine the impact of some possible options (the U.S. fiscal stimulus, U.S. monetary easing, and foreign official initiative to purchase U.S. treasury securities) on the economies of the U.S. and the rest of the world and on global imbalances by using the structural vector autoregression (SVAR) model.

Several important conclusions were derived from this analysis.

First, the empirical results show that an expansionary fiscal policy does not have significant impact on U.S. house prices, U.S. GDP, or overseas GDP. This is because the U.S. private net savings are likely to increase significantly. Therefore, the fiscal policy may not be a very reliable instrument for ushering in global economic recovery. In particular, U.S. households may not increase consumption because of fears with regard to the future.

Second, a reduction in the FF rate may increase the U.S. house price, U.S. GDP, and overseas GDP. On the other hand, the reduction in the FF rate will decrease the U.S. current account by further decreasing the U.S. private balance. The problem herein is that there is little room for any further cuts in the policy rate.

Third, an increase in the foreign official purchases of U.S. treasury securities can underpin U.S. house prices, U.S. GDP, and overseas GDP. Moreover, it can improve the U.S. current account by increasing the U.S. fiscal balance. This policy will significantly help bolster global demand without expanding the U.S. current account deficit.

Thus, the role of foreign monetary authorities is very important with regard to the recovery of the world economy.

However, many open questions remain.

First we need to consider the microeconomic factors behind the current crisis. We find that the crisis can be traced to a combination of multiple market failures as well as regulatory failures. The rapidly falling market values of credit instruments hit both the net worth and the profitability of the banking system.

Although the correction in U.S. house price is thought to be the source of continuing losses to the financial system in this paper, it will be important to investigate the negative feedback between deteriorating financial conditions and weakening economies for closer analyses. The continuous declines in house prices could increase solvency problems for banks. On the other hand, the deterioration of the quality of banks' balance sheets could lead to decreased lending activity, resulting in the drop in GDP. In this way, the greatest policy priority for ensuring a durable economic recovery is restoring the health of the financial sector (IMF, 2009).

Second, although our model did not include non-U.S. policy variables except purchases of U.S. treasury securities in this paper, we need to consider the various policy responses around the world in order to simulate the future paths of the global economy more strictly. Many central banks continue to ease credit conditions and provide liquidity. And most G20 countries have contributed to fiscal efforts.

Third, our analysis argues about the so-called conventional actions of the Fed and does not cover the impact of unconventional monetary policy reactions[15].

Better understanding is needed with regard to the impacts of the new U.S. monetary policy that increases the size of the Fed's balance sheet on the long-term interest rates and the economy. Further, the difference in the impacts of the purchases of U.S. treasury securities by the Fed and by the foreign monetary authorities on the government bond market also needs to be studied. These are left for future empirical studies.

Acknowledgments

The author gratefully acknowledges the valuable comments of Prof. Eiji Ogawa, Prof. Takashi Misumi and the seminar participants at the Graduate School of Commerce and Management in Hitotsubashi University. Any remaining errors are the author's own responsibility.

[15] The Fed decided on March 2009 to increase the size of the Federal Reserve's balance sheet further by purchasing up to an additional $750 billion of agency mortgage-backed securities, bringing its total purchases of these securities to up to $1.25 trillion this year, and to increase its purchases of agency debt this year by up to $100 billion to a total of up to $200 billion. Moreover, the FOMC announced plans to purchase up to $300 billion of longer-term Treasury securities over the next six months to help improve conditions in private credit markets

Data Appendix

HP is the U.S. house price index computed by the Office of Federal Housing Enterprise Oversight (OFHEO). Data are seasonally adjusted.

GOV is the U.S. fiscal balance to GDP ratio. The fiscal balance is constructed by gross government saving minus gross government investment obtained from National Income and Product Accounts (NIPA) table 5.1 at the Web site of the U.S. Bureau of Economic Analysis. Data are seasonally adjusted at annual rates.

PRI is the U.S. private balance to GDP ratio. The private balance is constructed by gross private saving minus gross private domestic investment obtained from National Income and Product Accounts (NIPA) table 5.1 at the Web site of the U.S. Bureau of Economic Analysis. Data are seasonally adjusted at annual rates.

FFR represents the effective federal funds rate. Data were obtained from the Web site of the Fed. .

BFO represents the outstanding of the U.S. treasury securities that the foreign official sector holds obtained from Flow of Funds of the United States in the Fed. Data are from Datastream. Although we estimated similarly using the flow data as a GDP ratio, our basic conclusion changed little.

Y represents the U.S. real GDP obtained from National Income and Product Accounts (NIPA) at the Web site of the U.S. Bureau of Economic Analysis. Data are seasonally adjusted.

OY represents the constant price GDP of the non-U.S. OECD countries calculated by OECD. Data are seasonally adjusted from Datastream.

References

Afonso.A., and Sousa, R. M.(2009). The Macroeconomic Effects of Fiscal Policy, *ECB Working Paper,* No.**991**.

Baxter,M., and King,R. (1993). Fiscal Policy in General Equilibrium, *American Economic Review,* **83**. 315-334.

Bems R., Dedola L., and Smets,F. (2007). U.S. Imbalances, The role of technology and policy. *ECB Working Paper,* No.**719**.

Bussiere M., Fratzscher,M., and Muller,G.J. (2007). Productivity Shocks, Budget Deficits and the Current Account. *Journal of International Money and Finance*, **26**(4), 523-545.

Christiano,L.,and Eichenbaum,M. (1992). Current Real Business Cycles Theories and Aggregate Labor Market Fluctuations, *American Economic Review,***82**. 430-450.

Cline,W.R. (2005). *The United States as a Debtor Nation: Risk and Policy Reform.* Institute for International Economics, Washington DC: Institute for International Economics.

Chinn M.D. (2005). Getting Serious about the Twin Deficits. *Council on Foreign Relations Special Report.*

Chinn M.D., and Ito, H. (2005). Current Account Balances, Financial Development and Institutions: Assaying the World Savings Glut. *LaFollette School Working Paper* No. 2005-023; October.

Erceg, C.J., Guerrieri,L., and Gust, C. (2005). Expansionary Fiscal Shocks and the Trade Deficit. *FRB International Finance Discussion Paper* No. **825**.

Ferguson, R.W. (2005). U.*S. Current Account Deficits: Causes and Consequences.* Remarks at University of North Carolina, April 20.

IMF (2008). *World Economic Outlook.* October.

IMF (2009). *World Economic Outlook.* April.

Jarocinski M., and Smets,F. (2008). House Price and the Stance of Monetary Policy, *ECB Working Paper* No **891**.

Kim, S. and Roubini, N. (2008). Twin Deficits or Twin Divergence ? Fiscal Policy, Current Account, and Real Exchange Rate in the U.S., *Journal of International Economics* **74**, 362-383.

Nishigaki,H. (2009). How will the related variables change if global imbalances unwind? , *Economic Modelling* **26**(1) 206-212.

Warnack, F. E. and Warnack,V.C. (2006). International Capital Flows and U.S. Interest Rates, *FRB International Finance Discussion Paper* No. **840**.

In: Financial Markets and the Global Recession ISBN: 978-1-60741-921-1
Editors: B. Naas and J. Lysne

Chapter 5

VOLATILITY MODELS: FROM GARCH TO MULTI-HORIZON CASCADES

***Alexander Subbotin*[1,2,*], *Thierry Chauveau*[1,†] *and Kateryna Shapovalova*[1,‡]**
[1]University of Paris-1 (Panthèon-Sorbonne), France
[2]Higher School of Economics, France

Abstract

We overview different methods of modeling volatility of stock prices and exchange rates, focusing on their ability to reproduce the empirical properties in the corresponding time series. The properties of price fluctuations vary across the time scales of observation. The adequacy of different models for describing price dynamics at several time horizons simultaneously is the central topic of this study. We propose a detailed survey of recent volatility models, accounting for multiple horizons. These models are based on different and sometimes competing theoretical concepts. They belong either to GARCH or stochastic volatility model families and often borrow methodological tools from statistical physics. We compare their properties and comment on their practical usefulness and perspectives.

*E-mail address: alexander.subbotin@univ-paris1.fr
†E-mail address: thierry.chauveau@univ-paris1.fr
‡E-mail address: kateryna.shapovalova@univ-paris1.fr

Keywords: Volatility modeling, GARCH, stochastic volatility, volatility cascade, multiple horizons in volatility.

J.E.L. Classification: G10, C13.

1. Introduction

Modeling stock prices is essential in many areas of financial economics, such as derivatives pricing, portfolio management and financial risk follow-up. One of the most criticized drawbacks of the so-called "modern portfolio theory" (MPT), including the diversification principle of Markowitz (1952) and the capital asset pricing model by Sharpe (1964) and Lintner (1965), is the non-realistic assumption about stock price variability. Clearly, stock returns are not *iid* distributed Gaussian random variables, but alternatives to this assumption are numerous, sometimes complicated and application-dependent. In this paper we review empirical properties of stock price dynamics and various models, proposed to represent it, focusing on the most recent developments, concerning mainly multi-horizon and multifractal stochastic volatility processes.

The subject of this study is the variability of stock prices, referred to as volatility. Usually introduction of scientific terminology aims at making a general concept more precise, but this is rather an example of the contrary. Depending on the context and the point of view of the author, the term "volatility" in finance can stand for the variability of prices (in this sense we used it above), an estimate of standard deviation, financial risk in general, a parameter of a derivative pricing model or a stochastic process of particular form. We will continue using it in the most general sense, that is as a synonym of variability. Before reviewing volatility models, we examine in more detail the evolution of the notion itself. This will help for a better understanding of the logic of the evolution of the corresponding models.

One of the first interpretations of the term "volatility" is due to the fact that the name of variability phenomenon itself has been identified with the most elementary method of its quantitative measurement - standard deviation of stock returns. This interpretation is logically embedded in the concept of MPT, also called mean-variance theory, because under its assumptions these two parameters contain all relevant information about stock returns, distributed normally[1].

[1]In MPT a simplifying assumption, alternative to the normality of returns, is the quadratic form of the utility function of investors. However, the latter can hardly be justified.

Note that in Markowitz (1952) risk is modeled statically: returns on each stock are characterized by constant volatility (variance or standard deviation) and co-variances with the returns on other assets. So volatility can be seen as synonym for standard deviation, or as an estimate of a constant parameter in the simplest model of stock returns. This definition of volatility has deep roots and is still widely used among asset management professionals.

The appearance in 1973 of the option pricing models by Black and Scholes (1973) and Merton (1973) led to significant changes in the understanding of volatility. A continuous-time diffusion (geometric Brownian motion) is used to model stock prices:

$$\frac{dS_t}{S_t} = \mu dt + \sigma dW_t \tag{1}$$

with S_t the stock price, μ the drift parameter and W_t a Brownian motion. The parameter σ is called volatility because it characterizes the degree of variability. Since the log-returns, computed from stock prices that follow equation (1), are normally distributed, this model is also called a log-normal diffusion.

Very soon it became obvious that equation (1) poorly describes reality. Its parameters unambiguously define option prices for given exercise dates and strikes, so that volatility parameter can be inferred from observations of option prices by using the inverse of the Black-Scholes formula. An estimate obtained in this way is called implicd volatility as opposed to historical volatility, measured as the standard deviation of returns. Contrary to the predictions of the Black and Scholes model empirical results show that implied volatility varies for option contracts with different parameters. This phenomenon is known as volatility smile. Its name is due to a characteristic convex form of the plot of the estimate of σ as function of the option exercise price.

The above remark does not mean that implied volatility is useless. It has been shown that it contains information about future variability of returns and thus it is often used in forecasting. In derivatives pricing implied volatility is important because it allows to extrapolate the observed market data, e.g. option prices, for the evaluation of other financial instruments, e.g. over-the-counter options (see Dupire, 1993, 1994; Avellaneda et al., 1997). Despite these partial successes, a more adequate model than log-normal diffusion could still be useful in both derivatives pricing and asset management applications. In Merton (1973) volatility parameter is already allowed to vary in time. Even earlier Mandelbrot (1963) points to the empirical properties of stock returns that to not correspond to the log-normal diffusion model and proposes a wider class of

Levy-stable probability distributions. Further developments in the led to the understanding of volatility as a stochastic process and not merely as a parameter, even time-varying.

The meaning of the term "volatility" in finance has come full circle: from a general term for variability phenomenon to a statistical estimate, then a model parameter and finally a stochastic process, which again is supposed to characterize the whole structure of the stock price variability. More technically, the modern understanding of volatility can be characterized as a time structure of conditional second-order moments in the distribution of returns. In the simplest case of log-normal diffusion this structure is described by one parameter and in more complicated cases, by a separate stochastic process.

This paper starts with an overview of empirical properties of volatility, the so-called "stylized facts". Then we briefly discuss traditional approaches to its modeling - conditional heteroscedasticity and stochastic volatility, that reproduce empirical properties to some extent. Though many models are good enough to describe separate stylized facts, we show that none of them is quite sufficient to represent the whole structure of stock price variability. In particular, most traditional models do not allow for representing returns dynamics on multiple time horizons (e.g. from minutes to days and months) simultaneously, which is important both practically and theoretically. Stylized facts themselves have features specific to the frequency, at which price dynamics is observed. We analyze and compare recently proposed models of conditional heteroscedasticity and stochastic volatility, based on the multi-horizon approach, and discuss the main unsolved problems, related to them.

2. Empirical Properties of Volatility

Many empirical studies show that financial time series satisfy a number of general properties, referred to as stylized facts. A realistic model for prices is expected to reproduce these properties. We characterize them briefly, for a detailed survey on the subject see Cont (2001).

- **Excessive volatility.** The observed degree of variability in stock prices can hardly be explained by variations in fundamental economic factors. In particular, returns of large magnitude (positive and negative) are often hard to explain by arrival of new information about future cash flows (Cutler et al., 1989).

- **Absence of linear correlations in returns**. Stock returns, computed over sufficiently long time periods (several hours and more) display insignificant linear correlation. This results is in accordance with the stock market efficiency hypothesis by Fama (1970) and the main results of MPT, using martingale measures.

- **Clustering of volatility and long memory in absolute values of returns**. Time series of absolute values of returns is characterized by important autocorrelation, and the autocorrelation function (ACF) decays slowly with time lags (slower than geometric decay). Long periods of high and low volatility are observed (Bollerslev et al., 1992; Ding et al., 1993; Ding and Granger, 1996).

- **The link between the trading volume and volatility.** Volatility of returns is positively correlated with the trading volume, and the latter time series displays the same long memory properties as in the absolute returns (Lobato and Velasco, 2000).

- **Asymmetry and leverage in the dynamic structure of volatility**. Positive and negative returns of the same magnitude, observed over the past period, have different effects on current volatility (asymmetry). Current returns and future volatility are negatively correlated (leverage). Presence of the leverage effect implies the asymmetry but the inverse does not hold (Black, 1976).

- **Heavy tails in the distribution of returns.** Unconditional probability distribution of daily returns is characterized by heavy tails, i.e. high probability of observing extreme values, compared to the normal distribution (Mandelbrot, 1963; Fama, 1965).

- **The form of the probability distribution of returns varies across time intervals, over which returns are computed** (Ghashghaie et al., 1996; Arneodo et al., 1998). Distributions of log-returns over long time intervals are relatively close to the normal law, while returns over short time intervals (5 - 30 minutes) have very heavy tails.

Among these stylized facts we shall be particularly interested in the properties related to the ACF of returns and the form of the probability distribution of returns and their magnitudes. We start with a definition of the above-mentioned long memory phenomenon in terms of ACF.

A stationary stochastic process X_t with finite variance has long memory (or long-range dependence) if its autocorrelation function $C(\tau) = \text{corr}(X_t, X_{t-\tau})$ at $\tau \to \infty$ decays with the time lag according to the power low (i.e. at hyperbolic speed):

$$C(\tau) \sim \frac{L(\tau)}{\tau^{1-2d}}, \tag{2}$$

where $0 < d < \frac{1}{2}$ and where $L(\cdot)$ is some continuous function that for $\forall x > 0$ and $\tau \to \infty$ satisfies $\frac{L(xt)}{L(t)} \to 1$. The process has short memory if its ACF decays exponentially (with geometric speed), so that:

$$\exists A > 0, c \in (0,1) : |C(\tau)| \leq Ac^{\tau} \tag{3}$$

In this definition the technical condition, imposed on the function $L(\cdot)$, implies that for infinite lag τ this function changes infinitely slowly. Notice that the definition refers to the theoretical ACF of the time series model and not to its sample estimate. As we will see, in many cases the sample ACF has properties, similar to those implied by definition (2), but the theoretical ACF does not satisfy this definition.

Alternatively, long memory can be characterized by the power law divergence of the spectral density of the time series X_t at the origin:

$$\Psi_x(u) \sim c_\Psi |u|^{-\alpha} \tag{4}$$

with $\Psi_x(\cdot)$ - spectral density function, α - scaling parameter and c_Ψ - a constant.

To illustrate the empirical properties of returns we use two types of stock index data: high frequency (intraday) observations over a relatively short time period (French CAC40 index) and daily observations for very long time period (Dow Jones Industrial Average Index, DJIA). We will see that the main empirical patterns are similar for these very different examples.

The return at time $t \in 1 \ldots T$ over the interval τ is defined as the change in the logarithm of price S:

$$r_t = \ln(S_t) - \ln(S_{t-\tau}). \tag{5}$$

As a measure of volatility we take the magnitude of return $|r_t|$. Note that similar results could be obtained for squared returns and, most generally, for $|r_t|^\alpha$

(Bollerslev et al., 1992; Ding et al., 1993; Ding and Granger, 1996), but for $\alpha = 1$ the long memory properties are more pronounced (Ding et al., 1993; Ghysels et al., 2006; Forsberg and Ghysels, 2007).

Figures 1 and 2 represent the time series of index values and returns, computed over different time intervals. For the CAC40 index we compute 15-minutes, daily and weekly returns, and for the DJIA index - daily, monthly and quarterly returns. On both data sets the phenomenon of volatility clustering can be easily identified: long-lasting and persistent periods of returns with high magnitude (positive and negative) alternate with low volatility periods. High volatility is rarely observed on up-going market trend. Large fluctuations are characteristic of trend reversals and slumps.

Now consider the form of the probability distribution of returns, computed over different time intervals (Figures 3 and 4). For 15-minutes returns on the CAC40 index the distribution is clearly leptokurtic: the deviation from the normal curve in the tails is significant. As the frequency of observations is reduced this deviation decreases. This can be interpreted as an effect of the central limit theorem, though the the adequacy of hypotheses underlying its various forms is subject to debate among researchers[2]. For weekly returns fat tails are still observed, especially in the left side of the distribution, corresponding to negative returns. However, a relatively small number of observations at this frequency (590) does not allow a precise judgment about the distribution of extreme values in returns. For the DJIA case we have a larger sample (2953 observations). As in the previous case, extreme negative returns are observed much more frequently than the normal probability model predicts. For monthly returns the deviation in tails is smaller, but the size of the sample is not sufficient for final conclusions.

We find that, as the time horizon of returns increases, the distribution approaches to the normal law, but this convergence is very slow. Indeed, monthly logarithmic returns are obtained by summing up more than six hundred 15-minutes returns, so if assumptions of the classical central limit theorem were satisfied, the distribution would have been very close to Gaussian. But fat tails do not disappear even at that horizon. As we will show later, the question of whether a sufficiently long horizon, at which returns are normal, exists is important for building models of volatility at multiple horizons. Clearly, a strict

[2]The distribution of logarithmic returns at finite horizons can hardly be expected to follow the normal law exactly due to the fact that the support of normal distribution is the whole real line, while realizations of infinite prices of assets are impossible

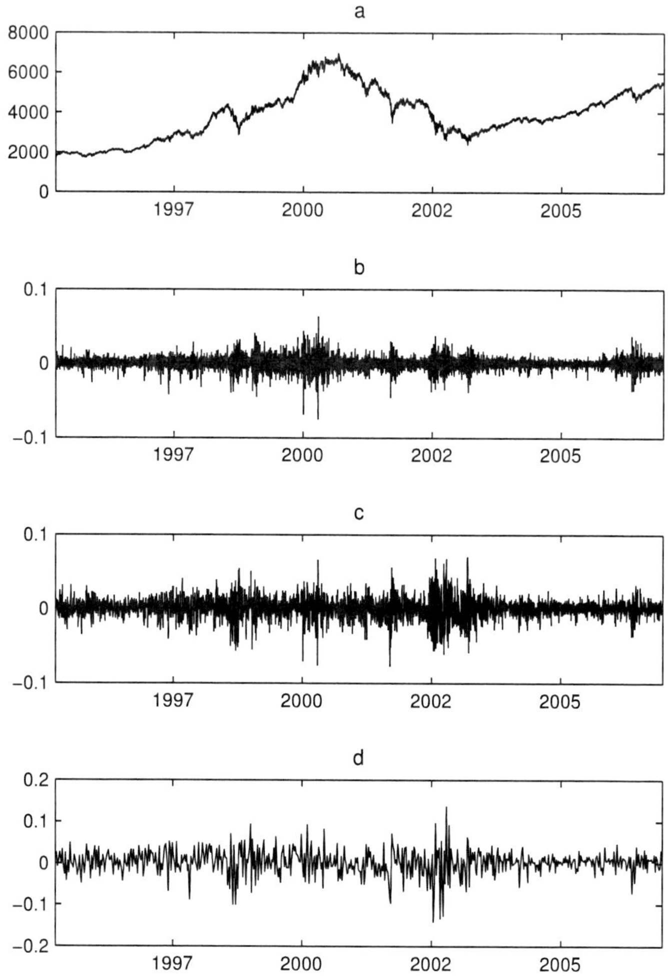

Source: Euronext, CAC40 index from 20/03/1995 to 29/12/2006 at 15-minutes intervals, 100881 observations. the figure shows a: index values; b: 15-minute returns, 100880 observations; c: daily returns, 2953 observations; d: weekly returns, 590 observations.

Figure 1. Returns on the CAC40 Index.

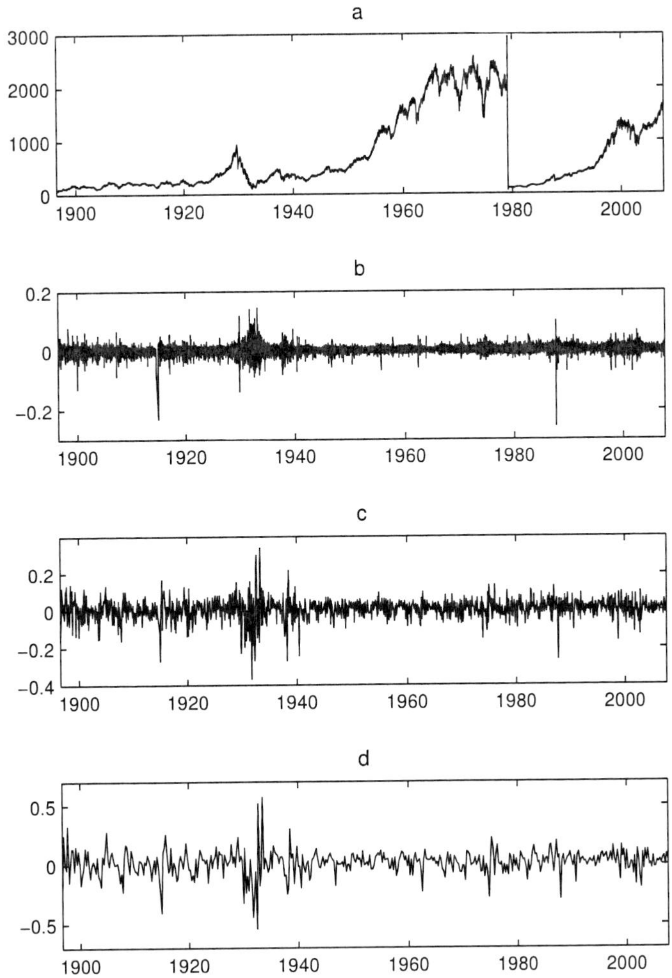

Source: Dow Jones Indexes, daily values of the DJIA index from 26/05/1896 to 10/10/2007, 28864 observations. The figure shows a: index values (for visualization purposes the values of index are reset to 100 at the beginning of the period and then again at 01/01/1979); b: daily returns, 28863 observations; c: monthly returns, 2953 observations; d: quarterly returns, 444 observations.

Figure 2. Returns on the DJIA Index.

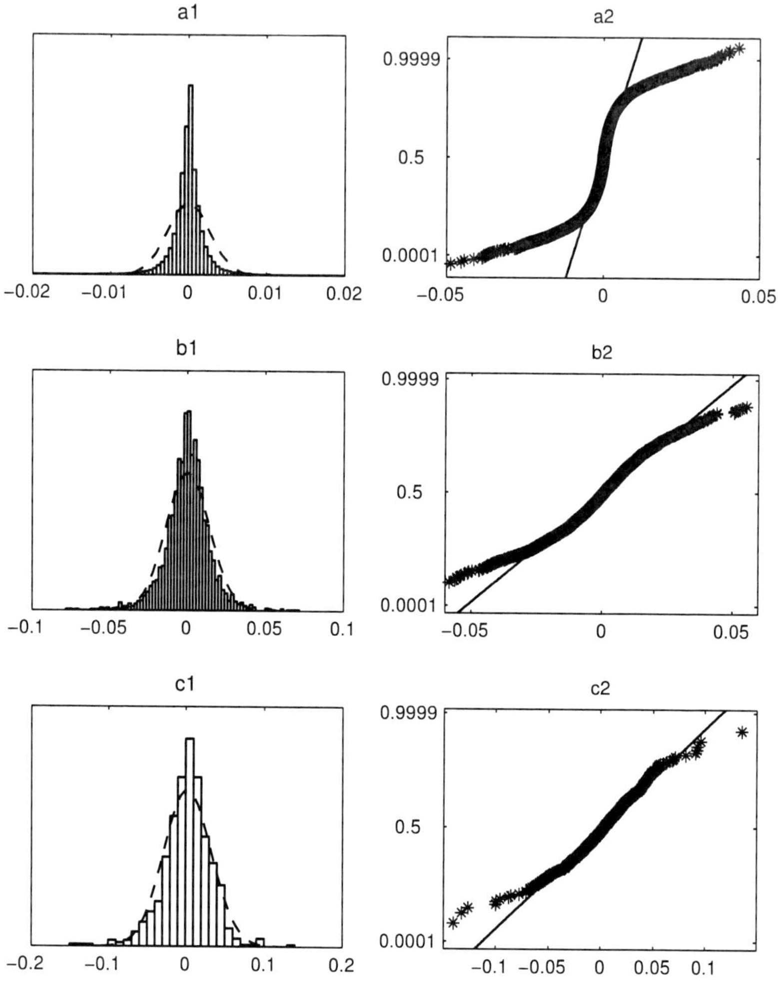

Source: Euronext, values of index CAC40 from 20/03/1995 to 29/12/2006 at 15-minutes intervals, 100881 observations. The figure shows a1: histogram of the distribution density and its log-normal approximation for 15-minutes returns, 100880 observations; a2: probability plot for the same data, i.e. empirical cumulative distribution function (cdf), compared with the theoretical normal cdf (if the normal distribution perfectly approximates the empirical distribution, all points are on the diagonal straight line); b1,2: the same for daily returns, 2953 observations; c1,2: the same for weekly returns, 590 observations.

Figure 3. Probability Distribution of Returns on the CAC40 Index.

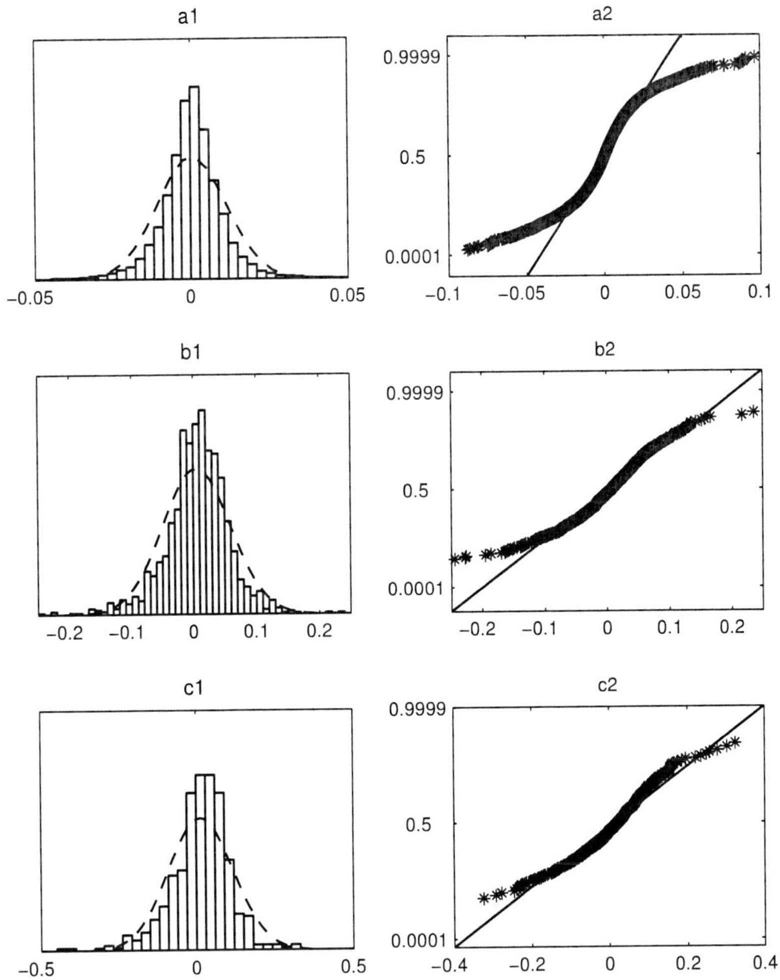

Source: Dow Jones Indexes, daily values of the DJIA index from 26/05/1896 to 10/10/2007, 28864 observations. The figure shows a1: histogram of the distribution density and its log-normal approximation for daily returns, 28863 observations; a2: probability plot for the same data, i.e. empirical cumulative distribution function (cdf), compared with the theoretical normal cdf (if the normal distribution perfectly approximates the empirical distribution, all points are on the diagonal straight line); b1,2: the same for monthly returns, 2953 observations; c1,2: the same for quarterly returns, 590 observations.

Figure 4. Probability Distribution of Returns on the DJIA Index.

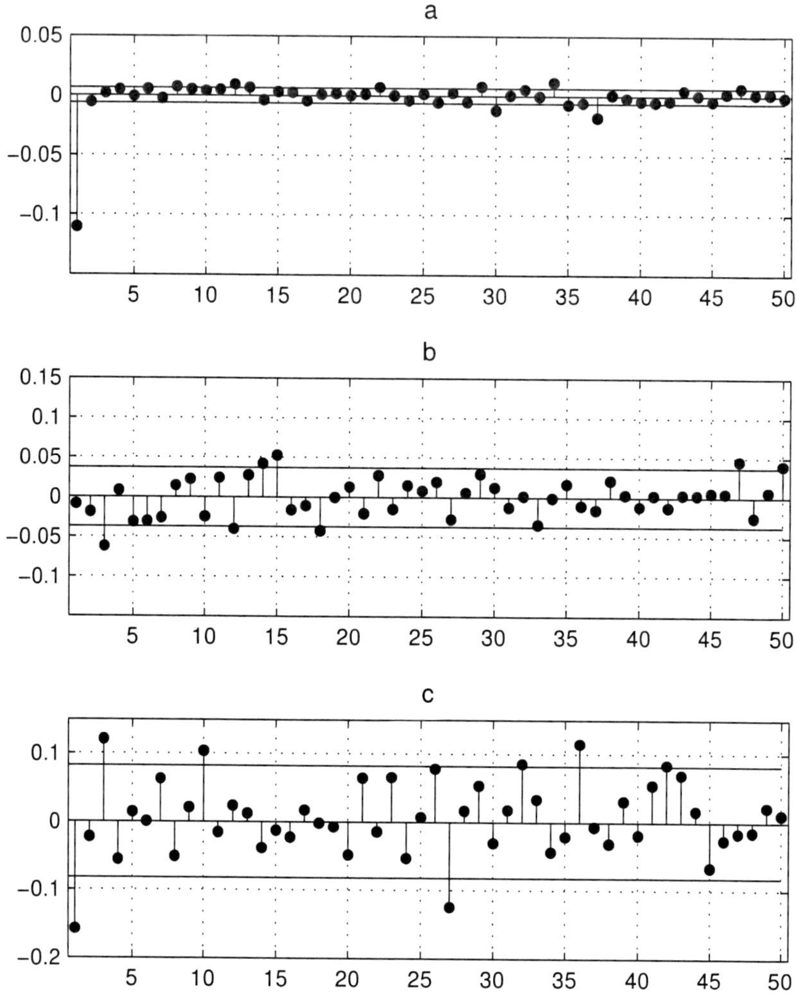

Source: Euronext, values of index CAC40 from 20/03/1995 to 29/12/2006 at 15-minutes intervals, 100881 observations. The figure shows a: ACF for 15-minutes returns, 100880 observations; b: the same for daily returns ,2953 observations; c: the same for weekly returns, 590 observations. Horizontal solid lines show confidence intervals for autocorrelations, computed under assumption that returns are normal white noise.

Figure 5. Sample ACF for the Returns on the CAC40 Index.

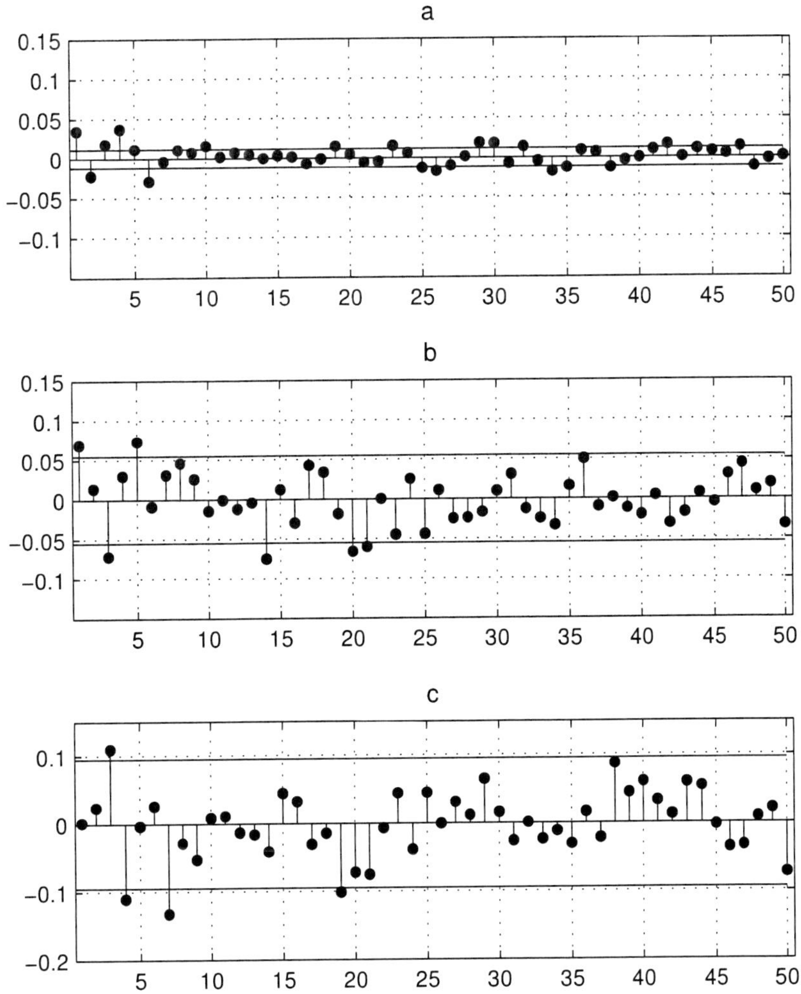

Source: Dow Jones Indexes, daily values of the DJIA index from 26/05/1896 to 10/10/2007, 28864 observations. The figure shows a: ACF for daily returns, 28863 observations; b: the same for daily returns ,2953 observations; c: the same for quarterly returns, 590 observations. Horizontal solid lines show confidence intervals for autocorrelations, computed under assumption that returns are normal white noise.

Figure 6. Sample ACF for the Returns on the DJIA Index.

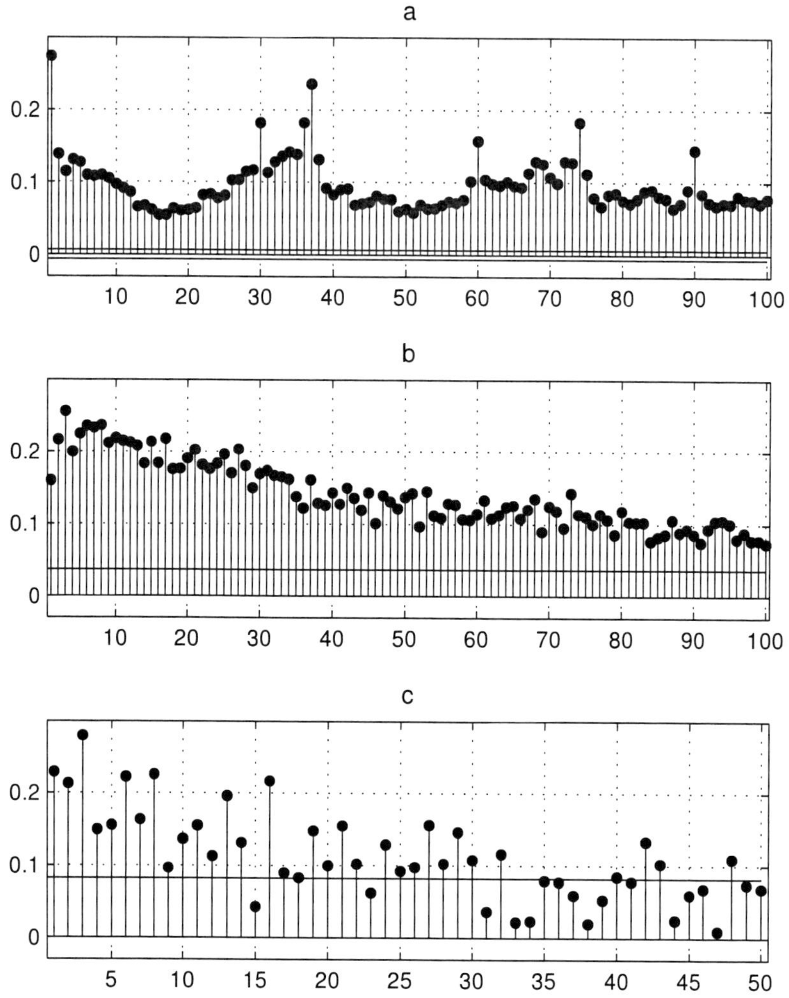

Source: Euronext, values of index CAC40 from 20/03/1995 to 29/12/2006 at 15-minutes intervals, 100881 observations. The same as on Figure 5, but instead of returns their absolute values are used.

Figure 7. Sample ACF for the Magnitudes of Returns on the CAC 40 Index.

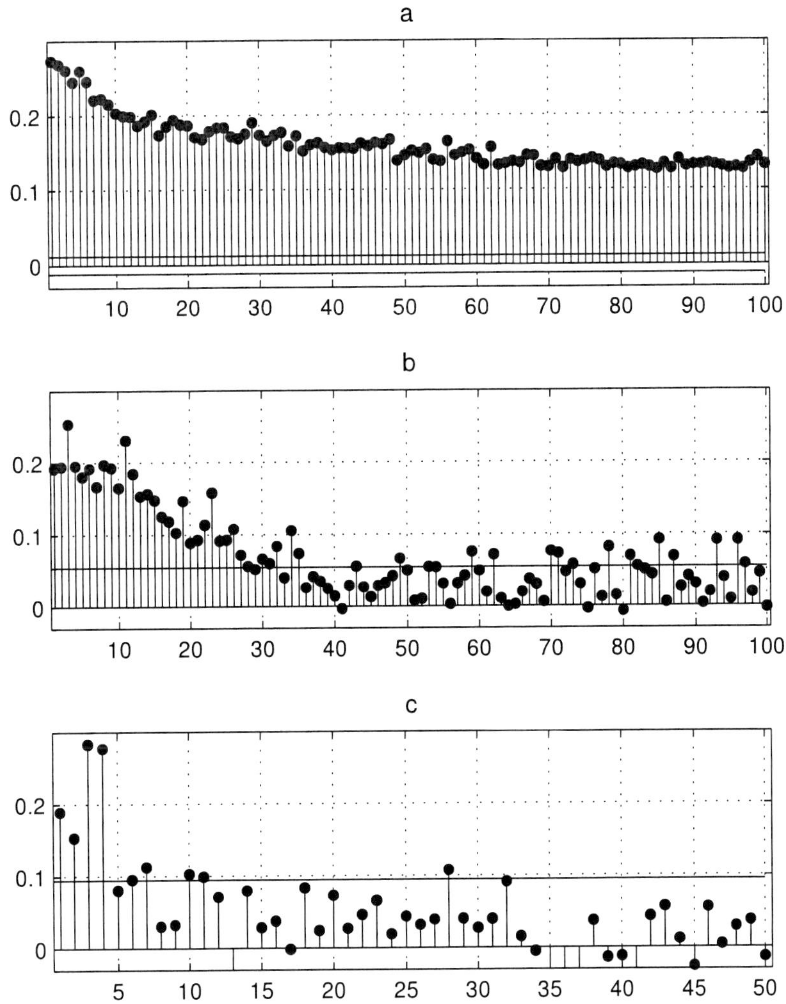

Source: Dow Jones Indexes, daily values of the DJIA index from 26/05/1896 to 10/10/2007, 28864 observations. The same as on Figure 6, but instead of returns their absolute values are used.

Figure 8. Sample ACF for the Magnitudes of Returns on the DJIA Index.

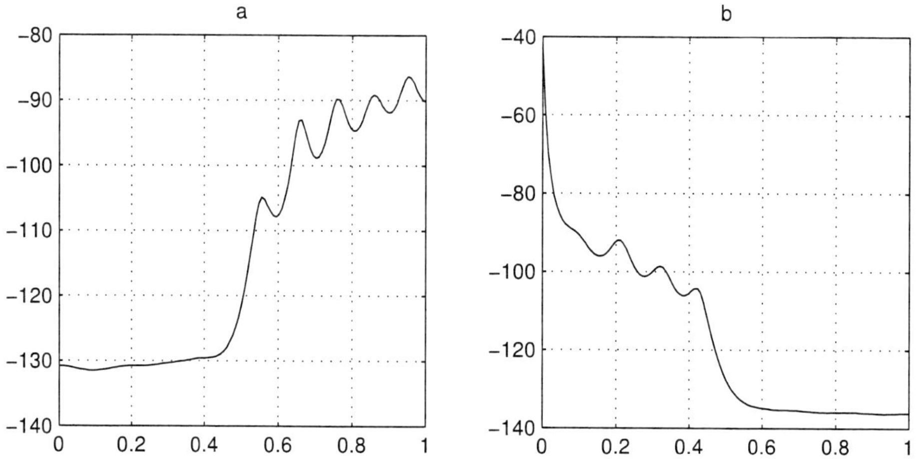

Source: Euronext, values of index CAC40 from 20/03/1995 to 29/12/2006 at 15-minutes intervals, 100881 observations. the figure shows a: pseudospectrum for 15-minutes returns, 100880 observations; b: pseudospectrum for absolute values of returns. The spectral density is estimated by the eigenvectors of the correlation matrix method with maximum lag 10 (Marple, 1987, p.373-378). On the X-axis: normalized frequencies (in radians per sample length), on the Y-axis: pseudospectrum values in decibels.

Figure 9. Sample Spectrum Density Function for the Returns on the CAC40 Index and their Magnitudes.

empirical answer to this question cannot be obtained: if such horizon exists, it should be very long (longer than 3 month), but we do not dispose of sufficiently long samples to accurately carry out normality tests at such horizons. In fact, the DJIA time series is the longest time series currently available in financial economics.

The analysis of the dependence structure in returns confirms the intuitions from the visual observation of time series profiles. First, autocorrelations in returns are weak at all frequencies (Figures 5 and 6). We only notice significant positive autocorrelation between consecutive 15-minutes returns, which are induced by the microstructure effects, falling out of the scope of this study (see Zhou, 1996, for details). For the CAC40 index we also record small negative autocorrelation in consecutive weekly returns, which can probably be explained

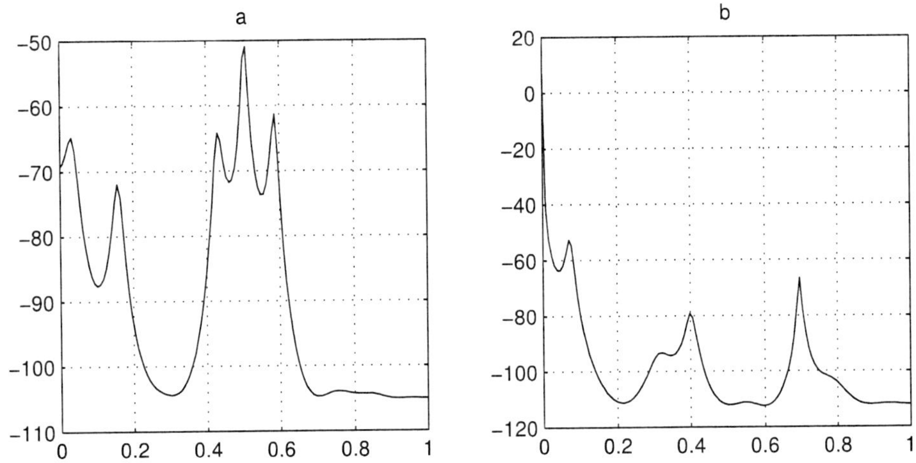

Source: Dow Jones Indexes, daily values of the DJIA index from 26/05/1896 to 10/10/2007, 28864 observations. The same as on Figure 9, but using daily returns.

Figure 10. Sample Spectrum Density Function for the Returns on the CAC40 Index and their Magnitudes.

by the "contrarian" effect[3], and positive correlation for lag 3 in weekly returns, which is probably a statistical artifact. For the returns on DJIA index no significant autocorrelations in returns are found.

The ACF computed for the absolute values of returns presents a big contrast (Figures 7 and 8). For magnitudes of returns on CAC40 positive autocorrelations are persistently significant up to very large lags at all frequencies of observation (15-minutes, daily and even weekly). Thus, at a 100-days lag correlations in daily volatilities are still significant, and for weekly returns they vanish no sooner than at lag 30 weeks (more than half of a year). The form of ACF can hardly be described by exponential decay, which characterizes the ARMA (autoregressive moving average) models. This illustrates long-range dependence in volatility. Daily volatilities of DJIA index display even stronger autocorrelations - they are still significant at 100-days lag and exceed 10% level. Autocorrelations in weekly absolute returns disappear at lags over 35 weeks,

[3]Contrarian strategy consists in selling stock that outperformed in past and buying those that underperformed, expecting trend reversal (see Conrad et al., 1997, and other behavioral finance literature)

and in quarterly absolute returns - at 4 quarters. So long-range dependence can be observed both in high-frequency and in daily observations of volatility.

Figures 9 and 10 show the estimated spectrum of fluctuations of returns and their absolute values (data are taken at the highest available frequency). The spectral density is estimated by the eigenvectors of the correlation matrix method with maximum lag 10 (Marple, 1987, p. 373-378). Normalized frequencies (in radians per sample length) are shown on the X-axis and pseudospectrum values in decibels are on the Y-axis. The spectrum of fluctuations in returns' magnitudes (volatility) has a peak at frequency close to zero, so that a significant part of the variation in volatility corresponds to the fluctuations, whose duration is comparable with the sample length. This observation also characterizes long memory: if the ACF decays at linear speed, the longest fluctuations' "cycle"[4] that can be observed equals the length of the sample.

Our empirical results illustrate the presence of long memory in volatility time series and the non-Gaussian character of the distribution of returns, especially at high observation frequencies. In the next section we explain how these properties can be reproduced by the models proposed in financial literature.

3. ARCH/GARCH Family of Volatility Models and Extensions

The key feature of the models proposed for stock price dynamics, has always been their capacity to reproduce the empirical properties of volatility in financial time series, and above all, the phenomenon of volatility clustering. It is appropriate to start the survey with autoregressive conditional heteroscedasticity (ARCH) models, used for the first time by Engle (1982) to represent inflation and later by Engle and Bollerslev (1986) for stock and FX market data. Returns in the ARCH model are represented as the sum of their conditional expectation and a Gaussian[5] disturbance of varying magnitude:

$$r_t = E(r_t|I_{t-1}) + \sigma_t \epsilon_t \tag{6}$$

with $\varepsilon_t \sim iid\ N(0,1)$, I_t the information set at date t, defined as the natural filtration of the price process, and σ_t the magnitude of the disturbance term,

[4]In this context the term "cycle" is used in stochastic sense rather than in strict deterministic sense.

[5]In general, normality condition for the noise is not necessary

satisfying:

$$\sigma_t^2 = \alpha_0 + \alpha_1 r_{t-1}^2 + \ldots + \alpha_q r_{t-q}^2 \tag{7}$$

with $\alpha_0 > 0, \alpha_i \geq 0$ for $\forall i > 0$ and $\sum_{i=1}^{q} \alpha_i < 1$. The parameter q specifies the depth of memory in the variance of the process.

A natural extension of ARCH is the generalized ARCH model (GARCH), first proposed in Bollerslev (1986) and widely used until know in the context of volatility forecasting (for example, see Bollerslev, 1987; Bollerslev et al., 1992; Hansen and Lunde, 2005). The model reads:

$$\sigma_t^2 = \alpha_0 + \sum_{i=1}^{q} \alpha_i r_{t-i}^2 + \sum_{i=1}^{p} \beta_i \sigma_{t-i}^2 = \alpha_0 + \alpha(L,q) r_t^2 + \beta(L,p)\sigma_t^2 \tag{8}$$

with L^n the lag operator of order n and $a(L,n)$ the operator of the form $\sum_{i=1}^{n} a_i L^i$, applied to a time series. So $a(L,q)X_t$ stands for $\sum_{i=1}^{q} a_i X_{t-i}$ and equation (8) can be rewritten:

$$[1 - \alpha(L,q) - \beta(L,p)]\, r_t^2 = \alpha_0 + [1 - \beta(L,p)]\left(r_t^2 - \sigma_t^2\right), \tag{9}$$

which corresponds to an ARMA model for the squared returns with parameters $\max\{p,q\}$ and p because $E(r_t^2 - \sigma_t^2 | I_{t-1})$ is an *iid* centered variable. To provide for the stability of the process, i.e. finite variation of the disturbances $\sigma_t \varepsilon_t$, all roots of the equations $\alpha(L_q) = 0$ and $1 - \alpha(L_q) - \beta(L_p) = 0$ must lie outside the unit circle. For GARCH(1,1) this constraint takes a simple form $\alpha + \beta < 1$. Sufficient and necessary conditions of strict stationarity, ergodicity and existence of moments of the GARCH-models are studied in Ling and McAleer (2002a,b).

GARCH models reproduce volatility clustering, observed empirically in financial time series (this is why volatility clustering is sometimes called GARCH-effect). The theoretical ACF of the process GARCH(1,1) decays at geometric speed, given by the sum $\alpha + \beta$. The closer this sum gets to unity, the more persistent autocorrelations are. In practice the estimates of $\alpha + \beta$ are often close to unity (Bollerslev et al., 1992). So the sample ACF for GARCH(1,1) is hard to distinguish from the long memory case, for which property (2) is verified.

The parameters of ARCH/GARCH models are usually estimated by the maximum likelihood method. The log-likelihood function for the Gaussian error case reads:

$$\ln L = -\frac{1}{2}\sum_{t=1}^{T}\left(2\ln\sigma_t + \varepsilon_t^2\right) \tag{10}$$

If the normality assumption is violated, a quasi-maximum likelihood (QML) estimation procedure is possible (the prefix "quasi" means that statistical inference is made under possible model misspecification). QML estimates of parameters are consistent under finite variance of disturbances (i.e. if $\alpha + \beta < 1$) and asymptotically normal if the fourth moment of disturbances is finite (Ling and McAleer, 2003).

The main drawback inherent to GARCH(1,1) is that its memory is not long enough, because the ACF decreases too fast, though possibly from high values of autocorrelation. When $\alpha + \beta$ is not very different from one, GARCH(1,1) degenerates to a process, called integrated GARCH by Engle and Bollerslev (1986). This model is non-stationary and implies permanent (non-vanishing) effect of initial conditions on the price dynamics and thus can hardly pretend to correctly represent reality.

An alternative approach consists in using processes, whose theoretical properties imply the presence of long memory. An early example of such process is the fractal Brownian motion of Mandelbrot and Van Ness (1968). It is a continuous-time Gaussian process with zero drift, whose ACF has the form:

$$C(\tau) = E(W_t^H W_{t-\tau}) = \frac{1}{2}\left(|t|^{2H} + |t-\tau|2H - |\tau|^{2H}\right), \tag{11}$$

where W_t^H denotes a fractional Brownian motion with parameter $H \in (0,1)$ at time $t \in [0,T], t \in \Re$, such as $0 \leq \tau \leq t \leq T$. The spectral density of the process reads:

$$\Psi(x) = 4\sigma^2 c_H \sin^2(\pi x) \sum_{i=-\infty}^{\infty} (|x+i|)^{-2H-1} \tag{12}$$

with $-\frac{1}{2} \leq x \leq \frac{1}{2}$, σ^2 the variance of the process and c_H a positive constant. It is easy to notice that with $H = \frac{1}{2}$ the process degenerates to an ordinary Brownian motion and with $H > \frac{1}{2}$ it has stationary dynamics with long memory.

In the ARCH/GARCH framework the fractionally integrated process proposed in Granger and Joyeux (1980); Hosking (1981) is a discrete analogue of the fractional Brownian motion and it is defined by:

$$(l - L)^d X_t = \varepsilon_t \tag{13}$$

with $\varepsilon_t \sim iid\ N(0, \sigma_\varepsilon^2)$ and operator $(l-L)^d, 0 < d < 1$ is an infinite series of the below form:

$$(l - L)^d = \sum_{i=0}^{\infty} \frac{\Gamma(i-d)}{\Gamma(-d)\Gamma(k+1)} L^i, \tag{14}$$

where $\Gamma(\cdot)$ stands for the Gamma-function. The spectral density of the process reads:

$$\Psi(x) = \frac{\sigma_\varepsilon^2}{\left(4\sin^2(\pi x)\right)^d} c_H \sin^2(\pi x) \sum_{i=-\infty}^{\infty} \left(|x+i|\right)^{-2H-1} \tag{15}$$

with $-\frac{1}{2} \leq x \leq \frac{1}{2}$. For $|d| < \frac{1}{2}$ the process has stationary dynamics with hyperbolic decay of the ACF, thus displaying long memory.

Fractional Brownian motion was proposed as a model of price dynamics in Mandelbrot (1971) and later in many studies that aimed at estimating the parameter H in (11) empirically (see Mandelbrot and Taqqu, 1979)). But taking this approach means to accept the presence of long-range correlations in returns themselves and not only in their magnitudes. As shown in Heyde (2002), to generate long-range dependence in magnitudes of returns the memory parameter of the process must satisfy $\frac{3}{4} \leq H \leq 1$, which clearly contradicts empirical evidence.

As follows from the above discussion, models that straightforwardly exhibit long-range dependence in magnitudes of returns rather than in returns themselves could be more realistic. One of the most popular models of this kind is fractionally integrated GARCH (FIGARCH) proposed in Baillie et al. (1996) and Bollerslev and Mikkelsen (1996). The process for the variance of returns is given by:

$$[1-\beta(L,p)]\,\sigma_t^2 = \alpha_0 + \left[1-\beta(L,p)-\phi(L)(1-L)^d\right] r_t^2 \tag{16}$$

with $\phi(L) = [1-\alpha(L,q)-\beta(L,p)]\,(1-L)^{-1}$. If d tends to one the model degenerates to IGARCH, discussed above.

A large number of other models, belonging to the GARCH family, were proposed to improve the forecasting power of GARCH(1,1). Among these models, the GARCH-in-mean first proposed by Engle et al. (1987) supposes that expected return increases with volatility and thus takes into account the effect of the varying risk premium. Other models include the effects of asymmetry and leverage, introduced in section 2.. Among the most influential models we can mention the GJR model (from Glosten-Jagannathan-Runkle), proposed in Glosten et al. (1992), the exponential GARCH with leverage effect, in addition eliminating some undesirable constraints on the values of parameter estimates (Nelson, 1991) and generalized quadratic ARCH (GQARCH) by Sentana (1995). Non-linear extensions of GARCH (often called NGARCH) have also been proposed. They generalize the form of dependence of current variance on past observations of returns. This class includes models where volatility switches between "high" and "low" regimes (Higgins and Bera, 1992; Lanne and Saikkonen, 2005). The study by Hansen and Lunde (2005) of the predictive power of ARCH-models uses 330 various specifications. A more detailed description of some of them can be found in Morimune (2007). Derivatives pricing under the GARCH-like dynamics of the underlying asset is discussed in Duan (1995); Ritchken and Trevor (1999); Barone-Adesi et al. (2008).

Among all extensions including the jump component in the price dynamics is of particular importance (Bates, 1996; Eraker et al., 2003). This generates fat tails in the distribution of returns, a property that is characteristic of empirical data. As early as in 1960s, Mandelbrot proposed to use stable Levy processes (power law processes with infinite variance) for this purpose (Mandelbrot, 1963). The properties of long memory processes, in which innovations are generated by Levy processes, are studied in Anh et al. (2002). Chan and Maheu (2002) proposed a rather general model, in which the intensity of price jumps is modeled by an ARMA process and volatility exhibits GARCH-effect.

All the above-mentioned extensions of GARCH are defined in discrete time. A continuous-time analogue of GARCH(1,1) was first studied by Drost and Werker (1996). They establish a link between GARCH and stochastic volatility models, which are are discussed in the next section. It is important that the estimates of the parameters of the discrete time GARCH(1,1) in, obtained for arbitrary chosen frequency of observation, can be converted to the parameters of a continuous process. This result is related to the time aggregation property of GARCH models that will be discussed in section 6.. Continuous-time GARCH models with innovations driven by jump processes are described in Drost and Werker (1996) and more recently in (Klüppelberg et al., 2004).

Portfolio management and basket derivatives pricing applications motivate the study of multi-dimensional conditional heteroscedasticity models, accounting for correlations between assets. The first model of this kind, called constant conditional correlation model (CCC), was developed by Bollerslev (1990). The returns on each asset follow a one-dimensional GARCH process and conditional correlations are constant. So any conditional covariance is defined as the product of a constant correlation by the time-varying independent standard deviation of returns. The main advantage of CCC is the simplicity of estimation and interpretation. The main drawback is the absence of interdependence in conditional volatilities of assets. Besides, it does not account for leverage, asymmetry and, clearly, for possible changes in correlations. A more general model with constant correlations, introducing asymmetry, is studied in Ling and McAleer (2003). Engle (2002) further generalized CCC, allowing for GARCH-like dynamics in correlations. The model was named DCC, standing for dynamic conditional correlations. The dynamics of correlations in DCC is similar for all assets. This constraint is weakened in Billio et al. (2006).

4. Stochastic Volatility Models

Conditional heteroscedasticity models have only source of randomness. The variance of the returns process is some function of its past realizations (for example, a linear combination of lagged squared returns). An alternative approach is to set up a simple model for returns, for instance given by (1). Instead of considering σ as a parameter, one can model it as a separate stochastic process. Two sources of randomness thus emerge. This idea is the concept of stochastic volatility.

The first stochastic volatility model was proposed in Taylor (1982). It assumes that log-volatility is an AR(1) process:

$$\begin{aligned} r_t &= \mu\sigma_t\varepsilon_t \\ \ln\sigma_t^2 &= \phi\ln\sigma_{t-1}^2 + \nu_t, \end{aligned} \tag{17}$$

where μ is some positive constant, included in the model to get rid of the constant term in the volatility process, and ϕ is the autoregression parameter that determines memory in volatility. The properties of the autoregressive stochastic volatility (ARSV) models were studied by Andersen (1994); Taylor (1994); Capobianco (1996). In particular, under the constraint of the log-volatility process being stationary, the distribution of returns is fat-tailed and symmetric Bai et al. (2003). Returns are uncorrelated (but clearly not independent). The ACF for returns and squared returns decays at geometric speed, a characteristic of ARMA models.

Stochastic volatility have become popular in applications, related to pricing and hedging of financial derivatives. The returns are always given by a relation analogous to (1) where volatility is given by $\sigma_t = f(X_t)$. Usually X_t is an Ito process, so the whole model reads:

$$\begin{aligned} \frac{dS(t)}{S} &= \mu dt + \sigma dW(t) \\ \sigma_t &= f(X_t) \\ dX_t &= \theta(\psi - X_t)dt + g(X_t)dB_t \\ < W, B >_t &= \rho t \end{aligned} \tag{18}$$

with θ and ψ two constant parameters, $f(\cdot)$ and $g(\cdot)$ two continuous functions, verifying some regularity conditions (depending on the concrete specification), and ρ the correlation parameter, used to model the dependence between two Brownian motions that drive the price dynamics. Hull and White (1987) use the specification $f(X_t) = X_t$ with $\theta < 0, \mu = 0$ and $g(X_t) = \nu X_t$, which corresponds to the geometric Brownain motion for volatility. This model allows for easy derivation of closed-form formulas for option prices, but its properties are far from being realistic: the variance of returns is not bounded because the volatility process is not stationary.

An alternative specification proposed in Scott (1987) uses an Ornstein-Uhlenbeck (OU) process for volatility, taking $f(X_t) = X_t, g(X_t) = \nu$, so that, after a shock, volatility converges to its long-term average ψ at speed θ with "volatility of volatility" ν. Another possibility is the exponential OU model (Stein and Stein, 1991) with $f(X_t) = \exp X_t \;\; g(X_t) = \nu$, which is a continuous time analogue of ARSV(1) . Perhaps, the most popular is the Heston (1993) model, where $f(X_t) = \sqrt{X_t}, g(X_t) = \nu\sqrt{X_t}$. In this case volatility is represented by a Cox-Ingersoll-Ross (CIR) model (see Cox et al., 1985).

The logic of the evolution of stochastic volatility models echoes the logic of GARCH extensions. Harvey and Shephard (1996) and later Jacquier et al. (2004) include the leverage effect in ARSV, letting two innovations in (17) be negatively correlated (in a continuous model of the form (18) this corresponds to the choice of $\rho < 0$). A stochastic volatility model with the effect of volatility on expected return, analogous to GARCH-M, is proposed in Koopman and Uspensky (2002). Jump component can be added to the stochastic volatility model by means of non-Gaussian processes. Instead of Brownian motion disturbances are generated by Levy processes (see Barndorff-Nielsen and Shephard, 2001; Eraker et al., 2003; Chernov et al., 2003; Duffie et al., 2003).

Various methods were proposed to incorporate long memory. Breidt et al. (1998); Harvey (1998) build discrete-time models with fractional integration,

Comte and Renault (1998) propose a continuous time model with fractional Brownian motion. Chernov et al. (2003) considers models, in which stochastic volatility is driven by various factors (components). Such models generate price dynamics with slow decay in sample ACF, a characteristic of long memory models, though the data generating processes themselves do not possess this property (LeBaron, 2001a). In Barndorff-Nielsen and Shephard (2001) long memory effect is produced by superposition if an infinite number of non-negative non-Gaussian OU processes, which incorporates long-range dependence simultaneously with jumps. Besides, long-range dependence in stochastic volatility can be achieved using regime-switching models (So et al., 1998; Liu, 2000; Hwang et al., 2007).

Multi-dimensional extensions of stochastic volatility models are also available. Their comparative surveys can be found in Liesenfeld and Richard (2003); Asai et al. (2006); Chib et al. (2006). For some particular cases, notably for the Heston (1993) model, the problem of the optimal dynamic portfolio allocation is solved (Liu, 2007). Finally, similar to the GARCH literature, methods of derivatives pricing are developed for the case, when the underlying asset has stochastic volatility (Heston, 1993; Hull and White, 1987; Henderson, 2005; Maghsoodi, 2005).

Notice that realizations of volatility process, defined by models of type (17) and (18), are not observable (with reservations, discussed below), so that for their estimation we have to use returns and their transformations. Estimation methods can either be based on the statistical properties of returns (efficient method of moments, quasi-maximum likelihood method, etc.) or on building linear model for squared returns. A detailed survey of these methods can be found in Broto and Ruiz (2004).

The interest in SV models especially increased in recent years because an unobservable variable volatility turned to be an "almost observable" one. This occurred thanks to the availability of the intraday stock quotations, making possible precise non-parametric estimation of volatility. The concept of realized volatility (RV), defined as the square root of the sum of squared intraday returns (Andersen et al., 2001; Barndorff-Nielsen and Shephard, 2002b; Andersen et al., 2003):

$$\hat{\sigma}_t^{RV} = \left(\frac{\sum_{i=1}^{M-1} r_{t,\delta}^2}{M-1} \right)^{\frac{1}{2}} \tag{19}$$

with $\hat{\sigma}_t^{RV}$ realized volatility of returns, $r_{i,\delta}$ logarithmic returns on the time interval $[i, i + \delta]$ с $\delta = \tau(M - 1)^{-1}$, τ the length of period, over which volatility is computed (for example, one day) and M the number of price observations, available for that period. If in formula (19) we omit squared root and normalization on the number of observations, we obtain a realized variance estimation over the period τ, which is also often used in practice (Barndorff-Nielsen and Shephard, 2002a; Hansen, 2005).

Using realized volatility and variance is complicated by the correlation of returns at high frequencies, induced by market microstructure effects (also called microstructure noise, see Biais et al., 2005)). Methods of correction of realized variance for this noise and of the optimal choice of sampling frequency were proposed in (Bandi and Russel, 2008) and partially in some earlier studies. But the simplest method, most frequently used in practice, is to compute returns over sufficiently long time intervals, where correlations are negligible, but short enough to benefit from the information, contained in high-frequency data. A survey of the properties of realized volatility and its use in the context of stochastic volatility models is given in McAleer and Medeiros (2008).

A alternative non-parametric estimation of volatility can be obtained by aggregation of artificially computed returns, corresponding to the difference between the maximal $H_{t,i}$ and the minimal $L_{t,i}$ values of stock price over K intervals of time length $[i, i + \Delta]$, onto which a time period of interest τ is divided (Alizadeh et al., 2002; Christensen and Podolskij, 2007; Martens and van Dijk, 2007):

$$\hat{\sigma}_t^{RR} = \frac{1}{4\ln 2} \sum_{i=1}^{M-1} \left(\ln H_{t,i} - \ln L_{t,i}\right), \tag{20}$$

where $\hat{\sigma}_t^{RR}$ is called realized range estimate. Clearly, the length of interval Δ must be chosen so as to contain several observations of prices. Statistical properties of the estimates, obtained in this way, can sometimes be better than those of realized variance. Another complement to realized variance is provided by the estimates with the process of bipower variation, which in particular allows estimation of the input of the jump component to the integrated variance (Barndorff-Nielsen and Shephard, 2002c; Woerner, 2005).

One of the main challenges in building volatility models has always been its forecasting (Andersen and Bollerslev, 1998; Andersen et al., 1999; Christoffersen and Diebold, 2000; Granger and Poon, 2003; Martens and Zein, 2004; Hansen and Lunde, 2005; Ghysels et al., 2006; Hawkes and Date, 2007). The development of non-parametric methods of estimation with intraday returns allowed, on the one hand, to increase the quality of forecasts, based on the time series of historical prices, compared to implicit volatility methods, based on options prices calibration (Martens and Zein, 2004) and, on the other hand, made it possible to compare various SV models, taking non-parametric estimate of volatility for its actually observed values (Brooks and Persand, 2003; Corradi and Distaso, 2006).

5. Aggregation of Returns in Time

In section 2. we compared returns on stock indices CAC40 and DJIA, computed from observations at different frequencies. We showed that the form of the probability distribution of returns changes across frequencies of observation. At the same time dynamic properties of volatility, such as long memory in absolute returns and absence of linear correlations in returns themselves, are common for time series, corresponding to different frequencies. A series of practically important questions arises in this context. In what way the long memory phenomenon is related to the properties of returns at different horizons? Can volatility models, calibrated on data of some frequency, reproduce the properties of returns at other frequencies? Does it make sense to make estimations at several time horizons for the same time series of stock prices, and if yes, how to reconcile the results?

The answer to the first question was largely given by Mandelbrot and Van Ness in 1968. They pointed out that for some class of stochastic processes, their properties eswtablished on short horizons allow to completely describe the properties at longer horizons. A process X_t is called self-affine if there exists a constant $H > 0$[6], such as for any scaling factor $c > 0$ random variables X_{ct} and $c^H X_t$ are identically distributed:

$$X_{ct} \stackrel{L}{=} c^H X_t \tag{21}$$

Fractal Brownian motion, defined through the form of its ACF in (11) is an example of self-affine process. When the condition $\frac{1}{2} < H < 1$ is verified, this process possesses long memory, and for $H = \frac{1}{2}$ it is a standard Brownian motion with independent increments.

[6]This parameter is called Hurst exponent. The name was given by Mandelbrot in honor of hydrologist Harold Hurst, who studied long-range dependence on the river Nile data.

Notice that in general self-affinity with $H > \frac{1}{2}$ does not imply presence of long-range dependence and vice versa. As a counter-example we can evoke L-stable processes, verifying self-similarity condition (21), whose increments are independent and generated by stationary random variables whose probability distribution satisfies $P(X > x) \sim cx^{-\alpha}$, with $0 < \alpha < 2$. These processes have discontinuous paths and thus are helpful to represent heavy tails in returns. Thus two very different phenomena - long-range dependence and extreme fluctuations - can be observed within the class of the self-affine processes.

Intuitively, saying that a probability distribution is L-stable means that the form of distribution does not change (i.e. is invariant upto a scaling parameter) when independent random variables, following this probability law, are summed up. In particular, the normal distribution is L-stable and Brownian motion is an example of an L-stable process. It is the only L-stable process with continuous trajectory and independent increments. As explained above, the independence property is lost for fractional Brownian motion. But random variables with heavy tails (infinite variance) can also be used to generate self-affine processes.

A generalization of the class of self-affine processes is the class of multifractal processes, for which the self-affinity factor is no longer constant, so that the aggregation property reads:

$$X_{ct} \stackrel{L}{=} M(c)X_t \tag{22}$$

with $M(\cdot)$ - independent of X positive random function of scaling factor c, such as $M(xy) \stackrel{L}{=} M(x)M(y)$ for $\forall x, y > 0$. For strictly stationary (i.e. stationary in distribution) processes the following local scaling rule is verified:

$$X_{t+c\Delta t} \stackrel{L}{=} M(c)\left(X_{t+\Delta t} - X_t\right) \tag{23}$$

In the multifractal case we can define a generalized Hurst exponent as $H(c) = \log_c M(c)$ and rewrite (22) in the form:

$$X_{ct} \stackrel{L}{=} c^{H(c)}X_t \tag{24}$$

From (22) we can obtain scaling rules for the moments of X_t:

$$E(|X_t|^q) = c(q)t^{\zeta(q)+1} \tag{25}$$

with $c(q)$ and $\zeta(q)$ deterministic functions. The function $\zeta(q)$ is particularly important and is called scaling function. Substituting $q = 0$ in 25, it is straightforward to notice that that the constant term in this function must be equal to one. For a self-affine process, which can also be called monofractal, the scaling function is linear and can be written $\zeta(q) = Hq - 1$. Applying Hölder inequality to (25) we can show that $\zeta(q)$ is always concave and that it becomes linear when $t \to \infty$. This implies that a multifractal process can only be defined for a finite time horizon, because beyond some horizon monofractal properties must prevail.

Alternatively (see Castaing et al., 1990) a multifractal process can be defined through the relation between the probability density functions of the increments of the process, computed for time intervals of different lengths l and L, such as $L = \lambda l$, $\lambda > 1$. This relation reads:

$$P_l(x) = \int G(\lambda, u) e^{-u} P_L(e^{-u} x) du \tag{26}$$

with $P_l(\cdot)$ the probability density function of the increments $\delta_l X_t$ of the process X_t at time horizon l, so that $x = \delta_l X_t = X_{t+l} - X_t$ (remember that for stationary processes $\delta_l X_t \stackrel{L}{=} X_l$). So if X_t is the logarithm of stock price, then the increments of the process represent returns at different time horizons. The function $G(\lambda, u)$, whose form depends exclusively on the relation between the lengths of two horizons, is called a self-similarity kernel. In the simplest case of a self-affine process it takes the form:

$$G(\lambda, u) = \delta(u - H \ln \lambda) \tag{27}$$

with $\delta(\cdot)$ the Dirac function[7]. In this monofractal case one point is enough to describe the evolution of the distributions, since P_l and P_L are different only by the scaling factor. This explains the degenerated form of (27).

In the general multifractal case equation (26) has a simple interpretation. The distribution P_l is a weighted superposition of scaled density functions P_L, with the weights defined by the self-similarity kernel. In other words, P_l is a geometric convolution between the self-similarity kernel and the density function P_L. Self-similarity kernel is also called propagator of a multi-fractal process. We will further need definition (26) to establish the multifractal properties of the multiplicative volatility cascade.

The scaling properties in stock prices and FX rates volatility have recently been studied in several papers. In particular, Schmitt et al. (2000) and

[7] The Dirac function $\delta(x)$ is equal to 0 in all points except $x = 0$, and to infinity at $x = 0$, so that the integral of the function is equal to 1.

Pasquini and Serva (2000) show that the non-linearity of the scaling function $\zeta(q)$, observed empirically, is incompatible with additive monofractal models of stochastic volatility, based on Brownian motion. So far this class of models has been most popular both among practitioners and researchers in finance. Multifractal properties can be due to a multiplicative cascade of disturbances (information flows or reactions to news), similar to the cascade used to model the turbulence in liquids and gazes. We discuss this issue later in more detail.

Interestingly, the time aggregation properties of simple models of the type GARCH and ARSV do not provide an adequate representation of stock returns at multiple horizons simultaneously. As regards the most popular GARCH(1,1) and its continuous time stochastic volatility analogue Drost and Nijman (1993) and Drost and Werker (1996) show that they verify the scale consistency property, i.e. if returns at some short scale follow GARCH(1,1), they must do so at any long scale with the same parameters. To prove this result the authors had to relax the assumption of the independence of errors in the model (8), assuming only that α and β are the best linear predictors of variance and that residuals ε_t are stationary (the so-called weak form of GARCH). Scale consistency is at the same time a strength and a weakness of the GARCH model. On the one hand, the results of statistic inference are independent of the frequency of observation. On the other hand, strict scale invariance does not allow reproducing the evolution in the form of the volatility distribution with time horizons and thus contradicts the empirical evidence.

The above arguments demonstrate the need for a model of volatility, that would not only reproduce long-range dependence and/or the presence of heavy tails in stock return, observed at some fixed frequency, but would give adequate results for other horizons. Ideally, this would give the possibility to model the change in the form of the probability distribution of returns at different time horizons and to reproduce the multifractal properties of the corresponding time series.

6. The Hypothesis of Multiple Horizons in Volatility

Up to now we discussed the time aggregation of returns from a purely statistical point of view. We noticed that the time series of returns, observed at different frequencies, have different properties. Can these properties be related to the real economic horizons, at which economic agents act?

The economic hypothesis of multiple horizons in volatility supposes that the heterogeneity in horizons of decision-taking by investors is the key element of explaining the complex dynamic of stock prices. For the first time the idea that price dynamics is driven by actions of investors at different horizons was advanced in Müller et al. (1997). They suppose that one can distinguish volatility components, corresponding to particular ranges of fluctuation frequencies, that are of unequal importance to different market participants. The latter include speculators that use intraday trades, daily traders, portfolio managers and institutional investors, each having its own characteristic time of reaction to news and frequency of operations on the market. From the economic point of view, frequencies of price fluctuations are associated with the periods between asset allocation decisions, or frequencies of portfolio readjustments by investors.

A parametric model of volatility at multiple horizons in the spirit of ARCH approach has been proposed in Müller et al. (1997) and further studied in Dacorogna et al. (1998). Current volatility is represented as a linear function of squared returns over different time periods in the past:

$$\sigma_t^2 = c_0 + \sum_{j=1}^{n} c_j \left(\sum_{i=1}^{j} r_{t-i} \right)^2 \tag{28}$$

with $c_k \geq 0$ for all $k = 0, ..., n$, so that for $k = 0$ and $k = n$ the inequality is strict, and with r_t the logarithmic return. Thus the expression $\sum_{i=1}^{j} r_{t-i}$ represents log-return over the period of length j. By construction the resulting heterogeneous ARCH (HARCH) model accounts for the hierarchical structure of the correlations in volatilities. The main problems of this model are a big number of parameters and high correlations between independent variables, that make its identification very complicated. The authors propose to reduce the dimension of the problem, using the principal components method. Later Corsi (2004) proposed a model, having the same form as HARCH, but using realized volatilities at different horizons (daily, monthly, weekly) as independent variables. This reduces correlations between regressors and the number of parameters.

Zumbach (2004) proposed to define current (or efficient) volatility as a weighted sum of several components, corresponding to different time horizons. He considers $n + 1$ representative horizons, whose length $\tau_k, k = 0 \ldots n$ increases dyadically: $\tau_k = 2^{k-1}\tau_0$. The component of volatility, corresponding to horizon k, is defined by the exponential moving average:

$$\sigma_{t,k} = \mu_k \sigma^2_{k,t-\delta t} + (1-\mu_k) r_t^2$$
$$\mu_0 = \exp(-\frac{\delta t}{\tau_0})\ \mu_k = \exp(-\frac{\delta t}{\tau_0 2^{k-1}}), k = 1 \ldots n \tag{29}$$

with r_t current return at the minimum time interval δt, at which prices are observed ($\delta t \leq \tau_0$). Supposing that time is measured in units of length δt, we choose for simplicity $\delta t = 1$. Then, using (29), we can obtain the expressions for returns and volatility at different horizons:

$$r_{t,k} = \frac{1}{\sqrt{\tau_k}} \left[\ln(S_t) - \ln(S_{t-\frac{\tau_k}{\tau_0}}) \right]$$
$$\sigma_{t,k} = \mu_k \sigma^2_{k,t-1} + (1-\mu_k) r^2_{t,k} \tag{30}$$

with the return $r_{t,k}$ at horizon $k = 2^{k-1}$ defined as the change in the logarithm of price, scaled to the minimal time period $\delta t = 1$. Finally, the resulting (efficient) volatility, corresponding to the unit time period, reads:

$$\sigma_t = \sum_{k=1}^{n} c\, 2^{-(k-1)\lambda}\ \sigma_{t,k} = \sum_{k=1}^{n} \omega_k \sigma_{t,k} \tag{31}$$

with $1/c = \sum_{k=1}^{n} 2^{-(k-1)\lambda}$, which provides $\sum_{k=1}^{n} \omega_k = 1$. The decay of weights in (31) according to the power law provides for long memory in the magnitudes of returns. This model is close to FIGARCH that uses the fractional differencing operator to create long-range dependence (see section 3.), but Zumbach's model has a clear interpretation in terms of multiple horizons hypothesis. Compared to HARCH, it uses less parameters (only four). Note, however, that empirical tests of (31) showed only a very slight increase in the forecasting power of the model, compared to GARCH(1,1).

Another model of volatility at multiple horizons, this time based on a modification of the ARSV model, was proposed in Andersen (1996) and Andersen and Bollerslev (1997). Here the heterogeneity of time horizons is interpreted in terms of different persistence of information flows that influence price variability. These information flows can be seen as factors of volatility, important to different types of investors. Current return is defined through the latent volatility, which is assumed proportional to the intensity of the aggregated information flow V_t:

$$r_t = V_t^{\frac{1}{2}} \xi_t \tag{32}$$

where ξ_t is an *iid* random process with zero expectation and unit variance. The information flow V_t is the result of simultaneous action of n different information flows $V_{t,j}$, each following a log-normal ARSV model of the type (17):

$$v_{t,j} = \alpha_j + v_{t-1,j} + \varepsilon_{t,j} \tag{33}$$

with $v_{t,j} = \ln V_{t,j} - \mu_j$, $\mu_j = E(\ln V_{j,t})$ and $\varepsilon_{t,j} \sim iid\ N(0, \sigma_j^2)$. The parameter α_j represents the persistence of the information flow j, supposed to be stationary $(0 \leq \alpha_j < 1)$. Aggregation of information flows is accomplished with the geometric mean rule:

$$\ln V_t = \sum_{i=1}^{N} v_{t,j} \sum_{i=1}^{N} \mu_j \tag{34}$$

According to this definition the spectrum of $\ln V_t$ is the mean spectrum of all autoregressive processes, defined by equations of the form (33).

Representing the heterogeneity of the parameter α_j by a standard β-distribution, the authors study the dynamics of returns' magnitudes and of the odd moments of returns, finding evidence in favor of long-range dependence. Besides, the process, obtained through the mixture of distributions, is self-affine. In particular, this implies that the ACF of volatility process decays at the same hyperbolic speed, whatever the frequency of returns observation.

Andersen and Bollerslev (1997) model has mostly explicative character (the authors try to explain long-range dependence by the heterogeneity of information flows), unlike the models described earlier that suppose identification of parameters and practical use in forecasting. It still does not explain the multifractality property, which is empirically observed in stock price volatility. Besides, the model does not have a direct microeconomic justification, based on decision-taking behavior of investors.

Explanation of the properties of volatility in the market microstructure models with heterogeneous investors is proposed in several studies. In particular, Brock and Hommes (1997) introduce the notion of adaptive rational equilibrium which is reached by investors, rationally choosing the predicting functions for future prices. The set of predictive functions is specified *a priori* and the criterion of choice is the quality of the forecasts, obtained by using these functions on historical data. Artificial markets of this type are also studied in Lux and Marchesi (2000), Chiarella and He (2001) and Anufriev et al. (2006), where investors choose between chartist (extrapolating the past) and fundamentalist strategies. Reproducing some of the empirical properties of stock prices, these models explain the paradox of excessive price volatility and volatility clustering to some extent. However, none of them accounts for the heterogeneity of time horizons. In a similar context LeBaron (2001b) studies the choice between strategies, based on historical data collected over different horizons. However, he does not explicitly model the rational choice of agents that rebalance portfolios at different frequencies.

Subbotin and Chauveau (2009) study the effect of multiple investment horizons on the price dynamics in a context of a pure exchange economy with one risky asset, populated with agents maximizing expected utility of wealth over discrete investment periods. Investors' demand for the risky asset may depend on the historical returns, so a wide range of behaviorist patterns is exploited. They establish necessary conditions under which the risky return can be an *iid* stationary process and study the compatibility of these conditions with different types of demand functions in the heterogeneous agents' framework. It is explicitly shown that conditional volatility of returns on the risky asset cannot be constant in many generic situations, especially if agents with different investment horizons exist on the market. So volatility clustering can be seen as an inalienable feature of a speculative market, which can be present even if all investors are so-called "fundametialists". Thus it is demonstrated that heterogeneity of investment horizons is sufficient to generate many stylized facts in returns' volatility.

A general weak point of artificial market models is the *a priori* character of assumptions about economic agents' behavior (which apparently has impact on the form of resulting market dynamics), and absence or insufficiency of analytic relation with the specification of volatility processes, used in practice. Thus, almost simultaneously with the model of artificial market, mentioned above, LeBaron (2001a) proposes a simple model of stochastic volatility with three factors, each given by an OU process (see section 4.) with different speed of mean reversion, which has no direct link to the former theoretical model. A similar stochastic volatility model with multiple horizons was proposed in Perello et al. (2004). Molina et al. (2004) study its estimation by the Monte Carlo Markov Chains method. Models with multiple factors, given by OU processes, can successfully reproduce long-range dependence and leverage effect, but are scale-inconsistent due to the finite (and small) number of factors and do not have any analytic relation to the economic microstructure models, which could justify multiple horizons. The model by Barndorff-Nielsen and Shephard

(2001) that uses a superposition of an infinite number of OU processes avoids the first of these two problems.

7. Modeling Multiple Horizons in Volatility and Econophysics Approach

The models of volatility at multiple horizons, described above, represent current volatility as a result of impact of factors (or components), varying at different frequencies. Such description of volatility has straightforward analogy in physics of liquids and gases. Hydrodynamics studies the phenomenon of turbulence, characterized by the formation of eddies of different sizes in the flows of fluids and gases, leading to the random fluctuations in thermodynamic characteristics (temperature, pressure and density). Most of the kinetic energy of a turbulent flow is contained in the eddies at large scales. Energy cascades from large scales to eddies structures at smaller scales. This process continues, generating smaller and smaller eddies, having hierarchical structure. The condition, under which laminar (i.e. normal) flow becomes turbulent, is determined by the so-called Reynolds number that depends on the viscosity of the fluid and on the properties of the flow. A statistical theory of turbulence was developed by Kolmogorov (1941), and a contemporaneous survey can be found, for example, in Pope (2000).

For the first time analogy between turbulence and volatility on the financial market was proposed in Ghashghaie et al. (1996). The authors noticed that the relation between the density of distribution of returns at various horizons is analogous to the distribution of velocity differentials for two points of a turbulent flow, depending on the distance between these points (so instead of physical distance, in finance we use distance in time). The cascade of volatility can be interpreted in terms of the multi-horizon hypothesis of Müller et al. (1997).

An analytical multiplicative cascade model (MCM) was proposed in Breymann et al. (2000). Volatility is represented as a product of disturbances at different frequencies. Denote S_t a discrete stochastic process for the stock price and $r_t = \ln S_t - \ln S_{t-1}$ the log-return. In MCM the returns are driven by equation:

$$r_t = \sigma_t \, \varepsilon_t, \tag{35}$$

with $\varepsilon(t)$ some *iid* noise, independent from the scale structure of volatility, and σ_t stochastic volatility process that can be decomposed for a series of horizons

$\tau_1, \ldots, \tau_n$ (here we suppose that τ_1 is the longest horizon), so that volatility at horizon $k \in \{2, \ldots, n\}$ depends on volatility at the longer horizon $k-1$ and some renewal process $X_{t,k}$:

$$\sigma_{t,k} = \sigma_{k-1}(t) X_{t,k} \tag{36}$$

So the multiplicative cascade for volatility reads:

$$\sigma_t = \sigma_{t,n} = \sigma_0 \prod_{k=1}^{n} X_{t,k} \tag{37}$$

At the initial time period t_0 all renewal processes $X_{t,k}$ are initialized as *iid* lognormal random variables with expectation $\mathrm{E}(\ln X_{t,k}) = x_k$ and variance $\mathrm{Var}(\ln X_{t,k}) = \lambda_k^2$. For transition from time t_n to time $t_{n+1} = t_n + \tau_n$ (recall that τ_n is the shortest time scale) we define:

$$X_{t_{n+1},1} = \left(1 - \mathbf{I}\left\{A_{t_{n+1},1}\right\}\right) X_{t_n,1} + \mathbf{I}\left\{A_{t_{n+1},1}\right\} \xi_{t_{n+1},1} \tag{38}$$

with $A_{t_{n+1},1}$ an event, corresponding to the renewal of process $X_{t,1}$ at time t_{n+1}, $\mathbf{I}\{\cdot\}$ the indicator function and $\xi_{t,1}$ lognormal *iid* random variables with expectation μ and variance λ^2. At any moment t_n the event $\{A_{t_{n+1},1}\}$ happens with probability p_1. By analogy $\{A_{t_{n+1},k}\}$ is defined as the renewal of process $X_{t,k}$ at moment t_{n+1}. The dynamics at horizons $k = 2, ..., m$ is defined iteratively by means of equation:

$$\begin{aligned} X_{t_{n+1},k} = \left(1 - \mathbf{I}\left\{A_{t_{n+1},k-1}\right\}\right) \left[(1 - \mathbf{I}\left\{A_{t_{n+1},k}\right\}) X_{t_n,k} + \right. \\ \left. \mathbf{I}\left\{A_{t_{n+1},k}\right\} \xi_{t_{n+1},k}\right] + \mathbf{I}\left\{A_{t_{n+1},k-1} \xi_{t_{n+1},k}\right\}, \end{aligned} \tag{39}$$

where for any k the random variables $\xi_{t,k}$ are *iid* log-normal with parameters μ and λ^2.

It follows from equation (39) that renewal at horizon k at moment t_{n+1} occurs if it has already occurred at the preceding, longer horizon $k-1$, or in case of the event $\{A_{t_{n+1},k}\}$ that happens withy probability p_k. Probabilities of renewal p_k must be calibrated so that the average interval between to renewal events would be equal to the length of the corresponding horizon τ_k. For simplicity we can consider only dyadic horizons, i.e. those satisfying $\tau_{k-1}/\tau_k = 2$ for $k \in \{2, \ldots, n\}$. Using the properties of Bernoulii process, one can easily show that:

$$p_1 = 2^{1-n}, \quad p_k = \frac{2^{k-n} - 2^{k-n-1}}{1 - 2^{k-n-1}}, \quad k = 2, \ldots, n \tag{40}$$

Empirical adequacy of the model is confirmed by the properties of ACF of returns and their absolute values at different horizons, defined in a standard way: $r_{t,k} = \ln S_t - \ln S_{t-\tau_k}$. Arneodo et al. (1998) shows that under MCM assumptions the ACF of logarithms of absolute values of returns at all horizons decays at logarithmic speed:

$$\mathrm{Cov}(\ln |r_{(t+\Delta t),k}|, \ln |r_{t,k}|) \cong -\lambda^2 \ln \frac{\Delta t}{\tau_1}, \ \Delta t > \tau_k \tag{41}$$

The last relationship can be used for identification of the "longest scale" in volatility (Muzy et al., 2001). From a practical point of view it is convenient to analyze MCM in an orthonormal wavelet basis, which simplifies simulations and allows to obtain analytical results of the the type of equation (41) (Arneodo et al., 1998).

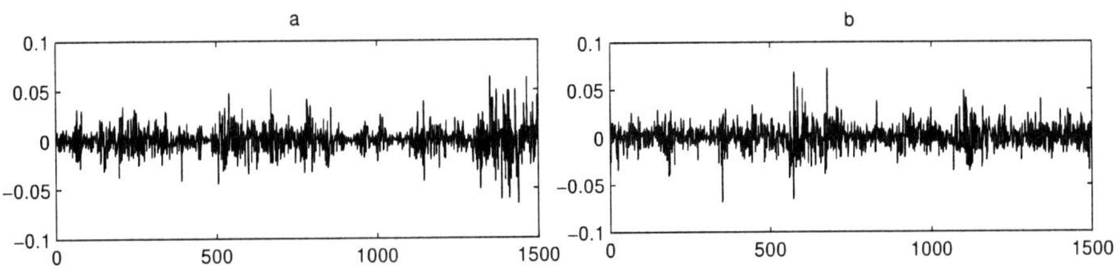

Left (a): daily returns on index CAC40 (source: Euronext, values of index CAC40 from 20/03/95 to 24/02/05). Right (b): daily returns, simulated with MCM at 14 horizons (from 15 minutes to 256 days). Returns are simulated for every 15 minutes and then are aggregated to daily time intervals.

Figure 11. Simulation with Multiplicative Cascade Model and Real Data: Daily Returns.

Figures 11 and 12 show the results of simulation of MCM, compared with real data of index CAC40. The number of horizons in simulation is equal to 14, which allows to fit the speed of decay in the ACF, and other parameters are calibrated so as to match unconditional long-term estimates of the first two sample moments in the returns' distribution. Note that the figure shows the ACF for returns, aggregated into daily intervals, whereas the simulation itself was carried out at 15-minutes frequencies. This illustrates the most important property of the volatility cascade: clustering of volatility and long-range dependence robust to time aggregation, i.e. coexisting at multiple horizons.

The MCM, described above, is called log-normal, because disturbances to volatility are log-normal. This does not mean that that the resulting distribution

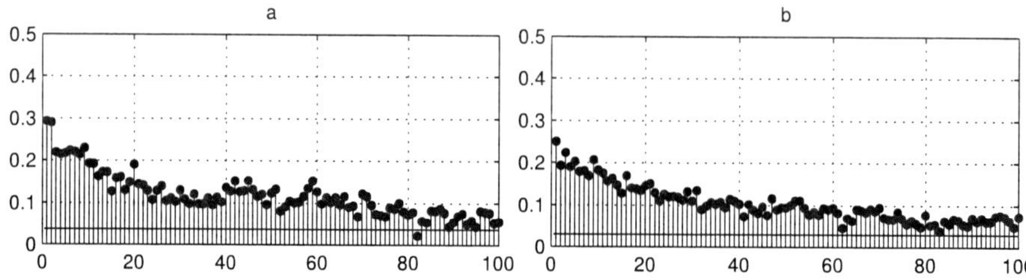

Left (a): sample ACF for the magnitudes of daily returns on index CAC40 (source Euronext, daily values of index CAC40 from 20/03/95 to 24/02/05). Right (b): sample ACF for data, simulated with MCM at 14 horizons (from 15 minutes to 256 days). Returns are simulated for every 15 minutes and then are aggregated to daily time intervals. ACF is computed for daily data.

Figure 12. Simulation with Multiplicative Cascade Model and Real Data: Sample ACF

of returns is log-normal. Nothing prevents from specifying the model in a way that provides for fat tails at short horizons (see more about it below). In a form described above MCM allows to simulate data, corresponding to the observed financial time series in many properties. But its practical use is complicated because of the absence of strict parametrization and estimation methods.

The link between MCM (here we talk about multiplicative cascade in more general sense, not focused on Breymann et al. (2000) specification, described above) and multifractal processes is studied in Muzy et al. (2000). Consider dyadic horizons of length $\tau_n = 2^{-n}\tau_0$. The increment of some process X_t on interval τ_k, denoted $\delta_k X_t$, is linked to the increment on the longest scale through equation:

$$\delta_k X_t = \left(\prod_{i=1}^{k} W_i\right) \delta_0 X_t \tag{42}$$

with W_i some *iid* stochastic factor. In MCM the stochastic volatility process was defined in a similar way. The expression (42) can be rewritten in terms of a simple random walk in logarithms of local volatility:

$$\omega_{t,k+1} = \omega_{t,k} + \ln W_{k+1} \tag{43}$$

with $\omega_{t,k} = \frac{1}{2}\ln(|\delta_k X_t|^2)$. Notice that equation (41) with new notations corresponds to $\mathrm{Cov}\,(\omega_{t+\delta t,k}, \omega_{t,k})$. If disturbances $\ln W_i$ are normally distributed

$N(\mu, \sigma^2)$, the distribution density $\omega_{t,k}$ denoted $P_k(\omega)$, satisfies:

$$P_k(\omega) = \left(N(\mu, \sigma^2)^{*k} * P_0 \right)(\omega) \tag{44}$$

with $*$ denoting the convolution operator, defined for two function $f(t)$ and $g(t)$ by the expression $(f * g)(t) = \int f(u)g(t-u)du$. Now it is straightforward to show that that equation (44) corresponds to the definition of multifractality in (26) with log-normal propagator of the form:

$$G_{\tau_k,\tau_0} = N(\mu, \sigma^2)^{*k} = N(k\mu, k\lambda^2) \tag{45}$$

In a similar way, a multifractal process, corresponding to (26), can be represented as a multiplicative cascade.

It follows from the above analysis that the MCM can be specified using a multi-fractal random walk. The class of these processes was proposed for volatility modeling in Bacry et al. (2001) and then generalized in Muzy and Bacry (2002); Pochart and Bouchaud (2002). A discrete version of MRW with step Δt can be obtained by summing up $t/\Delta t$ random variables:

$$X_{\Delta t}(t) = \sum_{k=1}^{t/\Delta t} \delta X_{\Delta t,k} \tag{46}$$

with $\delta X_{\Delta t,k}$ a noise, whose variance is given by stochastic process:

$$\delta X_{\Delta t,k} = \exp\left(\omega_{\Delta t,k}\right) \varepsilon_{\Delta t} \tag{47}$$

where $\omega_{\Delta t,k}$ is the logarithm of stochastic volatility, like in (43), and $\varepsilon_{\Delta t}$ is Gaussian noise, independent of ω. The definition of $\omega_{\Delta t,k}$ is based on the form of the autocovariance function, corresponding to the described above for MCM:

$$\begin{aligned} \mathrm{Cov}(\omega_{\Delta t,k}, \omega_{\Delta t,l}) &= \lambda^2 \ln \rho_{\Delta t,|k-l|} \\ \rho_{\Delta t,m} &= \frac{T}{(|m|+1)\Delta t}, \ |m| \leq \frac{T}{\Delta t} - 1 \\ \rho_{\Delta t,m} &= 1, \ |m| > \frac{T}{\Delta t} - 1 \end{aligned} \tag{48}$$

Here T is the integral time, i.e. the longest horizon, after which multifractal properties are no more observed. To provide for finite variance of the increments of the process $X_{\Delta t}(t)$ at transition to the continuous time by taking $\Delta t \to 0$, we need to define the mean log-volatility in the following way:

$$\mathrm{E}(\omega_{\Delta t,k}) = -\mathrm{Var}(\omega_{\Delta t,k}) = -\lambda^2 \ln\left(\frac{T}{\Delta t}\right) \tag{49}$$

The MRW model is identified by three parameters: the variance of the process $X_{\Delta t}(t)$, the variance of logarithmic volatility process (λ^2) and the integral time T. These parameters can be easily clibrated using the form of the spectrum and of the ACF. MRW can also be extended to multidimensional space (Muzy and Bacry, 2002). But the price to pay for the parsimony in parametrization of the model is the impossibility of direct and exact modeling of the interdependence between volatilities at different horizons, compared to the flexibility in this aspect, allowed by the HARCH or Zumbach model (see section 6.). Lynch and Zumbach (2003) study the volatility cascade empirically through the correlations of historical and realized volatility and find that the structure of this cascade is different from the one observed in turbulence. This can be explained by the existence of "characteristic" horizons, corresponding to the frequencies of market operations, specific to investors of different types (daily traders, portfolio managers, pensions funds, etc.). Compared to traditional models of stochastic volatility of the form (18), MRW processes do not allow for leverage effect. Besides, the intuitively attractive property of volatility reversion to its mean level, present in OU processes, is lost. Anteneodo and Riera (2005) proposes an additive-multiplicative model of cascade that enriches the one described in this section by the mean-reversion effect. But its complexity is considerably higher.

An alternative approach to studying the properties of volatility, related to econophysics, consists in direct estimation of the evolution of probability distribution at different horizons. A necessary assumption for such analysis is Markov property of the cascade. Consider a series of horizons $\tau_0 < \tau_1 < \ldots < \tau_n$ (in this case, unlike the description of MCM, it is more convenient to numerate horizons in increasing order) and a process $\delta_k X$ of increments at horizons τ_k, $k \in \{0, \ldots n\}$ of process X_t at some fixed time t (this can be a process of stochastic volatility or a trend-corrected price process, or its logarithm). By definition, Markovity for $\delta_k X$ means:

$$P_{k|k+1,\ldots,n}(x) = P_{k|k+1}(x), k = 0, \ldots, n-1, \tag{50}$$

where $P_{k|k+1}(\cdot)$ stands for the conditional density of the distribution of $\delta_k X$, given $\delta_{k+1}X$. Since

$$P_{k|k+1,\ldots,n}(x) = \frac{P_{k,\ldots,n}(x_k, \ldots, x_n)}{P_{k+1,\ldots,n}(x_{k+1}, \ldots, x_n)}, \tag{51}$$

it suffices to know the conditional densities at consecutive horizons and the distribution at the longest scale to define the joint distribution $P_{0,\ldots,n}$ of all increments. The last property is of special importance in finance. Using it, we can design an algorithm of simulation of a process with the same probability distribution of increments as in the empirical data (Nawroth and Peinke, 2006). Such algorithm can be useful for the implementation of a Monte Carlo algorithm in derivative pricing and portfolio management applications.

To verify if the Markov property is satisfied one can use the necessary condition, given by Chapman-Kolmogorov equation:

$$P_{m|k}(x) = \int P_{m|\delta_l X = u}(x)\, P_{l|k}(u) du, k < l < m \tag{52}$$

that can be checked for three different series of increments by direct comparison of the left and the right side of the equation. Empirical data for increments of exchange rates and stocks' volatilities are in good agreement with (52) and do not reject the Markovity hypothesis (Friedrich et al., 2000; Renner et al., 2001a; Ausloos and Ivanova, 2003; Buhbinder and Chistilin, 2005; Cortines et al., 2007). Notice that in MCM we did the Markov assumption implicitly, saying that volatility at each horizon is the result of adding multiplicative disturbance to the volatility at longer horizon.

For Markov processes conditional densities satisfy the Kramers-Moyal evolution equation (Risken, 1989, p.48-50):

$$-\tau \frac{\partial}{\partial \tau} P_{\tau|\tau_0}(x) = \sum_{k=1}^{\infty} \left(-\frac{\partial}{\partial x} \right)^k D_k(x, \tau) P_{\tau|\tau_0}(x) \tag{53}$$

Here we assume the length of horizons τ to be continuous. Coefficients $D_k(x, \tau)$ in Kramers-Moyal decomposition are defined as the limit at $\Delta_\tau \to 0$ of conditional moments $M_k(\delta_\tau X, \tau, \Delta\tau)$:

$$\begin{aligned} D_k(x, \tau) &= \lim_{\Delta\tau \to 0} M_k(x, \tau, \Delta\tau) \\ M_k(x, \tau, \Delta\tau) &= \frac{\tau}{k!\Delta\tau} \int (u - x)^k P_{\tau - \Delta\tau|\tau}(u) du \end{aligned} \tag{54}$$

In a general case all coefficients are different from zero, but according to Pawula's theorem, if $D_4(x,\tau) = 0$, then all coefficients in the decomposition starting from the third one are also equal to zero. This condition can also be verified empirically. If it is satisfied, (53) becomes a simple Fokker-Plank equation (also know as the second Kolmogorov equation):

$$-\tau\frac{\partial}{\partial\tau}P_{\tau|\tau_0}(x) = \left[-\frac{\partial}{\partial x}D_1(x,\tau) + \frac{\partial^2}{\partial x^2}D_2(x,\tau)\right]P_{\tau|\tau_0} \tag{55}$$

Unconditional density of the distribution of $\delta_\tau X$ at horizon τ satisfies the same differential equation.

Fokker-Plank equation describes the density of the stochastic process, given by Langevin equation:

$$-\tau\frac{\partial}{\partial\tau}x(\tau) = D_1(x,\tau) + \sqrt{D_2(x,\tau)}f(\tau) \tag{56}$$

with $f(\tau)$ the so-called Langevin force, which is usually modeled by Gaussian white noise. Thus, under a series of constraints, equation for stock prices and their volatilities can be obtained by estimation of Kramers-Moyal coefficients from (54) (Renner et al., 2001a; Buhbinder and Chistilin, 2005; Cortines et al., 2007). This unambiguously defines the evolution of the distribution from normal to fat tails. For example, Renner et al. (2001a) obtains the following form of coefficients, studying the increments in FX rates:

$$\begin{aligned} D_1(x,\tau) &= -\gamma x \\ D_2(x,\tau) &= \alpha\tau + \beta x^2 \end{aligned} \tag{57}$$

For a standard multifractal model of turbulent cascade (Castaing et al., 1990), described above, Kramers-Moyal coefficients take the form:

$$\begin{aligned} D_1(x,\tau) &= -\gamma(\tau)x \\ D_2(x,\tau) &= \beta(\tau)x^2 \end{aligned} \tag{58}$$

The resemblance of (58) and (57) evidences in favor of the analogy between turbulence and volatility. In Ausloos and Ivanova (2003) similar type of analysis is made for logarithmic returns on $S\&P500$ index. The results for D_2 are the same, but D_1 turned out to be very close to zero, which corresponds to the absence of the restoring force in terms of Langevin equation (i.e. no friction in the liquid). The last result is not confirmed in Cortines et al. (2007) on the logarithmic returns on the Brazilian index Ibovespa. Besides, the authors find significant linear trend in the equation for D_2 at horizons longer than one day. This is an important deviation from the classical multifractal model of turbulent cascade. Notice that the same deviation has been independently found on the empirical data for turbulence in liquids (Renner et al., 2001b).

In Buhbinder and Chistilin (2005) coefficients of Fokker-Plank equation are estimated for daily realized volatility of DJIA index, computed from 5-minutes returns. They find that the resulting estimates of Kramers-Moyal coefficients are well described by the equations:

$$\begin{aligned} D_1(\sigma,\tau) &= -\sigma(a_1 + a_2 \ln \sigma) \\ D_2(\sigma,\tau) &= b_1\sigma^2(\exp b_2\sigma) \end{aligned} \tag{59}$$

The first equation in (59) accounts for non-linearity in the coefficient of the restoring force at low volatility levels, the second models higher than quadratic speed of the increase in diffusion coefficient, observed at high volatility levels. With small σ replacing (59) in (55) results in the stochastic differential equation, corresponding to the exponential OU model of stochastic volatility. This model is also advocated in Masoliver and Perello (2006), based on entirely different considerations, related to the properties of ACF.

A huge number of methods and models that were proposed for describing volatility at multiple horizons evidences for rapid development of this research area in finance. It is too early to talk about a consistent theory, because for the moment there is no clear leadership among competing approaches. Besides, developing such a theory requires practical extensions, related to forecasting, optimal asset allocation and derivatives pricing. Some progress is made in each of these directions. Calvet and Fisher (2001) and Richrads (2004) propose methods of forecasting of multifractal time series. Some studies treat option prices under multi-horizon stochastic volatility, driven by a factor model (Fouque et al., 2003; Fouque and Han, 2004). Finally, solution of an asset allocation problem for the case when prices are driven by multifractal processes is given in Muzy et al. (2001).

Another direction of research, related to the multi-horizon models of volatility, deserves a special mention. Its aim is constructing indicators of volatility, that would represent the current state of the market, taking into account not only the magnitude of fluctuations, but also there frequency. As follows from the above theoretical arguments, considering volatility simultaneously at various horizons brings in important information, compared to measuring it at some particular horizon. This information can be used primarily for decision taking in dynamic portfolio management, based on volatility timing. Different multiple-horizon indicators, applicable to volatility measurement independently of the specification of the stochastic volatility process, were proposed in Zumbach et al. (2000); Maillet and Michel (2003); Maillet et al. (2007); Subbotin (2008). All of them are defined as probability transforms of volatility at different scales, based on an analogy with the Richter-Gutenberg scale in geophysics (Richter, 1958). Probability transform measures rareness of fluctuations of a given magnitude at the financial market. Thus by constructions they are universal in the sense that their values are comparable in time and over different assets. This is an important advantage from the practical point of view. The differences in indicators lie in how volatilities at multiple horizons are estimated, how the importance of each horizon is measured and how the results over different horizons are aggregated.

8. Conclusion

Modeling and measurement of stock price and exchange rate variability is one of the key elements of the theory and practice of investment portfolio management and other areas of finance. We discussed the notion of volatility and two approaches to its modeling in discrete and continuous time (conditional heteroscedasticity and stochastic volatility), pointing to the differences in how they capture the changes in the parameters of conditional returns' distribution. Evolution of these models has always been directed to reproduce more exactly the empirical properties in time series of prices, such as long-range correlations in magnitudes of returns, their absence in returns themselves and fat tails in returns distributions at short horizons.

Among all models we draw special attention to those that represent volatility at multiple horizons, because they seem to be the most promising. Multi-horizon representation allows to take into account the properties of returns, that manifested themselves when the latter are aggregated in time. The challenge is to capture the evolution in the form of the probability distribution of returns, computed over time intervals of different length. We described several classes of multi-scale models, from heterogeneous ARCH to multiplicative cascades. An important role in multi-horizon analysis belongs to methods and techniques, borrowed from hydrodynamics and other areas of statistical physics. Such borrowing became possible thanks to the discovery of the analogy (though possible incomplete) between volatility and turbulence in liquids and gases.

The concept of volatility at multiple horizons suggests the development of methods of its measurement, that account not only for the magnitude of fluctuations, but also for their frequency. Information, obtained from measurement at different levels of time aggregation (i.e. at various horizons) can be used jointly. This can be helpful, in particular, in asset management applications and in forecasting. An interesting further development may include forecasting volatility at multiple horizons simultaneously. Another important issue is the study of derivatives hedging strategies with regards to the frequency of operators' interventions on the market.

References

S. Alizadeh, M. Brandt, and F. Diebold. Range-based estimation of stochastic volatility models. *The Journal of Finance*, **57**(3):1047–1091, 2002.

T. Andersen. Stochastic autoregressive volatility: a framework for volatility modeling. *Mathematical Finance*, **4**:75–102, 1994.

T. Andersen. Return volatility and trading volume: An information flow interpretation of stochastic volatility. *Journal of Finance*, **51**(1):169–204, 1996.

T. Andersen and T. Bollerslev. Heterogeneous information arrivals and return volatility dynamics: Uncovering the long run in high frequency data. *Journal of Finance*, **52**:975–1005, 1997.

T. Andersen and T. Bollerslev. Answering the skeptics: Yes, standard volatility models do provide accurate forecasts. *International Economic Review*, **39**(4): 885–905, 1998.

T. Andersen, T. Bollerslev, and S. Lange. Forecasting financial market volatility: Sample frequency vis-a-vis forecast horizon. *Journal of Empirical Finance*, **6**(5):457–477, 1999.

T. Andersen, T. Bollerslev, F. Diebold, and P. Labys. The distribution of exchange rate volatility. *Journal of the American Statistical Association*, **96**: 42–55, 2001.

T. Andersen, T. Bollerslev, F. Diebold, and P. Labys. Modeling and forecasting realized volatility. *Econometrica*, **71**(2):579–625, 2003.

V. Anh, C. Heyde, and N. Leonenko. Dynamic models of long-memory processes driven by levy noise. *Journal of Applied Probability*, **39**:730–747, 2002.

C. Anteneodo and R. Riera. Additive-multiplicative stochastic models of financial mean-reverting processes. *Physical Review E*, **72**:026106, 2005.

M. Anufriev, G. Bottazzi, and F. Pancotto. Equilibria, stability and ssymptotic dominance in a speculative market with heterogeneous traders. *Journal of Economic Dynamics and Control*, **30**(9-10):1787–1835, 2006.

A. Arneodo, J. Muzy, and D. Sornette. Casual cascade in stock market from the 'infrared' to the 'ultraviolet'. *European Physical Journal B*, **2**:277–282, 1998.

M. Asai, M. McAleer, and J. Yu. Multivariate stochastic volatility: A review. *Econometric Reviews*, **25**(2-3):145–175, 2006.

M. Ausloos and K. Ivanova. Dynamical model and nonextensive statistical mechanics of a market index on large time windows. *Physical Review E*, **68**: 046122, 2003.

M. Avellaneda, C. Friedmen, R. Holmes, and D. Samperi. Calibrating volatility surfaces via relative-entropy minimization. *Apllied Mathematical Finance*, **4** (1):37–64, 1997.

E. Bacry, J. Delour, and J. Muzy. Multifractal random walk. *Physical Review E*, **64**:026103, 2001.

X. Bai, J. R. Russel, and G. Tiao. Kurtosis of garch and stochastic volatility models with non-normal innovations. *Journal of Econometrics*, **114**:349360, 2003.

R. Baillie, T. Bollerslev, and O. Mikkelsen. Fractionally integrated generalized autoregressive conditional heteroscedasticity. *Journal of Econometrics*, **74** (1):3–30, 1996.

F. Bandi and J. Russel. Microstructure noise, realized variance, and optimal sampling. *Review of Economic Studies*, **75**(2):339–369, 2008.

O. Barndorff-Nielsen and N. Shephard. Non-gaussian ornsteinuhlenbeck-based models and some of their uses in financial economics. *Journal of the Royal Statistical Society B*, **63**(2):167–241, 2001.

O. Barndorff-Nielsen and N. Shephard. Estimating quadratic variation using realized variance. *Journal of Applied Econometrics*, **17**(5):457–477, 2002a.

O. Barndorff-Nielsen and N. Shephard. Econometric analysis of realized volatility and its use in estimating stochastic volatility models. *Journal of the Royal Statistical Society: Series B*, **64**(2):253–280, 2002b.

O. Barndorff-Nielsen and N. Shephard. Power and bipower variation with stochastic volatility and jumps. *Journal of Financial Econometrics*, **2**(1): 1–37, 2002c.

G. Barone-Adesi, R. Engle, and L. Mancini. Garch option pricing model with filtered historical simulation. *Review of Financial Studies, forthcoming*, 2008.

D. Bates. Jumps and stochastic volatility: Exchange rate processes implicit in deutsche mark options. *Review of Financial Studies*, **9**:69–107, 1996.

B. Biais, L. Glosten, and C. Spatt. Market microstructure: A survey of microfoundations, empirical results and policy implications. *Journal of Financial Markets*, **8**:217264, 2005.

M. Billio, M. Caporin, and M. Gobbo. Applied financial economics letters. *Applied Financial Economics Letters*, **2**(2):123–130, 2006.

F. Black. Noise. *Journal of Finance*, **41**, 1976.

F. Black and M. Scholes. Pricing of options and corporate liabilities. *Journal of Political Economy*, **81**(3), 1973.

T. Bollerslev. Generalized autoregressive conditional heteroskedasticity. *Journal of Econometrics*, **31**(3):307–327, 1986.

T. Bollerslev. A conditionally heteroskedastic time series model for speculative prices and rates of return. *The Review of Economics and Statistics*, **69**(3): 542–547, 1987.

T. Bollerslev. Modeling the coherence in short-run nominal exchange rate: A multivariate generalized arch approach. *Review of Economics and Statistics*, **72**:498–505, 1990.

T. Bollerslev and O. Mikkelsen. Modeling and pricing long memory in stock market volatility. *Journal of Econometrics*, **73**(1):151–184, 1996.

T. Bollerslev, R. Chou, and K. Kroner. Arch modeling in finance : A review of the theory and empirical evidence. *Journal of Econometrics*, **52**(1-2):5–59, 1992.

F. Breidt, N. Crato, and P. de Lima. The detection and estimation of long memory in stochastic volatility. *Journal of Econometrics*, **83**(1-2):325–34, 1998.

W. Breymann, S. Ghashghaie, and P. Talkner. A stochastic cascade model for fx dynamics. *International Journal of Theoretical and Applied Finance*, 3: 357–360, 2000.

W. Brock and C. Hommes. A rational route to randomness. *Econometrica*, **65** (5):1059–1095, 1997.

C. Brooks and G. Persand. Volatility forecasting for risk management. *Journal of Forecasting*, **22**(1):1 – 22, 2003.

C. Broto and E. Ruiz. Estimation methods for stochastic volatility models: a survey. *Journal of Economic Surveys*, **18**(5):613–649, 2004.

G. Buhbinder and C. Chistilin. *An Empirical Model of Stochastic Volatility of Financial Fluctuations*. Proceedings of the VI Young Researchers' Conference in Mathematical Modeling and Information Technology, 29-31 October 2005, Kemerovo, Russia (in Russian), 2005.

L. Calvet and A. Fisher. Forecasting multifractal volatility. *Journal of Econometrics*, **105**(1):27–58, 2001.

E. Capobianco. State-space stochastic volatility models: a review of estimation algorithms. *Applied Stochastic Models and Data Analysis*, **12**:265279, 1996.

B. Castaing, Y. Gagne, and E. J. Hopfinger. Velocity probability density functions of high reynolds number turbulence. *Physica D*, **46**(2):177–200, 1990.

W. Chan and J. Maheu. Conditional jump dynamics in stock market returns. *Journal of Business & Economic Statistics*, **20**(3):377–389, 2002.

M. Chernov, R. Gallant, E. Ghysels, and G. Tauchen. Alternative models for stock price dynamics. *Journal of Econometrics*, **116**(1-2):225–257, 2003.

C. Chiarella and X.-Z. He. Asset price and wealth dynamics under heterogeneous expectations. *Quantitative Finance*, **1**(5):509 – 526, 2001.

S. Chib, F. Nardari, and N. Shephard. Analysis of high dimensional multivariate stochastic volatility models. *Journal of Econometrics*, **134**(2):341–371, 2006.

K. Christensen and M. Podolskij. Realized range-based estimation of integrated variance. *Journal of Econometrics*, **141**(2):323–349, 2007.

P. Christoffersen and F. Diebold. How relevant is volatility forecasting for financial risk management? *The Review of Economics and Statistics*, **82**(1): 12–22, 2000.

F. Comte and E. Renault. Long memory in continuous-time stochastic volatility models. *Mathematical Finance*, **8**(4):291–323, 1998.

J. Conrad, M. Gultekin, and G. Kaul. Profitability of short-term contrarian strategies: Implications for market efficiency. *Journal of Business & Economic Statistics*, **15**(3):379–386, 1997.

R. Cont. Empirical properties of asset returns: Stylized facts and statistical issues. *Quantitative Finance*, **1**(2):223–236, 2001.

V. Corradi and W. Distaso. Semi-parametric comparison of stochastic volatility models using realized measures. *Review of Economic Studies*, **73**(3):635–667, 2006.

F. Corsi. A simple long memory model of realized volatility. *Working Paper, University of Southern Switzerland*, 2004.

A. Cortines, R. Riera, and C. Anteneodo. From short to fat tails in financial markets: a unified description. *The European Physical Journal B*, **60**(3): 385–389, 2007.

J. Cox, J. Ingersoll, and S. Ross. An intertemporal general equilibrium model of asset prices. *Econometrica*, **53**:363–384, 1985.

D. Cutler, J. Poterba, and L. Summers. What moves stock prices? *Journal of Portfolio Management*, **15**:4–12, 1989.

M. Dacorogna, U. Muller, R. Dave, R. Olsen, and O. Pictet. *Modelling Short-term Volatility with GARCH and HARCH models*, pages 161–176. John Wiley, N.-Y., 1998.

Z. Ding and C. Granger. Modeling volatility persistence of speculative returns: a new approach. *Journal of Econometrics*, **73**:185–215, 1996.

Z. Ding, C. Granger, and R. Engle. A long memory property of stock market returns and a new model. *Journal of Empirical Finance*, **1**(1):83–106, 1993.

F. Drost and T. Nijman. Temporal aggregation of garch processes. *Econometrica*, **61**(4):909–927, 1993.

F. Drost and B. Werker. Closing the garch gap: Continuous time garch modeling. *Journal of Econometrics*, **74**(1):31–57, 1996.

J.-C. Duan. The garch option pricing model. *Mathematical Finance*, 5(1):1332, 1995.

D. Duffie, D. Filipovic, and W. Schachermayer. Affine processes and applications in finance. *Annals of Applied Probability*, **13**:984–1053, 2003.

B. Dupire. Pricing and hedging with smiles. *Proceedings of AFFI Conference, La Baule, June 1993*, 1993.

B. Dupire. Pricing with a smile. *Risk Magazine*, **7**(1):18–20, 1994.

R. Engle. Dynamic conditional correlation - a simple class of multivariate garch models. *Journal of Business and Economic Statistics*, **20**(3):339–350, 2002.

R. Engle. Autoregressive conditional heteroscedasticity with estimates of variance of united kingdom inflation. *Econometrica*, **50**:987–1008, 1982.

R. Engle and T. Bollerslev. Modelling the persistence of conditional variances. *Econometric Reviews*, **5**(1):1 – 50, 1986.

R. Engle, D. Lilien, and R. Robins. Estimating time varying risk premia in the term structure: The arch-m model. *Econometrica*, **55**(2):391–407, 1987.

B. Eraker, M. Johannes, and N. Polson. The impact of jumps in returns and volatility. *Journal of Finance*, **53**:1269–1300, 2003.

E. Fama. The behaviour of stock market prices. *Journal of Business*, **38**:34–105, 1965.

E. Fama. Efficient capital markets: A review of theory and empirical work. *Journal of Finance*, **25**:383–417, 1970.

L. Forsberg and E. Ghysels. Why do absolute returns predict volatility so well? *Journal of Financial Econometrics*, **5**(1):31–67, 2007.

J.-P. Fouque and C.-H. Han. Asian options under multiscale stochastic volatility. *Contemporary Mathematics*, **351**:125–138, 2004.

J.-P. Fouque, G. Papanicolaou, R. Sircar, and K. Solna. Multiscale stochastic volatility asymptotics. *Multiscale Modeling & Simulation*, **2**(1):22–42, 2003.

R. Friedrich, J. Peinke, and C. Renner. How to quantify deterministic and random influences on the statistics of the foreign exchange market. *Physical Review Letters*, **84**:5224 – 522, 2000.

S. Ghashghaie, W. Breymann, J. Peinke, P. Talkner, and Y. Dodge. Turbulent cascades in foreign exchange markets. *Nature*, **381**:767–770, 1996.

E. Ghysels, P. Santa Clara, and R. Valkanov. Predicting volatility: Getting the most out of return data sampled at different frequencies. *Journal of Econometrics*, **131**(1-2):59–95, 2006.

L. Glosten, R. Jagannathan, and D. Runkle. On the relation between the expected value and volatility of the nominal excess return on stocks. *Journal of Finance*, **46**:17791801, 1992.

C. Granger and R. Joyeux. An introduction to long memory time series models and fractional differencing,. *Journal of Time Series Analysis*, **1**:15–29, 1980.

C. Granger and S.-H. Poon. Forecasting volatility in financial markets: A review. *Journal of Economic Literature*, **41**(2):478–539, 2003.

P. Hansen. A realized variance for the whole day based on intermittent high-frequency data. *Journal of Financial Econometrics*, **3**(4):525–554, 2005.

P. Hansen and A. Lunde. A forecast comparison of volatility models: Does anything beat a garch(1,1). *Journal of Applied Econometrics*, **20**(7):873 – 889, 2005.

A. Harvey. *Long Memory in Stochastic Volatility*, pages 307–320. Butterworth-Heineman, Oxford, 1998.

A. Harvey and N. Shephard. Estimation of an asymmetric stochastic volatility model for asset returns. *Journal of Business & Economic Statistics*, **14**(4): 429–434, 1996.

R. Hawkes and P. Date. Medium-term horizon volatility forecasting: A comparative study. *Applied Stochastic Models in Business and Industry*, **23**(6):465 – 481, 2007.

V. Henderson. Analytical comparisons of option prices in stochastic volatility models. *Mathematical Finance*, **15**(1):49–59, 2005.

S. Heston. A closed-form solution for options with stochastic volatility with applications to bond and currency options. *Review of Financial Studies*, **6**: 327–343, 1993.

C. Heyde. On modes of long-range dependence. *Journal of Applied Probability*, **39**(4):882–888, 2002.

M. Higgins and A. K. Bera. A class of nonlinear arch models. *International Economic Review*, **33**(1):137–158, 1992.

J. Hosking. Fractional differencing. *Biometrika*, **68**:165–176, 1981.

J. Hull and A. White. The pricing of options on assets with stochastic volatilities. *Journal of Finance*, **42**(2):281–300, 1987.

S. Hwang, S. Satchell, and P. Pereira. How persistent is stock return volatility? an answer with markov regime switching stochastic volatility models. *Journal of Business, Finance and Accounting*, **34**(5-6):1002–1024, 2007.

E. Jacquier, N. Polson, and P. Rossi. Bayesian analysis of stochastic volatility models with fat tails and correlated errors. *Journal of Econometrics*, **122**(1): 185–212, 2004.

C. Klüppelberg, A. Lindner, and R. Maller. A continuous-time garch process driven by a levy process: Stationarity and second-order behaviour. *Journal of Applied Probability*, **41**(3):601–622, 2004.

AN Kolmogorov. The local structure of turbulence in incompressible viscous fluid for very large Reynolds numbers. *Proceedings of the USSR Academy of Sciences (in Russian)*, **30**:299–303, 1941.

S. Koopman and E. Uspensky. The stochastic volatility in mean model: Empirical evidence from international stock markets. *Journal of Applied Econometrics*, **17**(6):667 – 689, 2002.

M. Lanne and P. Saikkonen. Non-linear garch models for highly persistent volatility. *The Econometrics Journal*, **8**(2):251276, 2005.

B. LeBaron. Stochastic volatility as a simple generator of apparent financial power laws and long memory. *Quantitative Finance*, **1**(6):621–631, 2001a.

B. LeBaron. Evolution and time horizons in an agent-based stock market. *Macroeconomic Dynamics*, **5**:225–254, 2001b.

R. Liesenfeld and J. Richard. Univariate and multivariate stochastic volatility models: Estimation and diagnostics. *Journal of Empirical Finance*, **10**(4): 505–531, 2003.

S. Ling and M. McAleer. Necessary and sufficient moment conditions for the garch(r, s) and asymmetric power garch(r, s) models. *Econometric Theory*, **18**:722–729, 2002a.

S. Ling and M. McAleer. Stationarity and the existence of moments of a family of garch processes. *Journal of Econometrics*, **106**:109–117, 2002b.

S. Ling and M. McAleer. Asymptotic theory for a vector arma-garch model. *Econometric Theory*, **19**:278–308, 2003.

J. Lintner. The valuation of risk assets and the selection of risky investments in stock portfolios and capital budgets. *The Review of Economics and Statistics*, **47**(1):13–39, 1965.

J. Liu. Portfolio selection in stochastic environments. *Review of Finanical Studies*, **20**(1):1–39, 2007.

M. Liu. Modeling long memory in stock market volatility. *Journal of Econometrics*, **99**(1):139–171, 2000.

I. Lobato and C. Velasco. Long memory in stock market trading volume. *Journal of Business & Economic Statistics*, **18**(4):410–427, 2000.

T. Lux and M. Marchesi. Volatility clustering in financial markets: A microsimulation of interacting agents. *International Journal of Theoretical and Applied Finance*, **3**(4):675 – 702, 2000.

P. Lynch and G. Zumbach. Market heterogeneities and the causal structure of volatility. *Quantitative Finance*, **3**(4):320–331, 2003.

Y. Maghsoodi. Exact solution of a martingale stochastic volatility option problem and its empirical evaluation. *Mathematical Finance*, **17**(2):249265, 2005.

B. Maillet and T. Michel. An index of market shocks based on multiscale analysis. *Quantitative Finance*, **3**(2):88–97, 2003.

B. Maillet, T. Michel, and A. Subbotin. *A Revised Index of Market Shocks: A New Multi-horizon Richter Scale for Stock Markets*. 2007. JMA conference paper, Fribourg, Switzerland, 31 May - 1 June 2007.

B. Mandelbrot. The variation of certain speculative prices. *Journal of Business*, **36**:394–419, 1963.

B. Mandelbrot. When can price be arbitraged efficiently? a limit to the validity of the random walk and martingale models. *Review of Economics and Statistics*, **53**(3):225–236, 1971.

B. Mandelbrot and M. Taqqu. Robust r/s analysis of long run serial correlation. In Bulletin of the International Statistical Institute, Vol. 48, Book 2. *Proceedings of the 42nd session of the International Statistical Institute*, Manila 1979, pages 69–104, 1979.

B. Mandelbrot and J. Van Ness. Fractional brownian motion, fractional noises and applications. *SIAM Review*, **10**:422–437, 1968.

H. Markowitz. Portfolio selection. *Journal of Finance*, **7**(1):77–91, 1952.

S. Marple. *Digital Spectral Analysis*. Prentice-Hall, Englewood Cliffs, New Jersey, 1987.

M. Martens and D. van Dijk. Measuring volatility with the realized range. *Journal of Econometrics*, **138**(1):181–207, 2007.

M. Martens and J. Zein. Predicting financial volatility: High-frequency time-series forecasts vis-á-vis implied volatility. *Journal of Futures Markets*, **24** (11):1005–1028, 2004.

J. Masoliver and J. Perello. Multiple time scales and the exponential ornstein-uhlenbeck stochastic volatility model. *Quantitative Finance*, **6**(5):423 – 433, 2006.

M. McAleer and M. Medeiros. Realized volatility: A review. *Econometric Reviews*, **27**(1-3):10–45, 2008.

R. Merton. Theory of rational option pricing. *Bell Journal of Economics and Management Science*, **4**:141–183, 1973.

G. Molina, C.H. Han, and J.P. Fouque. *MCMC Estimation of Multiscale Stochastic Volatility Models*. 2004. Unpublished manuscript. University of Calfornia.

K. Morimune. Volatility models. *The Japanese Economic Review*, **58**(1):1–23, 2007.

U. Müller, M. Dacorogna, R. Dave, R. Olsen, O. Pictet, and J. Von Weizsacker. Volatilitics of different time resolutions - analyzing the dynamics of market components. *Journal of Empirical Finance*, **4**:213–239, 1997.

J. Muzy, J. Delour, and E. Bacry. Modelling fluctuations of financial time series: from cascade process to stochastic volatility model. *The European Physical Journal B*, **17**(3):537–548, 2000.

J.-F. Muzy and E. Bacry. Multifractal stationary random measures and multifractal random walks with log infinitely divisible scaling laws. *Physical Review E*, **66**(5):056121, 2002.

J.-F. Muzy, D. Sornette, J. Delour, and A. Arneodo. Multifractal returns and hierarchical portfolio theory. *Quantitative Finance*, **1**(1):131–148, 2001.

A. Nawroth and J. Peinke. Multiscale reconstruction of time series. *Physics Letters A*, **360**(2):234–237, 2006.

D. Nelson. Conditional heteroskedasticity in asset returns: A new approach. *Econometrica*, **59**:347–370, 1991.

M. Pasquini and M. Serva. Clustering of volatility as a multiscale phenomenon. *The European Physical Journal B*, **16**(1):195–201, 2000.

J. Perello, J. Masoliver, and J.-P.Bouchaud. Multiple time scales in volatility and leverage correlations: A stochastic volatility model. *Applied Mathematical Finance*, **11**:27–50, 2004.

B. Pochart and J.-P. Bouchaud. The skewed multifractal random walk with applications to option smiles. *Quantitative Finance*, **2**(4):303–314, 2002.

S.B. Pope. *Turbulent flows*. Cambridge university press, 2000.

C. Renner, J. Peinke, and R. Friedrich. Evidence of markov properties of high frequency exchange rate data. *Physica A*, **298**(3):499–520, 2001a.

C. Renner, J. Peinke, and R. Friedrich. Experimental indications for markov properties of small-scale turbulence. *Journal of Fluid Mechanics*, **433**:383–409, 2001b.

G. Richrads. A fractal forecasting model for financial time series. *Journal of Forecasting*, **23**(8):586 – 601, 2004.

C. Richter. *Elementary Seismology*. Freeman, San Francisco, 1958.

H. Risken. *The Fokker-Planck equation: Methods of Solution and Applications*. Springer-Verlag, Berlin, 1989.

P. Ritchken and R. Trevor. Pricing options under generalized garch and stochastic volatility processes. *Journal of Finance*, **54**(1):377–402, 1999.

F. Schmitt, D. Schertzer, and S. Lovejoy. Multifractal fluctuations in finance. *International Journal of Theoretical and Applied Finance*, **3**(3):361–364, 2000.

L. Scott. Option pricing when the variance changes randomly: Theory, estimation, and an application. *Journal of Financial and Quantitative Analysis*, **22**: 419–438, 1987.

E. Sentana. Quadratic arch models. *Review of Economic Studies*, **62**(4):639–661, 1995.

W. Sharpe. Capital asset prices: A theory of market equilibrium under conditions of risk. *Journal of Finance*, **19**(3):425–442, 1964.

M. So, K. Lam, and W. Li. A stochastic volatility model with markov switching. *Journal of Business & Economic Statistics*, **16**(2):244–253, 1998.

E. Stein and J. Stein. Stock price distributions with stochastic volatility: an analytic approach. *Review of Financial Studies*, **4**:727–752, 1991.

A. Subbotin. A multi-horizon scale for volatility. *CES Working Paper 2008.20, University of Paris-1*, 2008. 44 p.

A. Subbotin and T. Chauveau. Price volatility in a market with boundedly rational traders and heterogeneous investment horizons. *Forthcoming*, 2009.

S. Taylor. *Financial Returns Modelled by the Product of two Stochastic Processes a Study of the Daily Sugar Prices 1961-75*, volume 1, pages 203–226. North-Holland, Amsterdam, 1982.

S. Taylor. Modeling stochastic volatility: A review and comparative study. *Mathematical Finance*, **4**(2):183–204, 1994.

J. Woerner. Estimation of integrated volatility in stochastic volatility models. *Applied Stochastic Models in Business and Industry*, **21**(1):27 – 44, 2005.

B. Zhou. High-frequency data and volatility in foreign-exchange rates. *Journal of Business & Economic Statistics*, **14**(1):45–52, 1996.

G. Zumbach. Volatility processes and volatility forecast with long memory. *Quantitative Finance*, **4**(1):70 – 86, 2004.

G. Zumbach, M. Dacorogna, J. Olsen, and R. Olsen. Measuring shocks in financial markets. *International Journal of Theoretical and Applied Finance*, **3**(3):347–355, 2000.

In: Financial Markets and the Global Recession ISBN: 978-1-60741-921-1
Editors: B. Naas and J. Lysne

Chapter 6

LEADER MARKET INDEXES

Emanuele Canegrati
Catholic University of Milan, Italy

Abstract

I perform a multivariate time series analysis of 11 world market indexes in order to measure their relationships and to detect the presence of leader market indexes, defined as those indexes whose trend is followed by other indexes. By using the Johansen cointegration test I show that international financial markets are strongly cointegrated, meaning that a long-term relationship does exist. This evidence confutes the theory which supports portfolio strategies based on the international diversification, since in the presence of cointegrated markets the portfolio risk cannot be reduced without sacrificing the expected return. Furthermore, by performing the Granger causality test I assess the causality realtionships among world indexes, demonstrating how NIKKEI 225 can be considered as a leader market index.

1. Introduction

Is there a market index which reacts faster than other indexes to market events and whose reactions are followed by other indexes? In other words, is there a leader market index? This question has always been particularly attractive to market traders, investors and portfolio managers, who aim to detect market trends to increase their gains from trade. Finance journalism, which is the main provider of financial information, has always seemed to recognize the

existence of a linkage among the performances of world stock markets and it has believed that some stock exchange (e.g. Wall Street) are more influencing than others in tracing the market trends[1]. The matter is strongly related to the quest for the benefits of the international portfolio diversification, started by Grubel (1968), who affirmed that the international diversification of portfolios is the source of world welfare gains form international economic relations, theorizing the advantages of a diversification strategy to obtain higher rates of return in a mean-variance portfolio *à la* Markowitz (1952).The first works aiming to test the validity of Grubel's theory found that the correlation among market returns of national stock exchanges are surprisingly low and that national factors play a special role in the return-generating process. For instance, Granger & Morgenstern (1970) used a spectral analysis to demonstrate that "*contrary to widespread beliefs, there is little or no interrelationship between different stock exchanges around the world*". Also Lessard (1974), by using a simple correlation analysis between national indexes and alternative world factors, discovered that the diversification across countries reults in a greater risk reduction than the diversification across industries within countries.Nevertheless, these early works had never been worried about the long-term relationships among indexes but were mainly based on the short-term concept of correlation[2]. Contributions by Engle & Granger (1987), and Granger & Hallman (1991) provided new econometric methods, based on the core idea of "Granger-causality (G-causality)", which soon demonstrated the limits of the correlation analyses.
This concept of G-causality is often a source of misunderstandings. Granger wrote that the G-causality (and the statistic test which measures it) does not capture a *true* causality among series (e.g. series x_t is the cause of series y_t) but it simply measures the ability of a series to predict another series (e.g. series x_t predicts series y_t). Basically, Granger supposed that if x_t is the G-cause of y_t, then x_t must come before y_t (Hamilton, 1994), as causes logically happen before effects. This definition of causality, which abstracts from sophisticated philosophical conjectures and which is based exclusively on a mere temporal concept, seems to be very helpful to us, who aim to find an answer to our initial

[1]Just to mention two examples, one may read "Asian shares follow Wall Street lower", from the *Financial Times*' web site, 22nd October 2008; "Nikkei's 6.8% Fall Leads Asia Lower", from the *Wall Street Journal*'s web site, 22nd October 2008.

[2]Note that *correlation* and *cointegration* are two distinct concepts and that neither correlation implies cointegration nor cointegration implies correlation. Sometimes, asset returns series are cointegrated in the long-run even though they seem not to follow the same trends in the short run.

questions, since we are looking for an approach which enables us to understand what happens to an index when another one moves in a certain direction, regardless of why this happens. The problem is even more simple than that addressed in other disciplines (i.e. Labor Econometrics) where the goal is to understand why things happen. Smith et al. (1993) were among the first to exploit the Granger causality test in the analysis of international stock returns, examining the stationarity of the time series by using the Dickey-Fuller test. They exploited a bivariate Granger causality rolling test for U.S., Great Britain, West Germany and Japan stock returns and discovered that G-causality is short-lived and gains are still obtainable by diversifying the portfolio. Also Kwan et al. (1995) used a bivariate causality test and find that markets do not show any form of weak-form efficiency in the long run and find a strong presence of unidirectional and bidirectional causality among indexes. Chan et al. (1997) used a time series of monthly stock prices and found that they are integrated of order 1, highlighting the existence of a weak-form efficiency and that a small number of stock markets show evidence of cointegration with others. As a consequence, a diversification strategy may be effective. This study is important because it is one of the first to exploit the Johansen cointegration test, based on the Maximum Likelihood estimator of Johansen, also called *reduced rank model* (1988, 1991). This estimator provides asymptotically efficient estimates of the cointegrating vectors and of the adjustment parameters. Finally, works using the Vector Auto Regressive technique demonstrated the existence of an influence by some stock markets on others. For instance, Ched & Sandgal (1989) showed how the US stock market is the most influential in the world. A VAR model was also used by Mathur & Subrahmanyam (1990) to measure the interdependencies among the Nordic and U.S. Stock Markets.

In this chapter I introduce the definition of market index leader, specifying it as that index which Granger-causes other indices but it is not Granger-caused by any other index. I perform a multivariate time-series analysis to detect the existence of possible leader market indexes in world financial markets. Unit root tests are performed in order to detect the presence of random walk patterns and I also provide a short-term forecasting analysis for future returns.

2. Leader Market Indexes

First of all, it is necessary to introduce the following

Definition 1 *(Leader Market Index) an index is defined as a leader index if it G-causes another index and it is not G-caused by any other index.*

For example, let us take two indexes, say M and N. M is said to be a leader index, with respect to N, if it G-causes (and it is not G-caused by) N. In this contest, the term "leader" must be read as a synonym of "first mover", one whose trend is followed by other indexes. This definition respects the true meaning of the Granger causality, which should not be read as "an event M causes another event N" but as "if M occurs, so does N". Therefore, G-causality is a purely time concept, which helps to ordinate events according to their time ordering. This is exactly what we need to find which indexes move first and how the others react.

More formally, let us write two time series, $M = \{m_t, t, \mathbb{R}\}$ and $N = \{n_t, t, \mathbb{R}\}$, where elements m_t and n_t are values observed at time t; furthermore, let us introduce the history of a series up to t, with $M_t = \{m_{t-s}, s \geq 0\}$, $N_t = \{n_{t-s}, s \geq 0\}$. Denote by Γ_t the information set at t and suppose that

$$M_s \subseteq \Gamma_t \Longleftrightarrow s \leq t$$

$$N_s \subseteq \Gamma_t \Longleftrightarrow s \leq t$$

These two conditions formalize a logical intuition. If we take an information set at time s, we can deduct that this is contained in another information set which exists at a successive instant of time t. That is, information sets enrich themselves over time and contain all the past information, if we assume perfect memory retention.

Definition 2 *(Causality) If we are better able to "predict" m_t by exploiting Γ_t than by exploiting $\Gamma_{t-1} - N_{t-1}$, then N causes M. If we are better able to "predict" m_t by exploiting $\Gamma_{t-1} \cup n_t$ than by exploiting Γ_{t-1}, then N causes M instantaneously.*

Appendix 1 illustrates more in details the concept of causality and causal ordering.

3. Dataset

The dataset I use in this study comprehends the logarithmic stock returns[3] of 11 amongst the most important world market share indexes, divided by geographical macro-areas. Here below, I summarize all the indexes of the sample, with their relative Yahoo code. Time series of daily closing prices, expressed in local currencies, were downloaded from *Yahoo.Finance* web-site[4] for a period of time from January, 2nd 1991 to March, 4th 2009, with a total number of observations equal to 4,580. The indexes are the following:

3.1. United States

- Dow Jones Industrial Average (DJI): The average of the index is calculated from the stock prices of 30 of the largest and most widely held public companies listed on the York Stock Exchange (NYSE).

- NASDAQ (National Association of Securities Dealers Automated Quotations) (IXIC): is a electronic screen-based equity securities trading market with nearly 3,200 companies quoted.

- S&P 500 Index (GSPC): is a value weighted index of the prices of 500 large cap common stocks actively traded on the York Stock Exchange (NYSE) and NASDAQ. Almost all of the stocks included in the index are among the 500 American stocks with the largest market capitalizations.

3.2. Asia & Oceania

- All Ordinaries (AORD), Australia: contains nearly all ordinary shares listed on the *Australian Securities Exchange.* The market capitalization of the companies included in the All Ords index amounts to over 95% of the value of all shares listed on the ASX.

- Hang Seng (HSI), Hong Kong: is a freefloat-adjusted market capitalization-weighted index in Hong Kong, made by 45 companies representing about 67% of capitalization of the *Hong Kong Stock Exchange.*

[3]The logarithmic return is calculated as $r_t = \ln\left(\frac{P_t}{P_{t-1}}\right) = \ln(P_t) - \ln(P_{t-1})$

[4]http://finance.yahoo.com/

- Nikkei 225 (N225), Japan: contains the 225 biggest companies listed on the *Tokyo Stock Exchange* (TSE).
- Straits Times (STI), Republic of Singapore: is a weighted index encompassing the 30 biggest companies listed on the Singapore Stock Exchange.

3.3. Europe

- CAC 40 (FCHI), France: is a capitalization-weighted index of the 40 most significant values among the 100 highest market caps listed on the *Euronext Paris*.
- DAX (GDAXI), Germany: is a blue chip index containing the 30 major German companies listed on the *Frankfurt Stock Exchange*.
- Madrid Stock Exchange General Index (IGBM) (SMSI), Spain: is a capitalization-weighted index that measures the performance of a selected number of continuous market stocks.
- Financial Times Stock Exchange Index (FTSE 100) (FTSE), United Kingdom: is an index of the 100 most highly capitalized UK companies listed on the *London Stock Exchange*.

4. Results

4.1. Descriptive Statistics

Figures 1.1 through 1.11 provide the plots of stock prices for each index over the entire sample period. The diagrams depict how the majority of the indexes have followed the same trend. For instance, DJIA, S&P 500, CAC 40, DAX, SMSI and FTSE show an overall upward-sloping trend, with two peaks, related to the two financial crises which affected the markets as a consequence of the terrorist attacks (September 11st, 2001) and the sub-prime crisis (the end of 2007). Instead, NASDAQ shows a gigantic peak around year 2000, caused by the new-economy bubble and its subsequent burst. Instead, a downward-sloping trend has been followed by the NIKKEI, which reflects the retrenchment of the Japanese economy over the most recent years. We expect that this index does not show a high degree of shared price movement with the other indexes and we will see later that this is just the case.

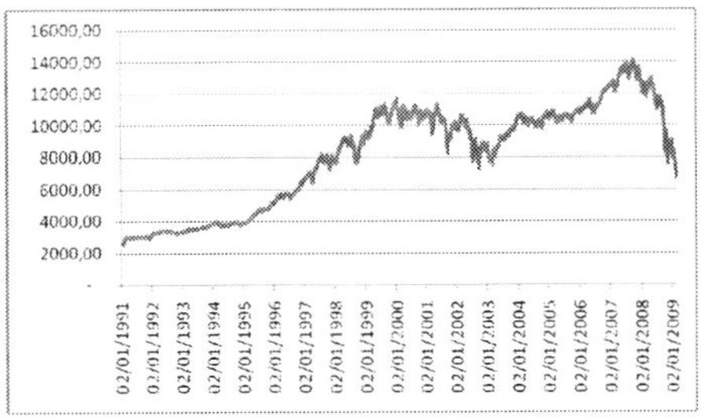

Figure 1.1. Dow Jones Industrial Average.

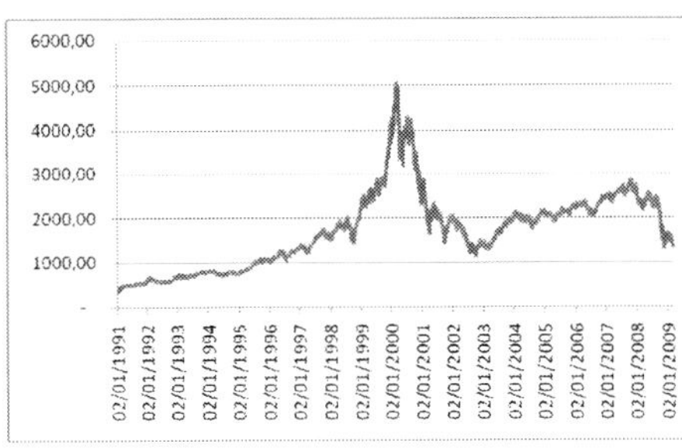

Figure 1.2. NASDAQ

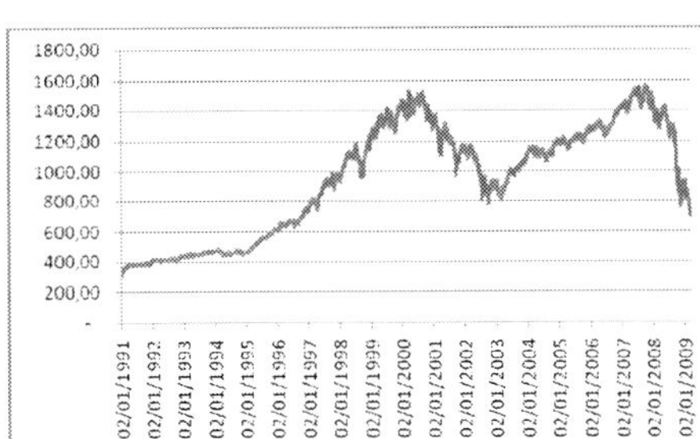

Figure 1.3. S&P 500.

Figure 1. Continued on next page.

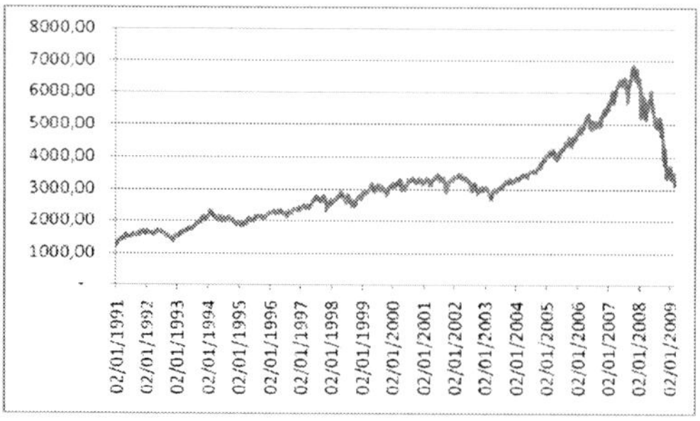

Figure 1.4. All Ordinaries.

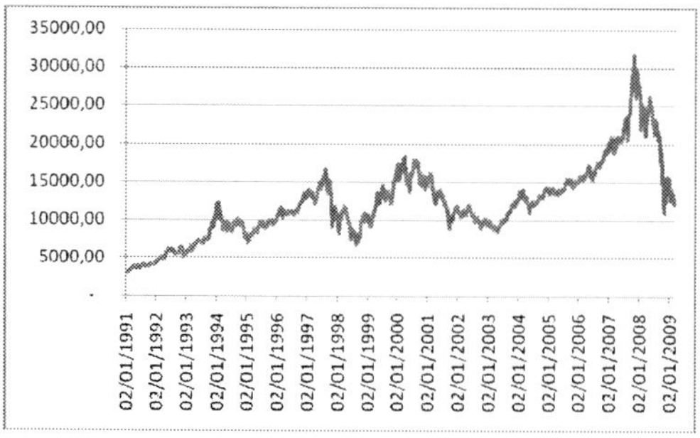

Figure 1.5. Hang Seng.

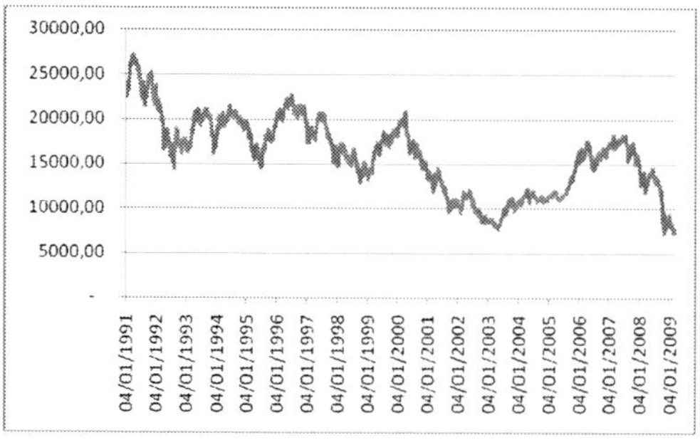

Figure 1.6. NIKKEI 225.

Figure 1. Continued on next page.

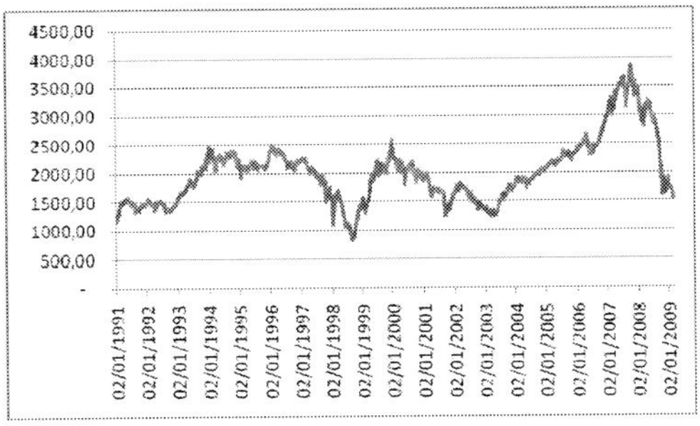

Figure 1.7. Straits Times.

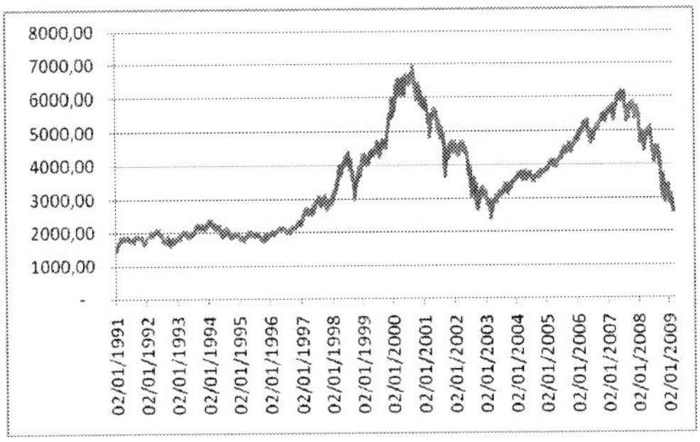

Figure 1.8. CAC 40.

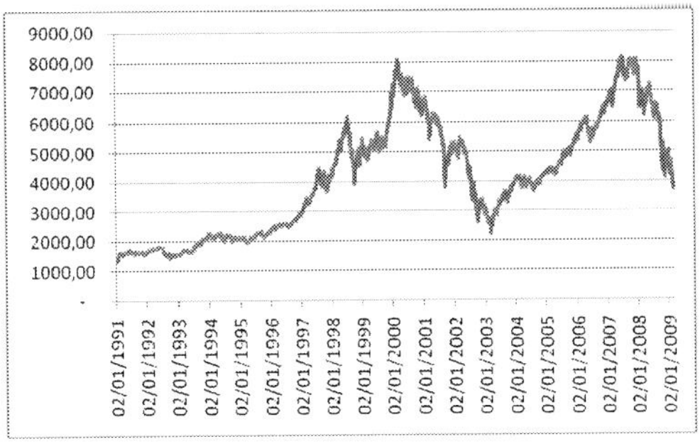

Figure 1.9. DAX.

Figure 1. Continued on next page.

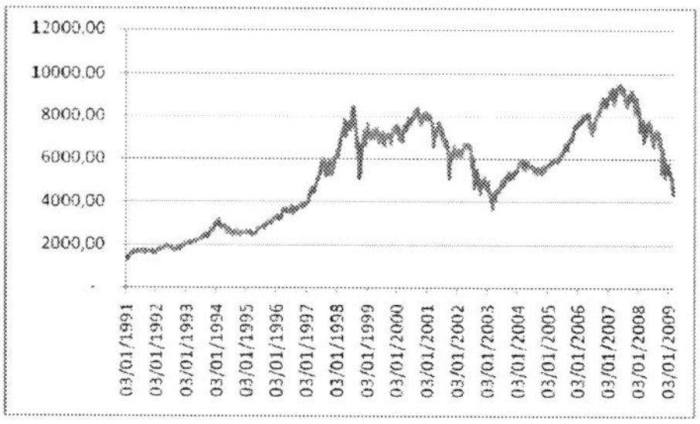

Figure 1.10. Madrid Stock Exchange General Index.

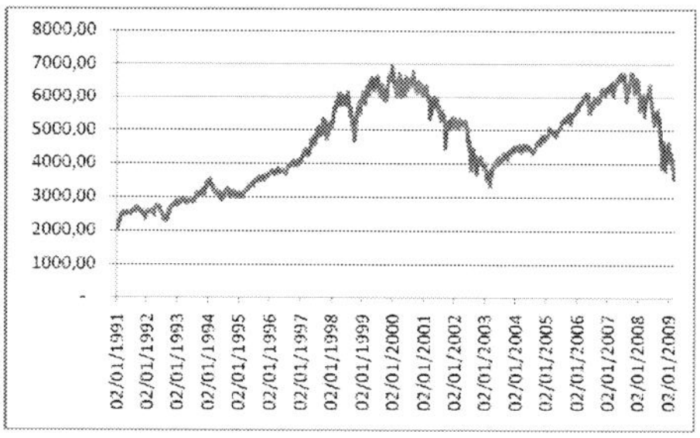

Figure 1.11. FTSE 100.

Figure 1. Stock Market trends.

Table 1 shows the summary statistics of world indexes. The mean of returns is almost the same across indexes, except for NIKKEI and SSMI, which show higher means (0.0064 and 0.0034, respectively). The variance can be taken as a suitable proxy to measure the riskiness of the market. NIKKEI and S&P 500 are characterized by the highest levels of variance, while the level of variance is particularly low for NASDAQ and STRAITS. The values of the skewness clearly show a strong asymmetry in the distribution of returns. The coefficients are all well greater than zero, meaning that the distribution is *right-skewed*, with a few relatively high returns. As for the kurtosis, we can easily see that all the distributions are leptokurtotic, with values of the excess kurtosis particularly high, which shows how more of the variance is generated by unusual extreme deviations.

Table 1. Summary Statistics on Daily Stock Market Returns

	Observations	*Mean*	*Variance*	*Skewness*	*Kurtosis*
DJI	4580	0.0019	0.0136	66.7272	4494.669
IXIC	4580	0.0015	0.0079	64.3982	4286.845
GSPC	4580	0.0014	0.0863	65.8201	4413.468
AORD	4580	0.0017	0.0112	66.8907	4509.374
HIS	4580	0.0021	0.0143	65.4488	4380.182
N225	4580	0.0064	0.0668	38.8138	1513.218
STI	4580	0.0015	0.011	65.7826	4410.074
FCHI	4580	0.0017	0.0118	65.9468	4424.742
GDAXI	4580	0.0018	0.0115	65.768	4408.755
SSMI	4580	0.0034	0.0229	47.3555	2258.286
FTSE	4579	0.0017	0.0129	66.6125	4484.041

4.2. Unit Root Tests

The unit root test is performed to ascertain whether the time series of an index is stationary, and it is a *necessary precondition* to perform the cointegration analysis. The existence of a unit root means that the process is non-stationary; this may cause a false interpretation about the existence of a substantial economic relationship. For example, we can observe that two nonstationary series are related, due to the fact that they both have a trend; this entails high R^2, significant values for the parameters and highly autocorrelated residuals. It is the phenomenon of the *spurious regressions* introduced by Granger & Newbold (1974). As demonstrated by Phillips (1986) when two series are integrated of order one $I(1)$, the error term will also be nonstationary and the OLS estimator will not converge in probability. In the literature on financial markets, the existence of a unit root means that market returns follow a random walk and, therefore, the existence of a weak-form efficiency is guaranteed[5].

Appendix 3 reports a description of the Augmented Dickey-Fuller test and

[5]In the presence of a unit root, a generic AR(1) process becomes $r_t = r_{t-1} + \varepsilon_t$, and since ε_t is IID, the return at day t will be exactly equal to that at the previous day, plus a random component.

Table 2. Augmented Dickey-Fuller Unit Root Test

	ADF First Differences	*ADF (with trend)*	*ADF (with drift)*
DJI	-4.562	-4.757	-4.562
IXIC	-5.923	-6.099	-5.923
GSPC	-5.479	-5.688	-5.479
AORD	-4.369	-4.535	-4.369
HIS	-4.157	-4.263	-4.157
N225	0.341	0.333	0.341
STI	-2.856	-3.003	-2.856
FCHI	-3.955	-4.054	-3.955
GDAXI	-3.679	-3.782	-3.679
SSMI	-1.819	-1.979	-1.819
FTSE	-3.444	-3.567	-3.444

its variants I used in the analysis. Results are presented in table 2[6]. It can be easily seen that the null hypothesis about the existence of a unit root is always rejected at the 1 percent level for every lagged value of the returns $\Delta r = r_t - r_{t-1}$, suggesting the existence of a stationary series of order 1 and satisfying the precondition for the cointegration analysis. As a consequence, the hypothesis about the existence of a weak-form efficiency is strongly rejected.

4.3. Granger Causality

4.3.1. Lag Lenght Selection Criteria

The determination of the optimal leg length of the variables, based on certain rules such as lag length selection criteria, is the precondition to perform the Granger causality test. In fact, in an auto-regressive process, the lag length q is always unknown and therefore has to be estimated. Selecting the right number of lags is fundamental in order to perform a correct analysis, because if the

[6]Critical values for ADF tests are: 1% -3.430; 5% -2.860; 10% - 2.570; Critical values for ADF tests (with trend) are: 1% - 3.960; 5% - 3.410; 10% -3.120; Critical Values for ADF tests (with drift) are: 1% - 2.327; 5% - -1.645; 10% -1.282.

Table 3. Selection Order Criteria

Lag	*FPE*	*AIC*	*HQC*	*BIC*
0	6.9e	39	56.646	56.6406
1	3.4e	43	66.5632	66.4979
2	2.6e	43	66.8508	66.7256*
3	2.5e	43*	66.877*	66.6918
4	2.5e	43	66.87	66.625

number of lags is too small the test is invalidate, while if it is too large it loses power. The lag length selection criteria I evaluated are

- *Akaike information criterion*, $AIC_q = -2T\left[\ln\left(\widehat{\sigma}_q^2\right)\right] + 2q$;
- *Hannan-Quinn criterion*, $HQC_q = \ln\left(\widehat{\sigma}_q^2\right) + 2T^{-1}q\ln\left[\ln\left(T\right)\right]$;
- the *final prediction error*, $FPE_q = \widehat{\sigma}_q^2\left(T-q\right)^{-1}\left(T+q\right)$ and
- *Bayesian information criterion*,
  $BIC_q \quad = \quad (T-q)\ln\left[(T-q)^{-1}T\sigma_q^2\right] \ + \ T\left[1+\ln\left(\sqrt{2\pi}\right)\right] \ +$
  $q\ln\left[p^{-1}\left(\sum_t r_t^2 - T\widehat{\sigma}_q^2\right)\right]$

where q denotes the number of parameters in the statistical model and $\widehat{\sigma}_q^2 = \sum_{t=1}^{T}\widehat{u}_t^2$ is the residual sum of squares. The choice on which criterion we should use is not easy. Liew (2004), by using simulated series, found that HQC is found to outdo the other criterion in correctly identifying the true lag length, while AIC and FPE should be considered a better solution if the sample is small. Since we have a large sample, the best choice is to use the HQC. Table 3 reports the results of the selection order criteria and we can see that the minimum HQC is related to a number of lags equal to 3. The asterisks denote the minimum values.

4.3.2. Vector Autoregressive Model (VAR)

To perform the Granger Causality Wald test a Vector Autoregression Model (VAR) is required. A VAR(q) is a model in which K variables are specified as linear functions of q own lags and q lags of the other $K-1$ variables, plus other possible exogenous variables, υ_t. Algebraically, this can be written as

$$\mathbf{r}_t = \mathbf{v} + \mathbf{B}_1 \mathbf{r}_{t-1} + \ldots + \mathbf{B}_q \mathbf{r}_{t-q} + \mathbf{C}\boldsymbol{\upsilon}_t + \mathbf{u}_t \qquad t \in \mathbb{Z} \tag{1}$$

where $\mathbf{r}_t = (r_{1t,\ldots,}r_{Kt})'$ is a $K \times 1$ vector of market returns, $\mathbf{B}_i$ are $K \times K$ matrices of parameters, $\boldsymbol{\upsilon}_t$ a vector of exogenous variables, $\mathbf{C}$ is a $K \times M$ matrix of coefficients, $\mathbf{v}$ a $K \times 1$ vector of parameters and $\mathbf{u}_t$ is a vector whose elements are "white noise"[7] components.

Table 4 shows the results of the analysis, with $q = 3$, as suggested by the lag lenght selection criteria[8].

After fitting a VAR I checked the *stability* of estimates, which is a stricter condition than the covariance stationarity, since stability implies covariance stationarity, while the converse is not true. A condition for stability was derived by Lutkepohl (1993) and Hamilton (1994), who demonstrated that if the modulus[9] of each eigenvalue of $\mathbf{B}$ is strictly less than one, then the estimated VAR(q) is stable.

The stability of a VAR system can be assessed by calculating the roots of the characteristic polynomial

$$\Pi(z) = \left(I_k - \mathbf{B}_1 z - \mathbf{B}_2 z^2 - \ldots\right)$$

obtained by applying the lag operator L to 1,

$$\left(I_k - \mathbf{B}_1 L - \mathbf{B}_2 L^2 - \ldots\right)\mathbf{r}_t = \Pi(L)\,\mathbf{r}_t = \mathbf{v} + \mathbf{C}\boldsymbol{\upsilon}_t + \mathbf{u}_t \tag{2}$$

Definition 3 *(Stationary Process) if the roots of* $|\Pi(z)|$ *lie all outside the unit circle the process is stationary.*

[7] $\mathbf{u}_t$ is white noise if and only if $E(u_t) = 0$, $Eu_t u_t' = \Sigma_{\mathbf{u}}$, nonsingular, and $Eu_t u_s' = 0$ if $s \neq t$.

[8] ***Significant at 1% of the confidence interval; **significant at 5% of the confidence interval; *significant at 10% of the confidence interval

[9] *Note*: Given a characteristic equation $ax^2 + bx + c = 0$, we know that the $\mathrm{x}_{1/2} = \frac{-b\pm\sqrt{b^2-4ac}}{2a} = \alpha + \beta i$, where $i = \sqrt{-1}$ and the modulus is $\sqrt{\alpha^2 + \beta^2}$.

Table 4. Vector Autoregressive Model

	DJI	*IXIC*	*GSPC*	*AORD*	*HSI*	*N225*	*STI*	*FCHI*	*GDAXI*	*SSMI*	*FTSE*
DJI											
L1.	-0.0154	-0.1168	-0.1004***	-0.0073	-0.0195	0.0446	3.76E-05	-0.0136	0.0008	-0.0009	-0.0314
L2.	-0.019	0.0793	0.0012	0.0488	0.0182	-0.9589	0.1012	0.1243*	0.0057	-0.0157	0.1270**
L3.	0.0558	0.0413	0.0418	0.0715	0.2682***	-0.9882	0.1059	0.0315	0.0052	0.045	0.0139
IXIC											
L1.	0.0503**	0.0825***	0.0390*	0.0398*	0.0588	0.1479	0.0144	-0.0041	0.0205	-0.0132	-0.0067
L2.	0.0227	-0.0069	0.0330*	0.0286	0.0284	-0.2275	0.0476	0.0669**	0.0766***	0.0235	0.0534**
L3.	0	0.0446	0.0132	0.0346	0.0976***	0.1838	0.0396	0.0283	0.0276	0.0227	0.0101
GSPC											
L1.	-0.3577***	-0.3504***	-0.2733***	-0.1373**	-0.2096	-0.6274	-0.0971	-0.0778	-0.0905	-0.0681	-0.044
L2.	-0.1478**	-0.2418***	-0.1725***	-0.1307*	-0.1116	0.716	-0.218	-0.2349***	-0.1242	-0.052	-0.2207***
L3.	-0.0528	-0.1132	-0.0554	-0.1384**	-0.3931***	0.1285	-0.1519	-0.0345	-0.0012	-0.0433	0.007
AORD											
L1.	0.4438***	0.5398***	0.4986***	-0.0101	-0.001	-0.4467	-0.0593	0.4477***	0.4278***	0.031	0.3754***
L2.	-0.1239***	-0.0885***	-0.0949***	-0.0932***	-0.1028**	0.4694	-0.1148	-0.0683**	-0.0564	0.1231***	-0.0661**
L3.	0.0777***	0.0619*	0.0780***	-0.0029	0.0547	-0.2305	0.0335	0.0634**	0.0831***	0.0284	0.0627**
HSI											
L1.	0.0444***	0.1022***	0.0569***	-0.013	0.0225	-0.1556	0.007	0.0576***	0.0438***	-0.0709***	0.0778***
L2.	-0.015	-0.0122	-0.0073	-0.0228*	-0.0221	0.0244	-0.0479***	0.0257	0.0181	0.0560***	0.0012
L3.	0.01285	0.0089	0.0038	0.0295**	0.0991***	0.1004	-0.0234	0.0511***	0.0512***	0.0605***	0.0434***
N225											
L1.	0.0023**	0.0028**	0.0020**	0.0015	0.0015	0.9936***	0.0031**	0.0066***	0.0043***	0.7115***	0.0035***
L2.	0.2518***	0.2135***	0.1840***	0.2392***	0.2949***	-0.1438	0.2710***	0.2326***	0.2189***	-0.0598***	0.2554***
L3.	-0.0232*	-0.0104	-0.0163	-0.0128	-0.0832***	-0.0169	-0.0485***	-0.0247	-0.0385**	-0.0342**	-0.0138

Table 4. Continued

	DJI	*IXIC*	*GSPC*	*AORD*	*HSI*	*N225*	*STI*	*FCHI*	*GDAXI*	*SSMI*	*FTSE*
STI											
L1.	0.0207	0.0462**	0.0168	0.0182	0.1192***	-0.0392	0.2242***	0.0334*	0.0369*	-0.0454**	0.0018
L2.	0.0064	-0.0146	0.0133	0.0335**	0.0912***	0.0329	0.0783***	-0.012	-0.0113	0.028	-0.0046
L3.	0.0214	0.0045	0.0085	0.0115	-0.02	0.0093	0.1070***	0.0005	0.0112	-0.0326*	0.0129
FCHI											
L1.	-0.0976***	0.0252	-0.0231	-0.1952***	-0.1724***	-0.6026*	-0.2123***	-0.1860***	-0.1170***	-0.1381***	-0.2310***
L2.	-5.80E-05	0.0073	-0.0093	-0.0024	-0.1007***	0.172	-0.0553*	-0.0522*	-0.0738**	-0.0934***	-0.0183
L3.	-0.0400*	-0.0516*	-0.0367*	-0.0111	-0.0109	0.6866**	-0.0426	-0.1038***	-0.0855***	-0.011	-0.0519
GDAXI											
L1.	-0.1887***	-0.1710***	-0.1542***	-0.1445***	-0.2213***	-0.2563	-0.1576***	-0.1395***	-0.2806***	0.0177	-0.1801***
L2.	0.0134	0.0491*	0.0226	0.0184	0.0294	0.1548	0.0352	0.0998***	0.0496*	0.0765***	0.0377*
L3.	0.0352	0.0439*	0.026	0.0143	0.0952***	-0.0778	0.0608**	0.0114	0.0093	0.0084	0.0217
SSMI											
L1.	0.7311***	0.5145***	0.5391***	0.6519***	0.6924***	0.2095	0.5900***	0.6759***	0.6852***	0.0897***	0.6967***
L2.	-0.0229	-0.0283	-0.0161	-0.037	0.007	-0.0967	-0.0055	-0.0433	-0.0506	0.0395	-0.0724***
L3.	0.0381*	0.0108	0.0321	0.0568**	0.0573	0.1993	0.044	0.027	0.0165	-0.0551*	0.0193
FTSE											
L1.	-0.0824***	0.011	-0.0067	-0.2567***	-0.2484***	0.3566	-0.2260***	-0.4299***	-0.3098***	-0.2201***	-0.3379***
L2.	0.0272	0.0486	0.0348	-0.0352	-0.0413	-0.1112	-0.0316	-0.1005***	-0.0428	0.0056	-0.0715***
L3.	-0.0166	0.0362	-0.0005	-0.0563**	-0.1234***	-0.1044	-0.0496	-0.0316	-0.0539	0.0384	-0.0955***

Equivalently, if the eigenvalues of the companion matrix of 1 are inside the unit circle the process is stationary[10].

Definition 4 *(Nonstationary Process) if one or more roots of* $|\Pi(z)|$ *lies on the unit circle, the process is nonstationary.*

Equivalently, if one or more eigenvalues of the companion matrix of 1 are on the unit circle the process is stationary.

Definition 5 *(Explosive Process) if one or more roots of* $|\Pi(z)|$ *lies inside the unit circle the process is explosive.*

Equivalently, if one or more eigenvalues of the companion matrix of 1 are outside the unit circle the process is stationary.

If we omit $\mathbf{C}\boldsymbol{v}_t$ and $\mathbf{u}_t$ from 2, the simplest (*homogeneous* or *trivial*) solution to $\Pi(L)\, r_t = \mathbf{v}$ is

$$\mathbf{r}_t = \mathbf{r}_{t-1} = \ldots = \overline{\mathbf{r}}$$

Otherwise, the nontrivial solution requires the calculation of the eigenvalues $\lambda \in \mathbb{C}$ and relative eigenvectors $\mathbf{c}_s$ to solve $|\lambda I - B| = 0$. After having calculated the nontrivial solution and having added it to the trivial solution, we obtained the complete solution

$$\mathbf{r}_t = \lambda_1 \mathbf{c}_1 + \ldots + \lambda_q \mathbf{c}_q + \overline{\mathbf{r}}$$

As t rises, $\mathbf{r}_t \longrightarrow \overline{\mathbf{r}}$ if $|\lambda| < 1$. Alternatively, we can solve the problem by using the companion matrix, solving

$$\begin{cases} \mathbf{r}_t = \mathbf{v} + \mathbf{B}_1 \mathbf{r}_{t-1} + \ldots + \mathbf{B}_q \mathbf{r}_{t-q} + \mathbf{C}\boldsymbol{v}_t + \mathbf{u}_t \\ \mathbf{r}_{t-1} = \mathbf{r}_{t-1} \\ \vdots \\ \mathbf{r}_{t-q+1} = \mathbf{r}_{t-q+1} \end{cases}$$

and

$$|\lambda I - B| = \left\| \begin{bmatrix} \lambda I & \cdots & 0 \\ \vdots & \ddots & \vdots \\ 0 & \cdots & \lambda I \end{bmatrix} - \begin{bmatrix} \mathbf{B}_1 & \cdots & \mathbf{B}_q \\ \cdots & \cdots & \cdots \\ I & \vdots & 0 \end{bmatrix} \right\| = 0$$

[10] The roots obtained by solving the characteristic polynomial are the inverse of the roots directly obtained by the companion matrix.

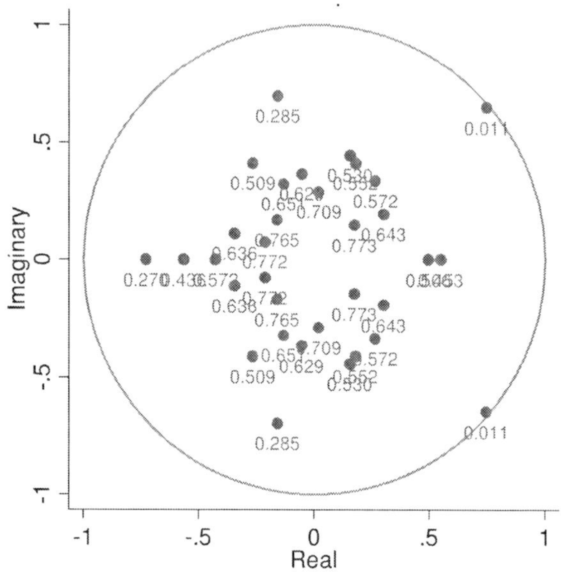

Figure 2. Stability Condition Test; Each point of the graph denotes the modulus of each eigenvalue, within the unit circle, and it is characterized by two coordinates, one imaginary (vertical axis) and another real (horizontal axis).

that is

$$\begin{vmatrix} \lambda - \mathbf{B}_1 & -\mathbf{B}_2 & \cdots & \cdots & -\mathbf{B}_q \\ -I & \lambda - I & 0 & \cdots & 0 \\ 0 & -I & \ddots & \ddots & \vdots \\ \vdots & \vdots & \ddots & \ddots & 0 \\ 0 & \cdots & \cdots & -I & \lambda \end{vmatrix}$$

[11] whose roots are given by the resolution of a q-order polynomial.

Figure 2 shows the results of the stability test. It is easy to see that the modulus of each eigenvalue is strictly less than one, so that the stability condition is fulfilled.

---

[11] Just to provide an example, suppose that $q = 3$. It must be $\begin{vmatrix} \lambda - \mathbf{B}_1 & -\mathbf{B}_2 & -\mathbf{B}_q \\ -I & \lambda - I & 0 \\ 0 & -I & \lambda \end{vmatrix} = 0$, which is equal to $(\lambda - \mathbf{B}_1)(\lambda - I)\lambda - \mathbf{B}_2 = 0$, which has three solutions in $\mathbb{C}$.

4.3.3. Forecasting

VAR can be seen as a way to costruct financial dynamic forecasts, in order to predict future market returns. A $g-$ day ahead forecast can be written as

$$\widehat{\mathbf{r}}_t(g) = \widehat{\mathbf{v}} + \sum_{i=1}^{q} \widehat{\mathbf{B}}_i \widehat{\mathbf{r}}_t(g-i) + \widehat{\mathbf{C}} \widehat{\boldsymbol{v}}_{t+g}$$

where this equation is recursive, meaning that the prediction at day g determines the prediction at day $g+1$. As demonstrated by Lutkepohl (1993) the asymptotic estimator of the covariance matrix for the prediction error can be written as

$$\widehat{\sum}_{\widehat{\mathbf{r}}}(g) = \widehat{\sum}_{\mathbf{r}}(g) + \frac{1}{T}\widehat{\Upsilon}(g)$$

with

$$\widehat{\sum}_{\mathbf{r}}(g) = \sum_{i=0}^{g-1} \widehat{\mathbf{\Phi}}_i \widehat{\sum} \widehat{\mathbf{\Phi}}_i'$$

and

$$\widehat{\Upsilon}(g) = \frac{1}{T}\sum_{t=0}^{T1}\left[\sum_{i=0}^{g-1} \mathbf{Z}_t'(\mathbf{B}')^{g-1-i} \otimes \widehat{\mathbf{\Phi}}_i\right] \sum_{\beta} \left[\sum_{i=0}^{g-1} \mathbf{Z}_t'(\mathbf{B}')^{g-1-i} \otimes \widehat{\mathbf{\Phi}}_i\right]'$$

$$\widehat{\mathbf{B}} = \begin{bmatrix} \mathbf{1} & \mathbf{0} & \mathbf{0} & \dots & \mathbf{0} & \mathbf{0} \\ \widehat{\mathbf{v}} & \widehat{\mathbf{W}}_1 & \widehat{\mathbf{W}}_2 & \dots & \widehat{\mathbf{W}}_{q-1} & \widehat{\mathbf{W}}_q \\ \dots & \dots & \dots & \dots & \dots & \dots \\ \mathbf{0} & & \vdots & \mathbf{I}_k & \vdots & \mathbf{0} \end{bmatrix}$$

$$\begin{aligned} \mathbf{Z}_t' &= (1, \mathbf{r}_t', \dots, \mathbf{r}_{t-q-1}') \\ \widehat{\mathbf{\Phi}}_0 &= \mathbf{I}_k \\ \widehat{\mathbf{\Phi}}_i &= \sum_{j=0}^{i} \widehat{\mathbf{\Phi}}_{i-j} \widehat{\mathbf{W}}_j \qquad i = 1, 2, \dots \\ \widehat{\mathbf{W}}_j &= 0 \qquad for \quad j > q \end{aligned}$$

Graphs 3.1 - 3.11 show the forecasts for each index, for a period of 4 days and show that the predictions are quite precise, since the forecast is always very close to the observed data and the 95% of the confidence interval band is not very far from the forecast line. Prediction slightly deteriorate only after the third day, as we observe that the 95% of the confidence interval band gets broader. All predicted returns follow a decreasing trend, which reflects the negative market sentiment at the time of the analysis. This results must be taken with accuracy and seen as an exercise whose attempt is to predict the future by looking the past. Which is reasonable, as long as we find that the random walk hypothesis is rejected.

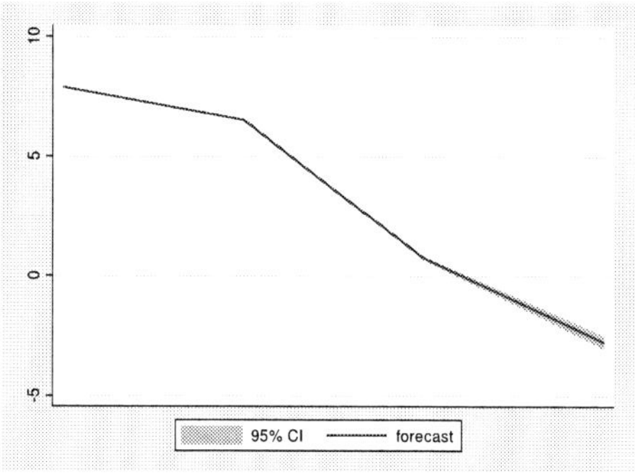

Figure 3.1. Dow Jones Industrial Average.

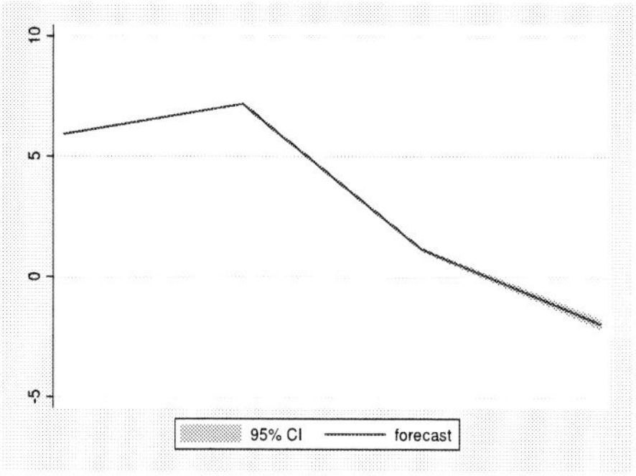

Figure 3.2. NASDAQ.

Figure 3. Continued on next page.

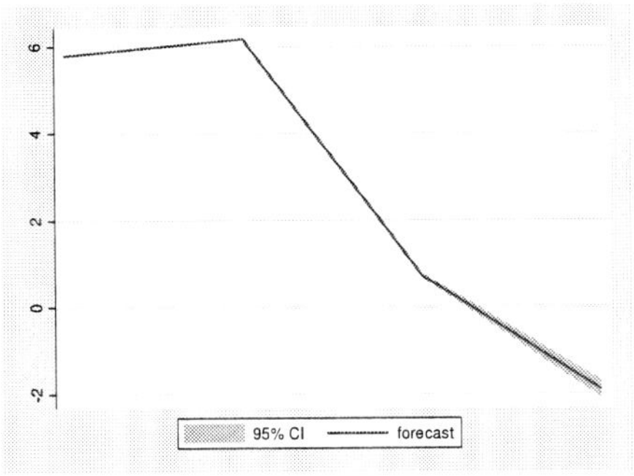

Figure 3.3. S&P 500.

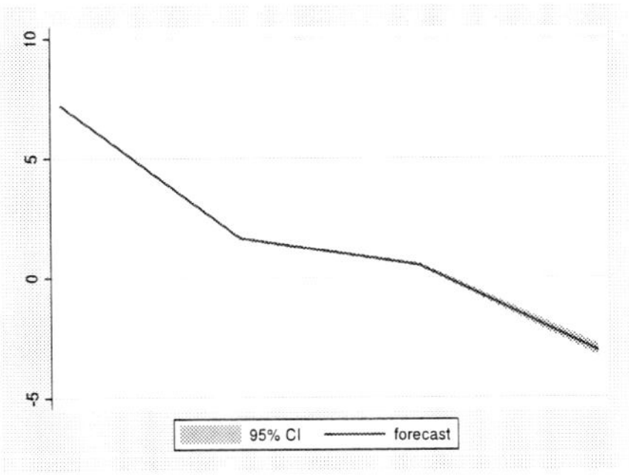

Figure 3.4. All Ordinaries.

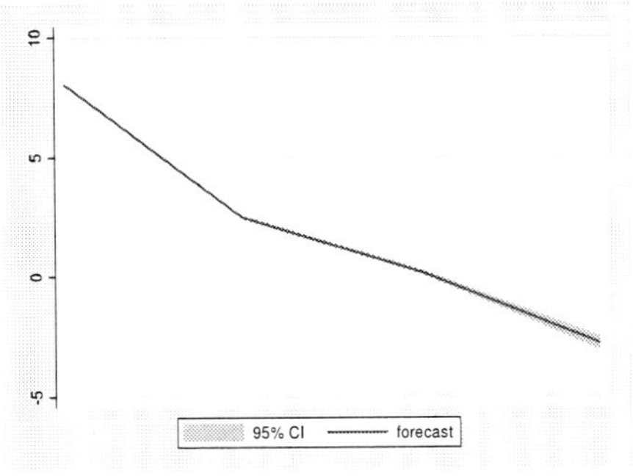

Figure 3.5. Hang Seng.

Figure 3. Continued on next page.

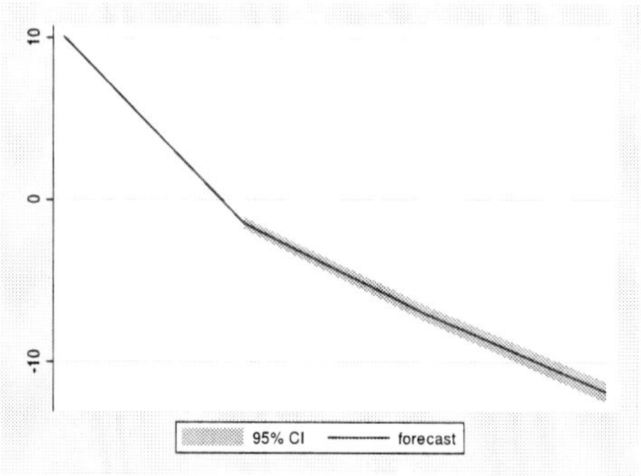

Figure 3.6. NIKKEI 225.

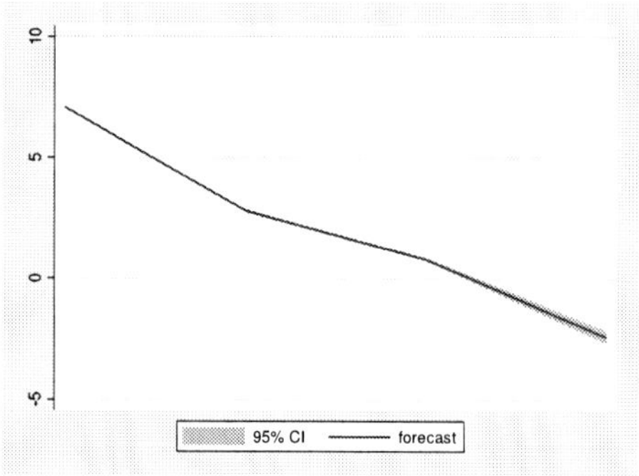

Figure 3.7. Straits Times.

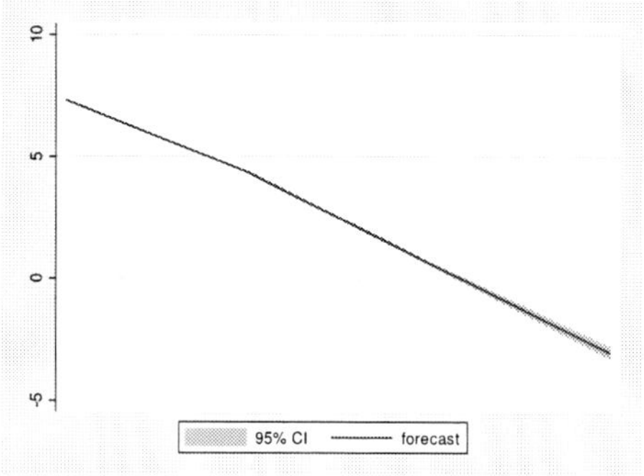

Figure 3.8. CAC 40.

Figure 3. Continued on next page.

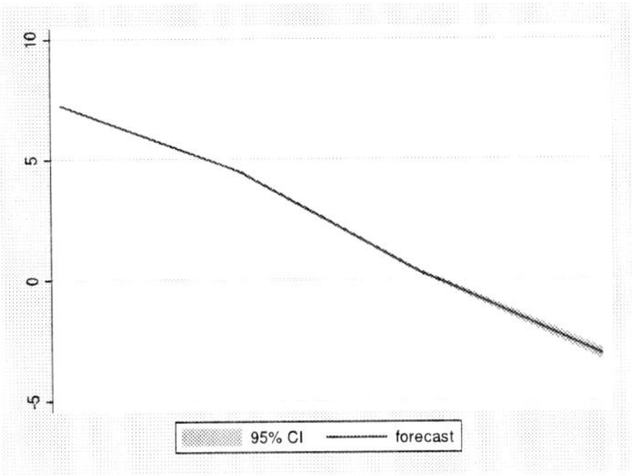

Figure 3.9. DAX.

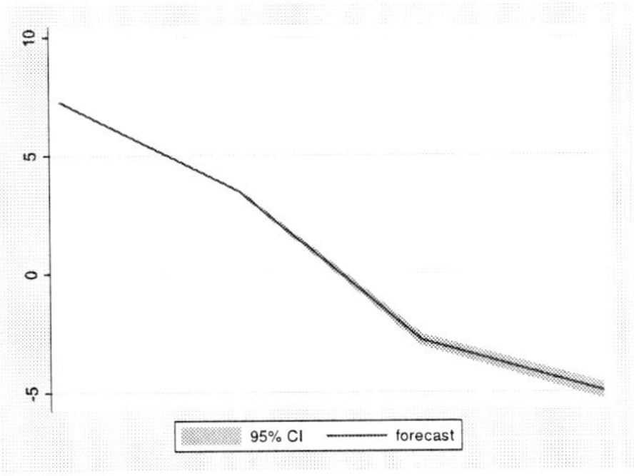

Figure 3.10. Madrid Stock Exchange General Index.

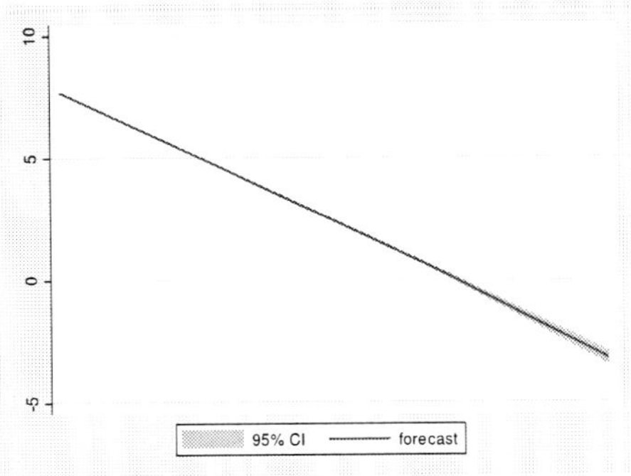

Figure 3.11. FTSE 100.

Figure 3. Stock Market Forecasts.

4.3.4. Granger causality Wald Test

Table 5 shows the results of the Granger causality Wald test. The test consists in regressing the stock returns of a given index on its own lagged values and on lagged values of the other indexes, and then testing the null hypothesis that the estimated coefficients on the lagged values of the other indexes are jointly equal to zero. If the null cannot be rejected, then we fail to reject the hypothesis that another index does not G-cause the given index. This process is made for every index. Finally, another test which set as null hypothesis that coefficients on the lags of all the other indexes are jointly zero. If the null cannot be rejected, we cannot reject that all the indexes, jointly, do not G-cause a given index.

Hereafter, I summarize tha main findings:

- **DJI** is G-caused by **GSPC, AORD, HIS, N225, FCHI, GDAXI, SSMI, FTSE** and **ALL** indexes at the 1% of the confidence interval, and by **IXIC** at the 10% of the confidence interval. Furthermore, it does not G-causes any other index.

- **IXIC** is G-caused by **GSPC**, **AORD**, **HIS**, **N225**, **GDAXI**, **SSMI**, and **ALL** indexes at the 1% of the confidence interval. Furthermore, it G-causes **AORD**, **HSI** and **GDAXI** at the 5% of the confidence interval, and **DJI** and **FCHI** at the 10% of the confidence interval.

- **GSPC** is G-caused by **AORD**, **HIS**, **N225**, **GDAXI**, **SSMI**, and **ALL** indexes at the 1% of the confidence interval. Furthermore, it G-causes **DJI**, **IXIC**, **AORD** and **HSI** at the 1% of the confidence interval and **STI, FCHI** and **FTSE** at the 5% of the confidence interval.

- **AORD** is G-caused by **GSPC**, **N225**, **FCHI**, **GDAXI**, **SSMI**, **FTSE** and **ALL** indexes at the 1% of the confidence interval and by **IXIC, HIS** and **STI** at the 5% of the confidence interval. Furthermore, it G-causes **DJI**, **IXIC**, **GSPC**, **STI, FCHI, GDAXI, SSMI** and **FTSE** at the 1% of the confidence interval and by **HSI** at the 5% of the confidence interval.

- **HSI** is G-caused by **GSPC**, **N225**, **FCHI**, **GDAXI**, **SSMI**, **FTSE** and **ALL** indexes at the 1% of the confidence interval and by **IXIC** and **AORD** and **STI** at the 5% of the confidence interval. Furthermore, it G-causes **DJI**, **IXIC**, **GSPC**, **FCHI**, **GDAXI**, **SSMI** and **FTSE** at the 1% of the confidence interval and **AORD** and **STI** at the 5% of the confidence interval.

- **N225** is G-caused by **ALL** indexes at the 1% of the confidence interval and by **FCHI** at the 5% of the confidence interval. Furthermore, it G-causes **DJI, IXIC, GSPC, AORD, HSI, STI, FCHI, GDAXI, SSMI** and **FTSE** at the 1% of the confidence interval.

- **STI** is G-caused by **AORD, N225, FCHI, GDAXI, SSMI, FTSE** and **ALL** indexes at the 1% of the confidence interval and by **GSPC** and **HIS** at the 5% of the confidence interval. Furthermore, it G-causes **AORD, HSI** and **SSMI** at the 5% of the confidence interval.

- **FCHI** is G-caused by **AORD, HIS, N225, GDAXI, SSMI** and **FTSE** at the 1% of the confidence interval and **GSPC** at the 5% of the confidence interval and **IXIC** at the 10% of the confidence interval. Furthermore, it G-causes **DJI, AORD, HSI, STI, GDAXI, SSMI** and **FTSE** at the 1% of the confidence interval and **N225** at the 5% of the confidence interval.

- **GDAXI** is G-caused by **AORD, HIS, N225, FCHI, SSMI, FTSE** and **ALL** indexes at the 1% of the confidence interval and by **IXIC** at the 5% of the confidence interval. Furthermore, it G-causes **DJI, IXIC, GSPC, AORD, HSI, STI, FCHI** and **FTSE** at the 1% of the confidence interval, and **SSMI** at the 5% of the confidence interval.

- **SSMI** is G-caused by **AORD, HSI, N225, FCHI, FTSE** and **ALL** indexes at the 1% of the confidence interval and **STI** and **GDAXI** at the 5% of the confidence interval. Furthermore, it G-causes **DJI, IXIC, GSPC, AORD, HSI, STI, FCHI, GDAXI** and **FTSE** at the 1% of the confidence interval.

- **FTSE** is G-caused by **AORD, HSI, N225, FCHI, GDAXI, SSMI** and **ALL** indexes at the 1% of the confidence interval, and by **GSPC** at the 5% of the confidence interval. Furthermore, **DJI, AORD, HSI, STI, FCHI, GDAXI** and **SSMI** at the 1% of the confidence interval.

Table 5. Granger Causality Wald Test

	DJI	*IXIC*	*GSPC*	*AORD*	*HSI*	*N225*	*STI*	*FCHI*	*GDAXI*	*SSMI*	*FTSE*
DJI	-	0.272	0.203	0.439	0.439	0.328	0.251	0.356	1	0.934	0.21
IXIC	0.072*	-	0.068	0.05**	0.05**	0.782	0.189	0.084*	0.04**	0.65	0.161
GSPC	0***	0***	-	0.005***	0.005***	0.806	0.02**	0.046**	0.415	0.742	0.031**
AORD	0***	0***	0***	-	0.016**	0.174	0***	0***	0***	0***	0***
HIS	0.001***	0***	0***	0.016**	-	0.758	0.017**	0***	0***	0***	0***
N225	0***	0***	0***	0***	0***	-	0***	0***	0***	0***	0***
STI	0.125	0.114	0.269	0.019**	0.019**	0.996	-	0.368	0.268	0.02**	0.882
FCHI	0***	0.298	0.217	0***	0***	0.034**	0***	-	0***	0***	0***
GDAXI	0***	0***	0***	0***	0***	0.684	0***	0***	-	0.032**	0***
SSMI	0***	0***	0***	0***	0***	0.647	0***	0***	0***	-	0***
FTSE	0.005***	0.371	0.544	0***	0***	0.756	0***	0***	0***	0***	-
ALL	0***	0***	0***	0***	0***	0.008***	0***	0.356	0***	0***	0***

Looking at the results, we can see that world financial markets are highly integrated and that the relation among world indexes is complex. In particular, two results emerge. First of all, the Dow Jones Industrial Average is G-caused by all the other indexes but does not G-cause any other index. This is surprising and goes against the common belief that the US financial market is the one which determines the trends of all the other indexes. Secondly, the Nikkei 225 clearly emerges as the leader market index, at least if we don't consider the effects of the variable ALL indexes: it is not G-caused by any other specific index and G-cause all the other indexes at the 1% of the confidence interval.

4.4. Johansen Multivariate Cointegration Tests

I use the Johansen (1988) multivariate cointegration tests to detect the number of common stochastic trends, that is, how many cointegrating vectors there are in the stock markets. Basically, the Johansen method furnishes a tool for the estimation of multivariate cointegrating systems based on the error correction mechanism of the basic VAR model with Gaussian errors. The Error Correction Model (VECM) explicates the autoregressive model

$$\mathbf{r}_t = \mathbf{B}_1\mathbf{r}_{t-1} + \ldots + \mathbf{B}_q\mathbf{r}_{t-q} + \mathbf{u}_t \tag{3}$$

into

$$\Delta\mathbf{r}_t = \sum_{i=1}^{q-1}\mathbf{\Gamma}_i\mathbf{r}_{t-i} + \mathbf{\Pi}_i\mathbf{r}_{t-q} + \mathbf{u}_t \tag{4}$$

with $\mathbf{\Gamma}_i = -\overbrace{(I - \mathbf{B}_1 - \mathbf{B}_i)}^{nxn}$ and $\mathbf{\Pi}_i = -\overbrace{(I - \mathbf{B}_1 - \mathbf{B}_q)}^{nxn}$ and I is the identity matrix. The number of distinct cointegrating vectors is determined by $rank\,(\mathbf{\Pi}_i)$ because it measures the number of linearly independent combinations of $\mathbf{r}_t$. As suggested by Fraser & Oyefeso (2005) the number of cointegrating vectors reveals the magnitude of integration among stock markets, because, if the matrix is full rank stochastic trends are absent and cointegration is not defined, while if the number of correlated cointegrating relationships between $\mathbf{r}_t$ is equal to zero, there are no stationary long-run relationships among the elements of $\mathbf{r}_t$. Denote $\ell^*\,(rank_i)$ the maximum of the likelihood of the VECM model under cointegration rank $rank_i$

$$\lambda_{LR}(rank_0, rank_1) = 2\left[\ln \frac{\ell^*(rank_0)}{\ell^*(rank_1)}\right] = -T\sum_{i=rank_0+1}^{rank_1} \ln(1-\lambda_i)$$

where λs are the ordered eigenvalues of a particular matrix used in the ML estimation of the VECM. The test statistic for the first $\lambda_{LR}(rank_0, k)$ is called *trace statistics*, and for the second $\lambda_{LR}(rank_0, rank_0+1)$ the *maximum eigenvalue statistic*. Under the null hypothesis Johansen demonstrated that

$$\lambda_{LR}(rank_0, k) \xrightarrow{d} trace(\Omega)$$

and

$$\lambda_{LR}(rank_0, rank_0+1) \xrightarrow{d} \lambda_{\max}(\Omega)$$

where

$$\Omega = \frac{\left(\int_0^1 \mathbf{\Lambda} d\mathbf{\Lambda}^{\mathbf{T}}\right)^{\mathbf{T}} \left(\int_0^1 \mathbf{\Lambda} d\mathbf{\Lambda}^{\mathbf{T}}\right)}{\left(\int_0^1 \mathbf{\Lambda}\mathbf{\Lambda}^{\mathbf{T}} ds\right)}$$

where $\dim(\mathbf{\Lambda}) = k - rank_0$ is a standard Wiener process.

Table 6 contains the Johansen test used to assess the rank of the cointegrating matrix in the VECM. Each row of the table tests a different null hypothesis that the number of cointegrating relationships is equal to r, reported in the maximum rank column. The alternative is that there are more than r cointegrating relationships. As a rule, the null hypothesis is rejected if the trace statistic is greater than the critical value reported in the last column. The first test is $H_0 : r = 1$ and so on until the test is not rejected. Critical values are from Johansen and Nielson (1993). The tests indicate 11 cointegrating equations.

Table 6. Johansen tests for cointegration

Maximum Rank	*Prms*	*LL*	*Eigenvalue*	*Trace Statistics*	*5% critical value*
None	242	81610.5	.	7987.08	255.27
At most 1 *	263	82198.2	0.36592	6811.69	212.67
At most 2 *	282	82669.2	0.3059	5869.62	175.77
At most 3 *	299	83114.8	0.29207	4978.45	141.2
At most 4 *	314	83538.6	0.28001	4130.87	109.99
At most 5 *	327	83939.2	0.26697	3329.61	82.49
At most 6 *	338	84317.7	0.25428	2572.61	59.46
At most 7 *	347	84677.2	0.2432	1853.66	39.89
At most 8 *	354	85028.2	0.23822	1151.65	24.31
At most 9 *	359	85335.2	0.21178	537.673	12.53
At most 10 *	362	85601.9	0.18679	4.2063	3.84
At most 11 *	363	85604	0.00163		

5. Considerations

5.1. Implications for Portfolio Allocation

In globalised financial markets, with free movements of capitals, traders, risk managers and international watchdogs are particularly interested in looking for tools which may help to disclose and forecast the interaction across financial markets. Being able to capture and predict market trends means being able to gain precision in pricing underlying assets and derivatives and to perform hedging strategies (Herwany & Febrien, 2008) and the measurement of the one-way and two-way causal relationships across market indexes is very helpful in developing portfolio strategies. In the presence of causality among indexes, the inclusion of those indexes would not lead to a diversified portfolio.

Granger & Hallman (1991) demonstrated how investment strategies exclusively based on short-term returns are harmful, since they simply neglect to consider long-term relationships. They also demonstrated how hedging strategies based on long-term relationships require less rebalancing of portfolio than those based on short-term relationships. A recent strand of literature followed by Alexander (2001) has started to simulate hedge fund strategies, substituting the concept of short-term correlation with the long-term cointegration, demonstrating that "this approach efficient market neutral long short hedge strategies may be achieved with relative few stocks and with much lower turnover rates compared to traditional market neutral strategies". In turn, the use of Granger-causality and cointegration analyses can lead to a more precise and parsimonious asset allocation.

Finally, the existence of highly cointegrated financial markets entails that a diversification strategy among national stock markets will not greatly reduce the portfolio risk, without sacrificing the expected return. The lack of interdependence across national stock markets has been presented as evidence supporting the benefits of international portfolio diversification, but our evidence shows that this is not the case. As a consequence, Grubel's theory is strongly confuted.

5.2. Leader Market Indexes and Efficient Market Hypothesis

According to the World Federation of Exchanges the three major Stock Exchanges in the world in terms of capitalization and total share turnover are the New York Stock Exchange (NYSE), the Tokyo Stock Exchange (TSE) and the Euronext[12]. Since Tokyo is eight hours ahead of West-European countries and fourteen hours ahead of New York, there is a two and one-half hour difference between the close of the Japanese Exchange and the open of Euronext, and eight and one-half hour difference between the close of Tokyo and the open of New York[13]. As a consequence, there is no overlapping periods of time in which Japanese, European and US markets are open. In the presence of efficient markets there should not exist a significant relationship between the open to close returns of these three markets since, over the day, new information flows into the market and prices instantly reflect all the available information so that, for example, the returns of NYSE should reflect all the new information flew into the market from the close of TSE on. The existence of cointegration among markets is clearly a violation of the efficiency hypothesis, since the information about TSE returns can be used to profitably trade in Euronext and NYSE markets. Furthermore, the absence of a unit root in the stochastic process, as captured by the Augmented Dickey-Fuller test, is a rejection of the Random Walk Hypothesis, since returns follow a trend and of the weak form of efficiency, which states that

[12]The market values of NYSE, TSE and Euronext are \$ 9,363,074 mln, \$ 2,922,616 mln and \$ 1,862,930 mln and the total share turnover is 1,517,615 mln, 301,781 mln and 146,173 mln respectively (all data are at the end of January 2009).

[13]The TSE opens at 12:00 p.m. GMT (Western Europe Standard Time) and closes at 6:00 a.m. GMT. The Euronext opens at 9:00 p.m. GMT and closes at 5:30 p.m. GMT. The NYSE opens at 2:30 p.m. GMT and closes at 10:00 p.m. GMT.

share prices exhibit no serial dependencies, meaning that processes are trendless and that future prices cannot be predicted by analyzing past prices[14]. Again, this evidence open a great dibate upon the possibility to use the Technical Analysis to detect the presence of market trends and to forecast, at least to a certain degree, future returns.

6. Conclusion

In this chapter I performed a multivariate time series analysis of 11 world market indexes in order to detect the presence of leader market indexes. I demonstrated that international financial markets are strongly cointegrated, meaning that a long-term relationship exists. This evidence confutes the theory which suggests the use of portfolio strategies based on the international diversification, since in the presence of cointegrated markets the portfolio risk cannot be reduced without sacrificing the expected return. Furthermore, I assessed the causality realtionships among world indexes, demonstrating how the Japanese index, instead of the US one, can be considered as a leader market index.

Appendix 1. Causality

Suppose to have a space of possible outcomes $\mathbb{C}$ and two sets of restrictions on these outcomes $M, N \subset \mathbb{C}$, with $(M \cap N) \subset \mathbb{C}$. x and y map $\mathbb{C}$ by the probabilistic functions $\Pr_x$ and $\Pr_y$. We write the set of the following 5 axioms which represents the steps to define the concept of causality. The expression $x \circlearrowright y$ must be read as "the couple (M, N) determines a causal ordering from x to y".

- Axiom of *Causal Ordering from x to y, $x \circlearrowright y$*

$$C1 := \left(\Pr_y(M) = M\right) \cap \left(\Pr_x(M \cap N) = \Pr_x(M)\right) \Rightarrow (M, N) \subset \mathbb{C} \quad x \circlearrowright y$$

[14]The random walk hypothesis entails that a first-order forecast $\widehat{r_h}(1) = E(r_{h+1}|r_h, r_{h-1}, \ldots) = r_h$, and generalizing, $\widehat{r_h}(l) = r_h$, for any forecast horizon $l > 0$.

- Axiom of *Acceptance of input X by N*

$$\begin{aligned} C2 \quad : \quad &= \left(\overset{-1}{\underset{x}{\Pr}} \left(\underset{x}{\Pr}(M) \right) = M, \quad \forall M \subset \mathtt{C} \right) \\ &\Longrightarrow C1 \end{aligned}$$

- Axiom of *Realilzability of N with X as input*

$$C3 := C2 \cap \left(\begin{array}{c} \Pr_{x_t}(M_1) = \Pr_{x_t}(M_2) \\ \Rightarrow \Pr_{y_s} \left(\Pr_{x_t}(M_1 \cap N) = \Pr_{x_t}(M_2 \cap N) \right), \\ \forall M_1, M_2 \subset \mathtt{C}, \forall t \geq s \end{array} \right)$$

- Axiom of *Structurality of N with x as input*

$$C4 := C3 \cap \left(\begin{array}{c} \text{\textit{any implemented}}\ C \subseteq \mathtt{C} \\ \Rightarrow \Pr_y \left(\Pr_x^{-1}(C) \cap B \right) = \mathbf{True} \end{array} \right)$$

- Axiom of *Causality*

$$C5 := C3 \Rightarrow C4$$

Appendix 2. Multi-variate Granger Causality Test

The standard multi-variate Granger causality test adopts an OLS approach of the following system of equations

$$\begin{aligned}
Y_t &= \mu_0 + \mu_1 Y_{t-1} + ... + \mu_k Y_{t-k} + \\
&+ \sum_{p=1}^{P} \left(\gamma_1^p X_{t-1}^p + ... + \gamma_k^p X_{t-k}^p\right) + u_t \\
X_t^1 &= \mu_0 + \mu_1 X_{t-1}^1 + ... + \mu_k X_{t-k}^1 + \gamma_1^1 Y_{t-1}^1 + ... + \gamma_k^1 Y_{t-k}^1 + \\
&+ \sum_{p=2}^{P} \left(\gamma_1^p X_{t-1}^p + ... + \gamma_k^p X_{t-k}^p\right) + u_t \\
&\vdots \\
X_t^p &= \mu_0 + \mu_1 X_{t-1}^p + ... + \mu_k X_{t-k}^p + \gamma_1^1 Y_{t-1}^1 + ... + \gamma_k^1 Y_{t-k}^1 + \\
&+ \sum_{p=1}^{P-1} \left(\gamma_1^p X_{t-1}^p + ... + \gamma_k^p X_{t-k}^p\right) + u_t
\end{aligned}$$

under the joint hypothesis

$$H_0 : \gamma_1^1 = ... = \gamma_{t-p}^1 \wedge ... \wedge \gamma_1^P = ... = \gamma_{t-p}^P = 0$$

which is tested by the meaning of a Wald test that the coefficients on the lags of the "excluded" variables are zero in the equation for the (assumed) dependent variable. Selection criteria, such as the Bayesian Information Criteria (BIC, Schwartz, 1978)) or the Akaike Information Criteria (AIC, (Akaike, 1974)), can be used to determine the appropriate number of lags.

The multivariate case of the Granger causality test brings forth more reliable results than the repeated pairwise analyses. Let us take the example depicted in Figure 4 (a): a pairwise analysis would not be able to clarify the connectivity patterns among the circle, the rectangle and the triangle. Instead, a multivariate approach is able to detect the causality nexus where the triangle is both caused by the circle and the rectangle. Suppose also, as depicted in Figure 4 (b), that the circle drives two outputs, the triangle and the rectangle with different time delays. A pairwise analysis would falsely derive a causal connection from the output "rectangle" to the output "triangle", whilst a multivariate Granger test would not provide this result.

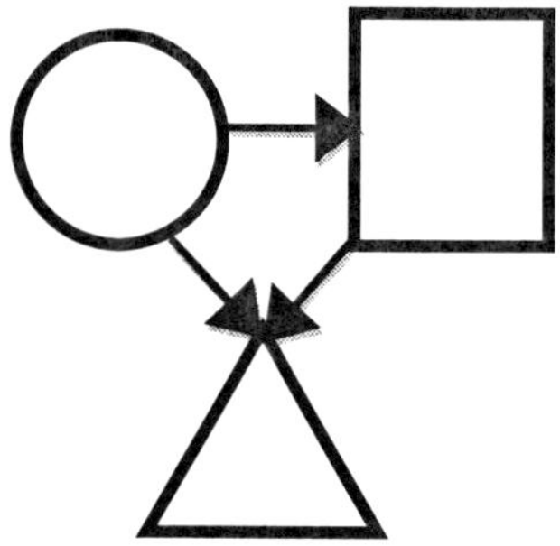

Figure 4. (a): Causality Ordering.

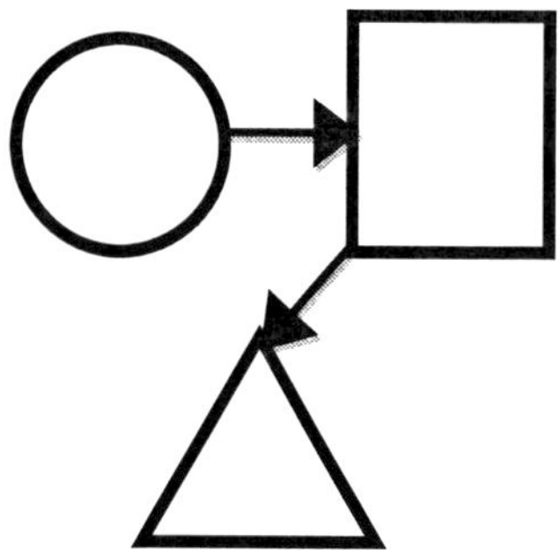

Figure 4. (b): Causality Ordering.

Appendix 3. Stationarity and Augmented Dickey-Fuller Test

Definition 6 *(Covariance Stationarity) A stochastic process y_t is said to be (covariance or weakly) stationary if the variances and covariances are finite and independent of time.*

For a stochastic process y_t to be stationary, three conditions must be satisfied:

1. $E[y_t] = const \quad \forall\, t;$
2. $Var[y_t] = const \quad \forall\, t;$
3. $Cov[y_t, y_{t+n}] = const \quad \forall\, t.$

An alternative definition of *strict stationarity* refers to the existence of an equality between the joint distribution $(y_{t_1}, \ldots, y_{t_h})$ and $(y_{t_1+t}, \ldots, y_{t_h+t})$ $\forall t$, with $h \in \mathbb{Z}^+$ and $(t_1, \ldots, t_k) \subset \mathbb{Z}^+$. That is, $(y_{t_1}, \ldots, y_{t_h})$ is invariant under time shifts.

For instance, assume that market returns of a given asset follow an autoregressive process of order one (AR(1))

$$r_t = \gamma r_{t-1} + \varepsilon_t \qquad \varepsilon_t \sim IID\,(0, \sigma_\varepsilon) \tag{5}$$

Using the Lag operator L, we can write 5 as

$$r_t = \gamma L r_t + \varepsilon_t \qquad \varepsilon_t \sim IID\,(0, \sigma_\varepsilon) \tag{6}$$

since $r_{t-1} = Lr_t$. We say that this process is stationary if and only if the polynomial $1 - \gamma L$ is *invertible*, that is if the root of the characteristic equation $1 - \gamma x = 0$ is larger than unity. It is easy to verify that we have only one root, $L = \frac{1}{\gamma}$, so that stationarity necessitates that $|\gamma| < 1$.

More generally, a given process ARMA(p, q), with p autoregressive terms and q moving average terms, written as

$$\gamma\,(L)\, r_t = \alpha\,(L)\, \varepsilon_t$$

is said to be stationary if and only if the elements of the solution vector $\mathbf{x} = (x_1, ..., x_p)$ to $\gamma\,(x) = 0$ are larger than the unity in absolute value. If this is the case the polynomial is invertible.

Definition 7 *(Orders of integration) If a series y_t becomes stationary after first differencing it is said to be integrated of order one and denoted by $y_t \sim I(1)$. More generally, if a series becomes stationary after n-differencing it is said to be integrated of order n and denoted by $y_t \sim I(n)$.*

The problem of finding a stationary process is the problem of testing for the existence of unit roots.

To detect the presence of unit roots, several tests were developed, where the most famous are the Dickey-Fuller (1979), the Augmented Dickey-Fuller, the Durbin-Watson and the Phillips-Perron (1987). The basic DF test is very suitable for AR(1) processes, but in the presence of AR(q) processes with autocorrelated errors the DF distribution is invalidate, because it is based on the assumption that ε_t is white noise.

Now, write a generic stochastic process in first differences with constant and trend

$$\Delta r_t = \gamma r_{t-1} + \sum_{i=1}^{q-1} \gamma_i \Delta r_{t-i} + \alpha + \beta t + \varepsilon_t \qquad \varepsilon_t \sim IID\left(0, \sigma_\varepsilon\right) \quad (7)$$

15

The Augmented Dickey-Fuller tests the null hypothesis $H_0 : \gamma = 1$, that is the hypothesis of a non-stationary (or stochastic) trend, against the alternative hypothesis $H_1 : \gamma = 0$, that is the hypothesis of a stationary (or deterministic) trend, by using the t-statistic

$$D_\tau = \frac{\widehat{\gamma} - 1}{se\left(\widehat{\gamma}\right)}$$

and

$$D_\gamma = \frac{T\left(\widehat{\gamma} - 1\right)}{1 - \widehat{\gamma}_1 - \ldots - \widehat{\gamma}_q}$$

References

[1] Akaike, H. (1974) A New Look at the Statistical Model Identification, *IEEE Trans. Autom. Control* **19**, 716-723

[2] Alexander, C. & Giblin, I. (2001) Cointegration and Asset Allocation: A New Active Hedge Fund Strategy, *ISMA Centre Discussion paper*

[3] Chan, C. K. et al. (1992) An Empirical Analysis of Stock Prices in Major Asian Markets and the U.S., *Financial Review* **27**, 289 – 307

[4] Chan, C. K. et al. (1992) Internation Stock Market Efficiency and Integration: a Study of Eighteen Nations, *Journal of Business Finance & Accounting*, **24**(6), 803 - 813

[15] We can also write a stochastic process which encompasses a MA component, but Dickey (1984) demonstrated how this process can be approximated by an AR(k) process, with k large enough.

[5] Engle, R. and Granger, C. W. J. (1987) Cointegration and Error-Correction: Representation, Estimation and Testing, *Econometrica*, March, 251 – 276

[6] Hamilton, J. D. (1994), *Time Series Analysis*, Princeton, Princeton University Press

[7] Herwany, A. & Febrian, E. (2008) Co-integration and Causality Analysis on Developed Asian Markets for Risk Management & Portfolio Selection, http://mpra.ub.uni-muenchen.de/10259

[8] Granger, C. W. J. (1969) Investigating Causal Relations by Econometric Models and Cross Spectral Methods, *Econometrica* **37**, 424-38

[9] Granger, C. W. J. & Newbold, P. (1974) Spurious Regressions in Econometrics, *Journal of Econometrics*, **35**, 143 - 159

[10] Granger, C. W. J. (1981) Some properties of time series data and their use in econometric model specification, *Journal of Econometrics* **16**, 121 – 130

[11] Granger, C. W. J. & Hallman, J. J. (1991), Long Memory Series with Attractors, *Oxford Bulletin of Economics and Statistics*, **53**, 11-26

[12] Granger, C. W. J. (2008), Personal Account by Clive Granger, from Scholarpedia, http://www.scholarpedia.org/article/Granger_causality

[13] Grubel, H. (1968) Internationally Diversified Portfolios: Welfare Gains and Capital Flows, *American Economic Review*, **58**, 1299 - 1314

[14] Granger, C.W.J. & Morgenstern, O. (1970) *Predictability of Stock Market Prices,* MA Lexington

[15] Gu, A. Y. & Annala, C. (2005) Leader and Follower Along Market Trends: A Granger Causality Test, *Journal of Accounting and Finance Research*, Vol. 13(5), 111-19

[16] Johansen, S. (1988) Statistical Analysis of Cointegrating Vectors, *Journal of Economic Dynamics and Control*, 12, 231-245

[17] Johansen, S. (1991) Estimation and Hypothesis Testing of Cointegration Vectors in Gaussian Vector Autoregressive Models, *Econometrica*, **59**, 1551 - 1580

[18] Harris, R. & Sollis, R. (2003) *Applied Time Series Modelling and Forecasting*, New York, John Wiley & Sons

[19] Kwan, A. Sim, A. & Cotsomitis, J. A. (1995) The Causal Relationships between Equity Indices on World Exchange, *Applied Economics*, **27**, 33 - 37

[20] Liew, V., (2004) Which Lag Length Selection Criteria Should We Employ?, *Economic Bulletin*, Vol. 3, No. 33 1-9

[21] Manning, N. (2002) Common Trends and Convergence, South East Asian Equity Markets, 1988, 1999, *Journal International Money Finance*, **21**, 183-202

[22] Markowitz, H. M. (1952) Portfolio Selection, *Journal of Finance*, **7** (1), 77-91

[23] Mathur, I. & Subrahmanyam, V. (1990) Interdependencies among the Nordic and U.S. Stock Markets, *Scandinavian Journal of Economics* **92** (4), 587-597

[24] Ramin et al. (2004) Relationship between Macroeconomic Variables and Stock Market Indices: Cointegration Evidence from Stock Exchange of Singapore's All-S Sector Indices, *Jurnal Pengurusan* **24**, 47-77

[25] Phillips, P. C. B. (1986) Understanding Spurious Regressions in Econometrics, *Journal of Econometrics*, **33**, 311 - 340

[26] Pan et al. (1999), Common Stochastic Trends and Volatility in Asian-Pacific Equity Markets, *Global Finance Journal*, **10**, 161-172

[27] Shwartz, G. (1978) Estimating the Dimension of a Model, *The Annual of Statistics* **5**, 461-464

[28] Smith, K. L., Brocato, J. & Rogers, J. E. (1993) Regularities in the Data between Major Equity Markets: Evidence from Granger Causality Tests, *Applied Financial Economics*, **3**, 55-60

[29] Tsay, R. (2002) *Analysis of financial time series*, New York, John Wiley & Sons

[30] Wiener, N. (1956) *The theory of prediction. In Modern Mathematics for Engineers*, vol. 1 (ed. E. F. Beckenbach). New York: McGraw-Hill.

In: Financial Markets and the Global Recession ISBN: 978-1-60741-921-1
Editors: B. Naas and J. Lysne

Chapter 7

THE CONTINUOUS-TIME DYNAMICS OF VIX AMID THE RECENT MARKET TURMOIL

*Minqiang Li**
College of Management,
Georgia Institute of Technology,
Atlanta, GA, USA

Abstract

The CBOE VIX index has been viewed as a gauge to measure investors' fear of market crash. The recent market turmoil has produced historically high volatility levels, in some cases around four times higher than their previous average levels. We take a new look at the continuous-time dynamics of VIX by including the recent market turmoil into the data. Two methodologies are utilized: the maximum likelihood estimation, and a parametric specification test. For data before year 2008, maximum likelihood estimation shows the need of stipulating a nonlinear drift function, similar to previous studies. However, inclusion of more recent data makes such a nonlinear drift less important. The parametric specification test nonetheless suggest that it is important to take into account both nonlinearity in the drift function and constant elasticity in the diffusion function when modeling the continuous-time dynamics of VIX. The results call for caution when adopting a particular parametric model for the continuous-time dynamics of the VIX index.

*E-mail address: minqiang.li@mgt.gatech.edu. Phone: (404)894-4926. Fax: (404)894-6030.

Keywords: CBOE VIX Volatility Index, Continuous-time Dynamics, Maximum Likelihood Estimation, Parametric Specification Test

JEL Classification: C60, G12, G13

I. Introduction

While the modern world financial markets have evolved for at least a few hundred years, the markets are still far from being complete. A complete market means that investors are able to hedge against any kinds of risk, such as traditional market risk, liquidity risk and credit risk, as well as nontraditional ones such as labor income risk, longevity risk, climate risk, etc. The process of financial engineering during the past half century can be thought of as an explosive effort by investors of trying to complete the markets.[1] A very significant boost in the process of completion took place in 1973, when CBOE introduced its first batch of exchange-traded stock options. Following that, there have been a plethora of new financial products both on exchanges and over the counter. These include single stock futures, credit derivatives, weather derivatives, freight derivatives, housing derivatives, economic derivatives, leveraged ETFs, catastrophe bonds, survival derivatives, etc.

Adding to the arsenal of financial innovations is the introduction of volatility derivatives, such as volatility futures, variance swaps, volatility options, etc. These products allow investor to hedge against and speculate on pure volatility risks. Most of the time, these products are built upon some volatility indices, the most well-known one being the CBOE VIX index introduced in 1993. This index has been mimicked by many other markets both inside the U.S. and outside. For example, CBOE also computes the volatility index VXN for Nasdaq 100 (NDX) and the index VXD for Dow Jones Industrial Average (DJIA). Outside the U.S., there is a growing list of volatility indices being introduced. For example, Deutsche Börse back calculated volatility index VDAX (as well as VDAX-NEW) based on the DAX from year 1992, while MONEP publishes VX1, VX6, and other related volatility indices based on CAC 40 since 1997. Two other examples are the VSTOXX and VSMI indices for the European markets.

[1] Of course, financial engineering serves some other purposes too, such as minimizing transaction costs, alleviating agency problems or information asymmetry, etc.

Derivative products are intrinsically related with volatility. Recently, direct bets on volatility have been introduced both on exchanges and over the counter. For example, the CBOE started trading VIX futures in March 2004. These products are welcome by market participants because they not only allow one to direct bet on the movement of volatility, but also allow one to isolate and hedge the volatility component in other derivative products. To reliably price volatility products and to calculate the optimal hedge positions, a good understanding of the dynamics of the volatility indices is essential. There are a few choices researchers can make. One could use a discrete-time process such as GARCH to model the volatility indices, or use a continuous-time process. In this paper, we focus on the second approach. Two earlier research papers are worth mentioning. In Bakshi, Ju, and Ou-Yang (2006), the authors employ maximum likelihood estimation to render a rank-ordering of various continuous-time models. A single volatility index (VXO) is used in their study.[2] Their results show that there is substantiate variance dynamics with nonlinear mean-reversion. Also, their results support the presence of a nonlinear diffusion coefficient structure. The combined specification of nonlinear drift and diffusion provides superior performance relative to its nested variants. Dotsis, Psychoyios, and Skiadopoulos (2007) further consider the addition of jumps in modeling the volatility dynamics. In addition to VIX, they also consider the VXO index, as well as several European volatility indices. However, because of the limitation of tractability, they have to restrict themselves to affine drift functions. This allows them to use a maximum likelihood estimation technique. With this restriction, their results show that it is necessary to add jumps to capture the evolution of implied volatility indices while (linear) mean-reversion is of second-order importance.

In this paper, we reexamine the continuous-time dynamics of various volatility indices. We have several motivations. First, most studies on volatility dynamics are completed before year 2007 and miss the recent market turmoil. For example, Bakshi, Ju, and Ou-Yang (2006) use a sample period from July, 1, 1988 to January 10, 2000, while Dotsis, Psychoyios, and Skiadopoulos (2007) use a sample period from October 14, 1997 to March 24, 2004. The year 2007 marks the dramatic downturn of the world financial markets and the subsequent dramatic increase of market volatility in 2008. For example, the maximum VIX level for the sample period in the study of Dotsis, Psychoyios, and Skiadopou-

[2]CBOE changed its methodology of computing VIX in 2003 and renamed the old VIX index to VXO. My private communications with the authors clarifies that the VIX index referred to in Bakshi, Ju, and Ou-Yang (2006) is actually the VXO index.

los (2007) is a little over 40 while it reached above 80 in 2008. This high volatility level is largely unexpected from the estimations in previous studies. Thus, it is useful to reexamine the volatility dynamics and to understand what have changed and what have not. For example, is it still important to incorporate nonlinearity in the volatility dynamics? Second, most previous studies have focused on the maximum likelihood estimation technique. Li (2009) studies diffusion processes whose diffusion functions are damped. Through Monte Carlo simulation, the author shows that the maximum likelihood estimation is often susceptible to finite sample bias. For example, it often misidentifies the damped diffusion with a nonlinear drift. Thus, in addition to maximum likelihood estimation, we also use a parametric specification test developed in Aït-Sahalia (1996b). This test is based on matching the invariant density of the volatility process with the one implied by the data. Thus, one can roughly view this estimation as matching various sample moments altogether at the same time, somewhat similar to the method of generalized moments. Loosely speaking, the maximum likelihood estimation cares more about the local behavior such as the transition probability at the next step, while the parametric specification test cares more about the global behavior. With large sample size, the two estimation methods have to give similar results because both are consistent. Thus, it is useful to see whether these two estimation techniques give similar results on the volatility dynamics. Conflicting results indicate the presence of finite sample bias and calls for caution when one wants to adopt a particular model. Finally, we study the volatility process directly instead of its squared variance process.

Several important results come out of our study. First, we perform two identical maximum likelihood estimations on the VIX index with and without including the two most recent years. We find that the inclusion of the recent market turmoil has a much larger effect on the estimated parameters in the drift function than those in the diffusion function. With the inclusion of the recent data, the mean-reversion in the drift function becomes weaker and less significant. However, the diffusion function is almost unchanged. Second, Our maximum likelihood estimation shows that nonlinearity parameters in the drift function are often insignificant or only marginally significant. Judging from the likelihood ratios, it suggests that we should not add the nonlinear parameters if we include more recent data. Our final result from a parametric specification test, however, contradicts the result obtained from the maximum likelihood estimation. The estimation unanimously rejects all models with only linear drift. The reason seems to be that the observed data seems to suggest a bimodal or multi-modal invariant density which a simple parametric specification does not seem to be able to deliver.

These results continue the debate on whether the existence or nonexistence of nonlinearity in the drift function estimated from various different methods is due to finite sample bias. A short list on papers examining this issue includes Aït-Sahalia (1996a, 1999), Chapman and Pearson (2000), Durham (2003), Li, Pearson and Poteshman (2004), and Takamizawa (2008). That maximum likelihood and parametric specification tests yield conflicting conclusions with regard to the inclusion of nonlinearity in the drift function indicates the existence of finite-sample bias in either or both of these two methods. Without additional data, it is difficult to draw the final conclusion on this issue. A joint estimation together with observations on VIX derivative prices might offer more insights on this issue, although the need to specify volatility risk-premium might make this estimation difficult.

The paper is organized as follows. Section **??** describes the data we use. Section **??** studies the continuous dynamics of various indices using the maximum likelihood estimation technique. Section **??** studies the continuous dynamics of various indices using a parametric specification test. Section **??** concludes.

II. Data Description

The data employed in this paper include the time series for the VIX index. The VIX index is the volatility index introduced by the Chicago Board Options Exchange in 1993 based on the paper by Whaley (1993). The original volatility index (now with ticker symbol VXO) was based on model-specific implied volatilities of S&P 100 index options, while the new VIX index is a model independent measure of future volatility based on S&P 500 index options. Both can be regarded as measures of market's expectation of the stock market volatility with a 30-day constant maturity. A good analysis of the theoretical underpinnings of the two indices is carried out in Carr and Wu (2006). According to CBOE, "(s)ince its introduction in 1993, VIX has been considered by many to be the world's premier barometer of investor sentiment and market volatility." Since the VIX index is back calculated to year 1990, we use the time period January 2, 1990 to April 15, 2009, a total of 4859 daily observations. For the maximum likelihood estimation, we use VIX observed on every Wednesday in order to save computational cost, with a total of 995 observations. However, for the specification test, we use daily observations as it is less computationally costly.

Table **??** presents the summary statistics of the daily CBOE VIX index as well as its first-order difference. The mean of the VIX index from January 2, 1990 to April 15, 2009 is 20.05 while the median is 18.45. The mode (the most frequently occurring value) is much lower, with a value of 11.65. This mostly results from the prolonged low volatility levels in two subperiods, namely from 1992 to 1997 and from 2004 to 2007. The minimum of the VIX is 9.31, realized on December 22, 1993, while the maximum is 80.86 on November 20, 2008. This value of the maximum is quite large given that the standard deviation of the data VIX is only 8.37. The empirical distribution of the VIX index is quite different from normal, with a skewness of 2.15 and a kurtosis of 10.71. The VIX index is also highly autocorrelated. For the first-order difference of VIX, the mean, median and mode are all very close to 0. The change of VIX also has a very large kurtosis of 22.69, but the autocorrelation is now fairly small with a value of -0.09.

In addition to the VIX index, we also collect daily data for the underlying market index, namely, the S&P 500 index. The data is from Yahoo Finance historical data. Figure **??** plots the VIX index together with the S&P 500 index. The S&P 500 graph is "M-shaped" during the full sample period, with a strong run leading to the first peak around the middle of year 2000. Following the burst of the internet bubble, the S&P 500 index picked up again starting around the end of year 2002. However, starting from the middle of year 2007, we see a big continuous drop of the S&P 500 as a result of the subprime mortgage crisis and the following credit crunch. Both of these two market downturns have had significant impact on the behavior of the VIX. For example, the VIX rose up to around 80% during the recent market turmoil. In addition, the Asian currency crisis in 1997 and the Russian sovereign bond default in 1998 also had strong impacts on the VIX. Low values of VIX usually come with high market index values, with a sample correlation of the VIX index and the S&P 500 index about -0.49. On the other hand, increases in the market index usually result in decreases in the VIX index, with a sample correlation of the changes in VIX and S&P 500 about -0.80.

Table 1. Summary Statistics of the VIX Index

This table presents the summary statistics of the CBOE VIX index as well as its first-order difference.

	VIX	ΔVIX
Observations	4859	4858
Mean	20.05	0.00
Median	18.45	−0.04
Mode	11.65	0.00
Min	9.31	−17.36
Max	80.86	16.54
Std. dev.	8.37	1.48
Skewness	2.15	0.41
Kurtosis	10.71	22.69
Autocorr.	0.98	−0.09

III. Maximum Likelihood Estimation of Volatility Indices

We consider a one-dimensional diffusion process for a state variable X_t:

$$\mathrm{d}X_t = \mu(X_t;\theta)\mathrm{d}t + \sigma(X_t;\theta)\mathrm{d}W_t, \tag{1}$$

where $\mu(X_t;\theta)$ and $\sigma(X_t;\theta)$ are the drift and diffusion coefficients respectively, and θ is the parameter vector. Different from Bakshi, Ju, and Ou-Yang (2006), we use the state variable X_t to model the volatility indices themselves instead of the squared variance processes. The values of the indices are divided by 100 so that they are expressed in percentage terms. We will often suppress the

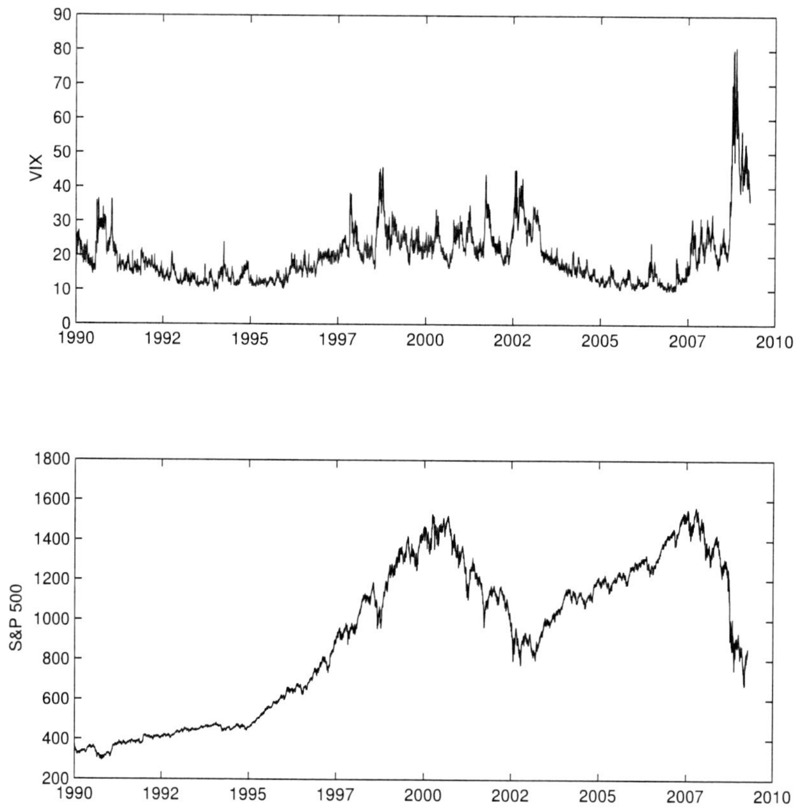

Figure 1. The S&P 500 index and the CBOE volatility index VIX. The index experienced a few downturns during this sample period, including the Asian current crisis, the Russian default, the internet bubble burst, and more recently the subprime mortgage crisis. All these events have led the volatility indices to surge, with the recent market turmoil having the strongest impact.

argument θ.

The processes we want to consider are the same ones as in Bakshi, Ju, and Ou-Yang (2006). They are a class of nested models with the following drift and diffusion functions proposed in Aït-Sahalia (1996a):

$$\mu(x;\theta) = \alpha_0 + \alpha_1 x + \alpha_2 x^2 + \alpha_{-1} x^{-1}, \tag{2}$$

$$\sigma(x;\theta) = \sqrt{\beta_1 x + \beta_2 x^{\beta_3}}. \tag{3}$$

Thus, for the full model, $\theta = (\alpha_0, \alpha_1, \alpha_2, \alpha_{-1}, \beta_1, \beta_2, \beta_3)$. We have chosen not to use a constant term β_0 in $\sigma(x;\theta)$ following Bakshi, Ju, and Ou-Yang (2006). Similar to their findings, we find that β_0 is often not significant and does not affect the likelihood function much. Different models are different restrictions of the parameter vector θ as listed below:

$$\text{AFF}: \quad \alpha_2 = \alpha_{-1} = 0, \;\; \beta_2 = 0, \;\; \beta_3 \text{ irrelevant} \tag{4}$$

$$\text{CEV-CD}: \quad \alpha_1 = \alpha_2 = \alpha_{-1} = 0, \;\; \beta_1 = 0 \tag{5}$$

$$\text{CEV-LD}: \quad \alpha_2 = \alpha_{-1} = 0, \;\; \beta_1 = 0 \tag{6}$$

$$\text{CEV-ND}: \quad \beta_1 = 0 \tag{7}$$

$$\text{SEV-CD}: \quad \alpha_1 = \alpha_2 = \alpha_{-1} = 0 \tag{8}$$

$$\text{SEV-LD}: \quad \alpha_2 = \alpha_{-1} = 0 \tag{9}$$

$$\text{SEV-ND}: \quad \text{no restrictions} \tag{10}$$

Here in naming the models, AFF stands for the "affine" model which is often referred to as the Cox-Ingersoll-Ross (CIR) model in finance. The shorthand notations CD, LD, and ND refer to constant drift, linear drift, and nonlinear drift, respectively. The notations CEV and SEV refer to constant elasticity of variance and stochastic elasticity of variance, respectively.

Let $p_X(\Delta, x|x_0)$ be the transition density of the process X_t after time period Δ from the current level of x_0 to future level x. To use the maximum likelihood estimation, one needs the transition density $p_X(\Delta, x|x_0)$. Except for a few special cases, explicit expressions for the transition densities do not exist. Fortunately, Aït-Sahalia (1999, 2002) has designed efficient and accurate analytical approximations. The method is based on a series expansion method by treating Δ small. More specifically, it first develops the part of the transition density that is singular in Δ and then uses a Taylor series expansion for the analytical part. The expansion coefficients were given iteratively in the original papers of Aït-Sahalia. The following proposition in Li (2009) simplifies the expansion by solving the iterations to the second order.[3] A brief proof is contained in Li (2009).

[3]Bakshi, Ju, and Ou-Yang (2006) solve the iteration to the fourth order for diffusion processes

Proposition 1 *Consider the process* $\mathrm{d}X_t = \mu(X_t)\mathrm{d}t + \sigma(X_t)\mathrm{d}W_t$ *with* $\sigma(\cdot) > 0$ *except possibly at the boundaries. Define* $\hat{\mu}(x) \equiv \frac{\mu(x)}{\sigma(x)} - \frac{1}{2}\sigma'(x)$ *and* $\lambda(x) \equiv -\frac{1}{2}(\hat{\mu}^2(x) + \hat{\mu}'(x)\sigma(x))$.
1. The approximate transition density $p_X^{(K)}(\Delta, x|x_0)$ *for the process* X_t *to order* $K = 2$ *in* Δ *is given by*

$$p_X^{(2)}(\Delta, x|x_0) = p_X^{(0)}(\Delta, x|x_0)(1 + c_1(x|x_0)\Delta + c_2(x|x_0)\Delta^2/2), \tag{11}$$

where

$$p_X^{(0)}(\Delta, x|x_0) = \frac{1}{\sqrt{2\pi\Delta}}\sqrt{\frac{\sigma(x_0)}{\sigma^3(x)}}\exp\left(\int_{x_0}^{x}\frac{\mu(u)}{\sigma^2(u)}\mathrm{d}u - \frac{1}{2\Delta}\left(\int_{x_0}^{x}\frac{1}{\sigma(u)}\mathrm{d}u\right)^2\right), \tag{12}$$

and for $x \neq x_0$,

$$c_1(x|x_0) = \frac{\int_{x_0}^{x}\lambda(u)/\sigma(u)\mathrm{d}u}{\int_{x_0}^{x}1/\sigma(u)\mathrm{d}u}, \qquad c_2(x|x_0) = c_1(x|x_0)^2 + \frac{\lambda(x) + \lambda(x_0) - 2c_1(x|x_0)}{\left(\int_{x_0}^{x}1/\sigma(u)\mathrm{d}u\right)^2}, \tag{13}$$

and for $x = x_0$, $c_1(x_0|x_0) = \lambda(x_0)$ *and* $c_2(x_0|x_0) = \lambda(x_0)^2 + (\sigma(\sigma\lambda')')(x_0)/6$.
2. The series approximation of $\log p_X(\Delta, x|x_0)$ *to order* $K = 2$ *in* Δ *is given by*

$$\log p_X^{(2)}(\Delta, x|x_0) = \log p_X^{(0)}(\Delta, x|x_0) + C_1(x|x_0)\Delta + \frac{1}{2}C_2(x|x_0)\Delta^2, \tag{14}$$

where $C_1(x|x_0) = c_1(x|x_0)$ *and* $C_2(x|x_0) = c_2(x|x_0) - c_1(x|x_0)^2$. *Writing out explicitly, we have*

$$C_1(x|x_0) = \frac{\int_{x_0}^{x}\lambda(u)/\sigma(u)du}{\int_{x_0}^{x}1/\sigma(u)du}, \quad C_2(x|x_0) = \frac{\lambda(x) + \lambda(x_0) - 2c_1(x|x_0)}{\left(\int_{x_0}^{x}1/\sigma(u)du\right)^2}. \tag{15}$$

---

with unit diffusion functions. However, we use a second-order expansion because it is already extremely accurate.

The above proposition allows the fast computation of the transition densities. To implement the second-order approximation, one just needs to compute three integrals, namely, $\int \mu/\sigma^2$, $\int \lambda/\sigma$, and $\int 1/\sigma$. For many models, these integrals can be computed explicitly. Even if explicit expressions are not available, they can be very efficiently computed using numerical integration such as quadrature method. This is the approach taken in this paper. Given discretely observed data x_i for $i = 0, 1, \cdots, n$ with fixed intervals Δ, the maximum likelihood estimation searches the optimal parameter values by maximizing the following log-likelihood function

$$\max_{\theta} \mathcal{L}[\theta] = \sum_{i=1}^{n} \log p_X(\Delta, x_i | x_{i-1}). \tag{16}$$

We use a simplex method for this maximization. Two different sample periods are considered. The first sample period is from January 1990 to December 2007, while the second sample period is from January 1990 to April 2009. Estimating these two sample periods together allow us to examine the effect of including the recent market turmoil into the data on parameter estimation.

Table **??** reports the results of the maximum likelihood estimation on the VIX index for the shorter sample period. There are a total of 927 weekly observations (Wednesdays) from January 2, 1990 to December 31, 2007. We use weekly observations to save computational time and our results do not change much if we use daily observations. We report the parameter estimates together with their standard errors in parentheses. To rank-order different models, likelihood ratio (LR) test statistic $-2(\mathcal{L}_R - \mathcal{L}_U)$ is used, when $\mathcal{L}_R$ and $\mathcal{L}_U$ refer to the likelihood functions of the restricted and unrestricted models respectively. The statistic is asymptotically chi-square distributed, with degree of freedom given by the number of restrictions. For readers' convenience, the 5% critical values of $\chi^2(df)$ with *df* equaling 1, 2, 3, and 4 are 3.84, 6.00, 7.82, and 9.50, respectively.

From Table **??** we see that the full model (SEV-ND) has the largest log-likelihood value, 2393.84. However, the LR test statistic between CEV-ND and SEV-ND is only 0.006, which is smaller than 3.84, the critical value of $\chi^2(1)$. Thus, the result favors CEV-ND over SEV-ND. Similar results hold for the LR statistics between the SEV-LD and CEV-LD pair, and the SEV-CD and CEV-CD pair. These results are consistent with the fact that the β_1's are insignificant in all three SEV models. The AFF model is clearly inadequate if we look at the LR statistic between the AFF and SEV-LD models. Among the

Table 2. Maximum Likelihood Estimation of the Continuous-time Dynamics of VIX (1990-2007)

This table reports the results of the maximum likelihood estimation on the VIX index for the shorter sample period. There are a total of 927 weekly observations (Wednesdays) from January 2, 1990 to December 31, 2007. We report the parameter estimates together with their standard errors in parentheses and the optimized log-likelihood function $\mathcal{L}$. To rank-order different models, likelihood ratio (LR) test statistic $-2(L_R - L_U)$ is used, when L_R and L_U refer to the likelihood functions of the restricted and unrestricted models respectively. The statistic is asymptotically chi-square distributed, with degree of freedom given by the number of restrictions. For comparison, the 5% critical values of $\chi^2(df)$ with df equaling 1, 2, 3, and 4 are 3.84, 6.00, 7.82, and 9.50, respectively.

Model	α_0	α_1	α_2	α_{-1}	β_1	β_2	β_3	$\mathcal{L}$
AFF	0.625	−3.303			0.122			2315.78
	(0.12)	(0.59)			(0.004)			
CEV-CD	0.106					2.420	2.841	2379.69
	(0.03)					(0.51)	(0.12)	
CEV-LD	0.453	−2.346				1.992	2.720	2385.92
	(0.11)	(0.69)				(0.41)	(0.12)	
CEV-ND	−10.034	55.660	−99.458	0.592		2.080	2.737	2393.81
	(2.89)	(16.09)	(28.19)	(0.16)		(0.44)	(0.12)	
SEV-CD	0.110				−0.025	1.667	2.483	2379.89
	(0.03)				(0.04)	(0.78)	(0.44)	
SEV-LD	0.481	−2.521			−0.102	0.955	1.873	2387.13
	(0.10)	(0.65)			(0.09)	(0.24)	(0.40)	
SEV-ND	−10.529	58.270	−103.715	0.621	0.010	2.542	2.922	2393.84
	(3.39)	(18.72)	(32.53)	(0.19)	(0.03)	(1.58)	(0.54)	

CEV models, the LR statistic between the CEV-CD and CEV-ND is 28.24 while the LR statistic between CEV-LD and CEV-ND is 15.78. Since both exceed the critical value of $\chi^2(3)$, the results favor the CEV-ND over either CEV-CD or CEV-LD. Therefore, the CEV-ND model seems to be the most favorable model among all seven models considered. The estimated drift function for the CEV-ND model is $\mu(x) = -10.034 + 55.660x - 99.458x^2 + 0.592/x$, with all four parameters statistically significant. Thus, similar to Bakshi, Ju, and Ou-Yang (2006), the nonlinearity in the drift function is important in capturing the strong mean-reverting behavior near both boundaries of the volatility process. On the other hand, a diffusion function with constant elasticity given by $\sigma(x) = \sqrt{2.080x^{2.737}}$ is sufficient.

The stationary density of the process X_t with drift and diffusion functions $\mu(x)$ and $\sigma(x)$ is given by (see Karlin and Taylor 1981)

$$\pi(x;\theta) = \frac{\xi(\theta)}{\sigma^2(x;\theta)} \exp\left(\int_0^x \frac{2\mu(u;\theta)}{\sigma^2(u;\theta)} du\right), \tag{17}$$

where $\xi(\theta)$ is a normalization constant so that $\pi(x;\theta)$ integrates to 1. For the CEV-ND model estimated in Table **??**, under the stationary density, there is a 0.003 probability that the the volatility level is above 0.4, 5×10^{-7} probability above 0.6, and around 10^{-11} probability above 0.8. Thus, using purely data before year 2007, the probability that the process would ever reach a level of 0.8 is extremely low and the sudden increase in VIX in 2008 was unexpected at the end of 2007 purely from the VIX data.

Table **??** reports the results from the maximum likelihood estimation of the VIX for the full sample period from January 2, 1990 to April 15, 2009. The general pattern is very similar to that of Table **??**. Again, the affine model AFF is insufficient. The SEV models all lose out to their CEV counterparts judging from the LR statistics. However, judging from the LR statistic between the CEV-LD and CEV-ND models, the CEV-LD model is weakly preferred over CEV-ND at 5% significance level. The LR statistic is $2 \times (2511.80 - 2509.07) = 5.46$ while the 5% critical value of $\chi^2(2)$ is 6.00. This is consistent with the fact that the nonlinear mean-reverting parameters α_2 and α_{-1} are not as significant as in Table **??**. This behavior is different from the one implied by the shorter sample period ending in 2007, where the nonlinear mean-reverting parameters are very important. The strength of nonlinear mean-reverting in the CEV-ND model is also much weaker for the whole sample period compared with the shorter sample period. On the other hand, the CEV-LD model is quite strongly preferred over the CEV-CD model for the full sample period, indicating that although there is no strong evidence for nonlinear mean-reverting, linear mean-reverting is still very important in describing the data.

It is interesting to look at the stationary density with parameters estimated from the full sample period. We consider both CEV-LD and CEV-ND models. For the CEV-LD model, under the stationary density, the probabilities that the volatility level is above 0.4, 0.6 and 0.8 are approximately 0.04, 0.01, and 0.004, respectively, while for the CEV-ND model, these three probabilities are 0.04, 0.003, and 0.0002, respectively. Judging purely from matching the tail probabilities, the CEV-LD seems to perform better than the CEV-ND model, consistent with the result of the LR test.

IV. Parametric Specification Tests of Volatility Models

The maximum likelihood estimation above shows that it is only marginally useful to stipulate a nonlinear drift function if we include the more recent data into the analysis. However, as Li (2009) shows, maximum likelihood estimation is subject to finite sample bias, especially when applied to parametric models. For example, Monte Carlo experiment in Li (2009) shows that when the true data-generating model is linear drift but with damped diffusion function, maximum likelihood estimation tends to mistake the damped diffusion with nonlinear drift function when the time series is of finite sample size. One possible indication of finite sample bias is that the tail probabilities under the stationary density implied by the estimated parameters do not match those implied by the sample. Therefore, in the following, we take a different approach, namely, the specification test for diffusion processes originally proposed in Aït-Sahalia (1996b).

The idea of the approach is fairly intuitive. For a given parameter vector, we could compute the theoretical stationary density. At the optimal parameter values, this theoretical density should be close to the stationary density implied by the data. Thus, the difference of these two densities could be used as a criterion for estimating the parameters. The actual procedure involves a few steps, as we now describe below. We do not repeat all the details below such as the assumptions on the processes, the optimal choice of the bandwidth parameters, etc. Readers are referred to the original paper by Aït-Sahalia (1996b).

1. Estimate the empirical stationary density $\hat{\pi}(X_i)$ nonparametrically for

Table 3. Maximum Likelihood Estimation of the Continuous-time Dynamics of VIX (1990-2009)

This table reports the results of the maximum likelihood estimation on the VIX index for the full sample period. There are a total of 995 weekly observations (Wednesdays) from January 2, 1990 to April 15, 2009. We report the parameter estimates together with their standard errors in parentheses. To rank-order different models, likelihood ratio (LR) test statistic $-2(\mathcal{L}_R - \mathcal{L}_U)$ is used, when $\mathcal{L}_R$ and $\mathcal{L}_U$ refer to the likelihood functions of the restricted and unrestricted models respectively. The statistic is asymptotically chi-square distributed, with degree of freedom given by the number of restrictions. For readers' convenience, the 5% critical values of $\chi^2(df)$ with df equaling 1, 2, 3, and 4 are 3.84, 6.00, 7.82, and 9.50, respectively.

Model	α_0	α_1	α_2	α_{-1}	β_1	β_2	β_3	$\mathcal{L}$
AFF	0.541	−2.659			0.136			2406.86
	(0.10)	(0.42)			(0.004)			
CEV-CD	0.109					2.163	2.782	2504.21
	(0.03)					(0.40)	(0.11)	
CEV-LD	0.395	−1.908				1.906	2.701	2509.07
	(0.10)	(0.64)				(0.34)	(0.10)	
CEV-ND	−3.131	14.755	−23.040	0.223		1.894	2.694	2511.80
	(1.57)	(7.54)	(11.23)	(0.10)		(0.36)	(0.11)	
SEV-CD	0.113				−0.023	1.635	2.485	2504.50
	(0.03)				(0.03)	(0.57)	(0.34)	
SEV-LD	0.408	−1.983			−0.047	1.249	2.215	2509.85
	(0.10)	(0.62)			(0.04)	(0.36)	(0.32)	
SEV-ND	−2.824	13.294	−20.998	0.204	−0.013	1.625	2.529	2511.86
	(1.61)	(7.72)	(11.31)	(0.10)	(0.03)	(0.63)	(0.38)	

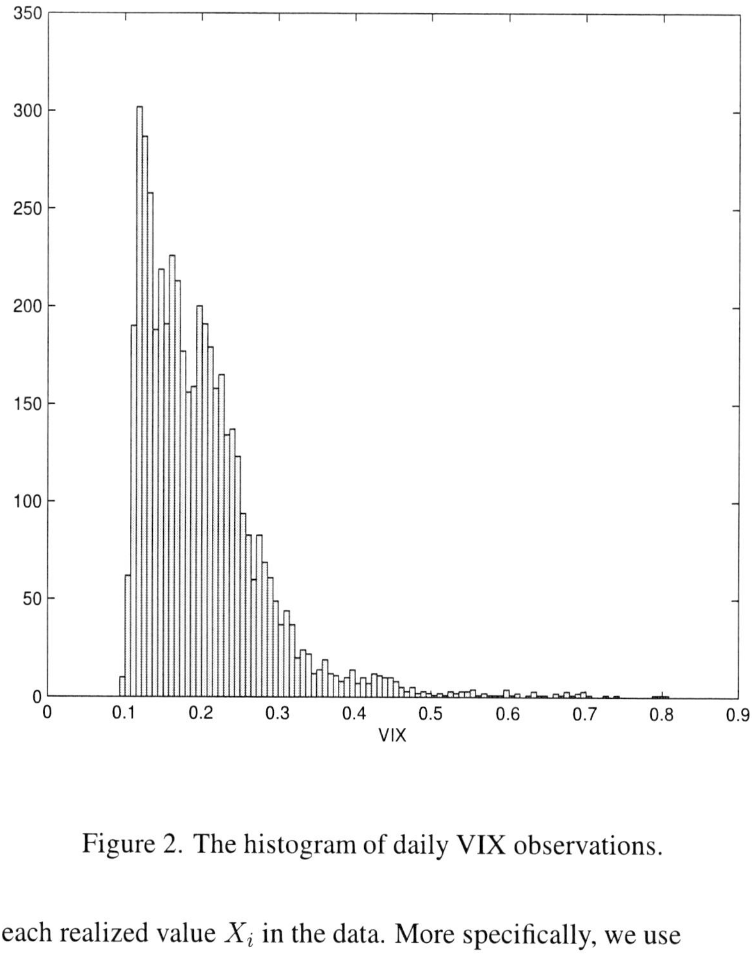

Figure 2. The histogram of daily VIX observations.

each realized value X_i in the data. More specifically, we use

$$\hat{\pi}(X_i) = \frac{1}{N} \sum_{j=1}^{N} \frac{1}{h_N} K\left(\frac{X_i - X_j}{h_N}\right), \tag{18}$$

where $K(x) = \exp(-x^2/2)/\sqrt{2\pi}$ is the normal density kernel function, and h_N is the bandwidth.[4] It is useful to take a look at the histogram of the daily VIX observations from January 2, 1990 to April 15, 2009, which

[4]More information on the kernel estimation technique can be found in Silverman (1986) and Wand and Jones (1994).

is plotted in Figure **??**. The estimated density $\hat{\pi}$ is a kernel smoothing of the histogram of the daily VIX observations after normalization. It seems that the empirical density is multi-modal, with a quite heavy right tail.

2. Given the model in equation (**??**), estimate the vector θ by minimizing the statistic

$$\hat{M} = \hat{M}(\theta) \equiv \frac{1}{N}\sum_{i=1}^{N} \hat{M}_i \tag{19}$$

where

$$\hat{M}_i \equiv N h_N \min_{\theta} \left(\pi(X_i;\theta) - \hat{\pi}(X_i)\right)^2, \tag{20}$$

where $\pi(x,\theta)$ is the model implied marginal density given by

$$\pi(x;\theta) = \frac{\xi(\theta)}{\sigma^2(x;\theta)} \exp\left(\int_0^x \frac{2\mu(u;\theta)}{\sigma^2(u;\theta)} \mathrm{d}u\right), \tag{21}$$

and $\xi(\theta)$ is the normalization constant so that $\pi(x;\theta)$ integrates to 1. Let the true marginal density of X be $\pi_0(X)$ and let $\mathbb{E}$ denote the expectation under this true marginal density. Then $\hat{M}$ is the empirical counterpart of the following distance measure

$$M \equiv \min_{\theta} \mathbb{E}\left[\left(\pi(X;\theta) - \pi_0(X)\right)^2\right]. \tag{22}$$

3. To test whether a particular parametric model should be accepted or rejected, we compare $\hat{M}$ with the critical value c_α. It is shown in Aït-Sahalia (1996b) that the test statistic $\hat{M}$ is asymptotically distributed as

$$h_N^{-1/2}\left(\hat{M} - E_M\right) \xrightarrow{d} N(0, V_M), \tag{23}$$

where

$$E_M \equiv \frac{1}{2\sqrt{\pi}} \int_0^{\infty} \pi_0^2(x)\,\mathrm{d}x, \tag{24}$$

$$V_M \equiv \frac{1}{\sqrt{2\pi}} \int_0^{\infty} \pi_0^4(x)\,\mathrm{d}x. \tag{25}$$

That is, at a given significance level α, a particular parametric model cannot describe data well if $\hat{M} \geq c_\alpha \equiv \hat{E}_M + h_N^{1/2} z_\alpha \hat{V}_M^{1/2}$. If $\alpha = 5\%$, then $z_\alpha \approx 1.645$.[5]

In our actual implementation, we will fix the values of α_0 for all the models considered. The fixed values of α_0 are those in Table **??** for the two different sample periods, respectively. The reason for doing this is as follows. A careful analysis of the implied marginal density $\pi(X;\theta)$ in equation (**??**) reveals that if we quadruple the drift function $\mu(X;\theta)$ and double the diffusion function $\sigma(X;\theta)$, then the marginal density does not change for any value of X. Therefore, depending on the particular functional forms of $\mu(X;\theta)$ and $\sigma(X;\theta)$, there could be an infinite set of parameters which minimize $\hat{M}$. For example, in the AFF model, without restricting the values of some parameters, if $(\alpha_0, \alpha_1, \beta_1)$ minimizes $\hat{M}$, then $(4\alpha_0, 4\alpha_1, 4\beta_1)$ would also minimize $\hat{M}$. Therefore, there is a need to fix some of the parameters in the drift or diffusion in order to get rid of the indeterminateness. This identification issue is also explained in Li (2009).

Table **??** presents the results from the specification tests of the continuous-time parametric models for the VIX index for the sample period from January 2, 1990 to April 15, 2009. It reports the estimated parameters, the test statistic $\hat{M}$, and the corresponding critical value c_α. All seven models are rejected by the specification tests, except for the CEV-ND and SEV-ND models. Also, the drift parameters for each of the models are quite close to the ones in Table **??** from the maximum likelihood estimation. However, for all the five rejected models, the the parameters for the diffusion functions are quite different from those in Table **??**. For these rejected models, the parameters estimated from the maximum likelihood function will give even larger values of $\hat{M}$, indicating that models without nonlinear drift are not able to match the theoretical and empirical stationary densities, even though the previous maximum likelihood estimation implies that nonlinear drift function is only of marginal importance. Since the two approaches give somewhat different results, a modeler has to exert caution if he has to choose between a model with linear drift and another one with nonlinear drift. Model risk has to be taken into account if these models in turn are used to price volatility derivatives.

Figure **??** plots the goodness of fit for the AFF model (the left two panels) and the CEV-ND model (the right two panels). In the top two panels, the

[5]Notice that there is a typo in equation (14) of Aït-Sahalia (1996b).

Table 4. Specification Tests of the Continuous-time Parametric Models for VIX

This table presents the results from the specification tests of the continuous-time parametric models for the VIX index for the sample period from January 2, 1990 to April 15, 2009. It reports the estimated parameters, the test statistic $\widehat{M}$, and the corresponding critical value c_α. All seven models are rejected by the specification tests, except for the nonlinear drift CEV-ND and SEV-ND models.

Model	α_0	α_1	α_2	α_{-1}	β_1	β_2	β_3	$\widehat{M}$	c_α
AFF	0.541	−2.960			0.157			9.20	2.83 reject
CEV-CD	0.109					10.311	3.690	22.10	2.76 reject
CEV-LD	0.395	−2.083				0.210	1.646	8.43	2.83 reject
CEV-ND	−3.131	19.773	−40.371	0.176		1.598	2.555	2.40	2.93 cannot reject
SEV-CD	0.113				0.039	35.299	4.612	17.90	2.77 reject
SEV-LD	0.408	−2.135			−0.067	0.296	1.269	8.26	2.83 reject
SEV-ND	−2.824	17.878	−36.473	0.158	0.00004	1.555	2.605	2.38	2.92 cannot reject

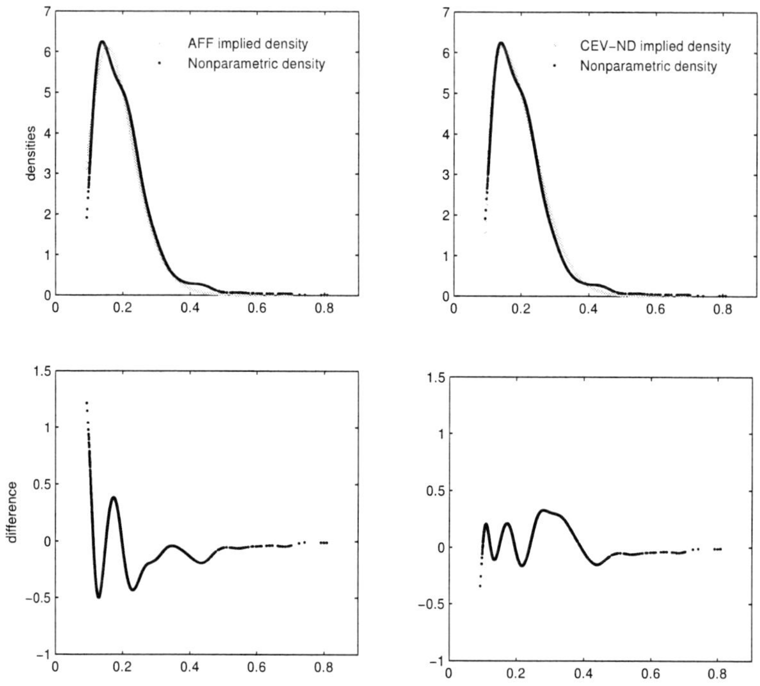

Figure 3. Density comparison for the AFF and CEV-ND models under the parametric specification test. This figure plots the goodness of fit for the AFF model (the left two panels) and the CEV-ND model (the right two panels). In the top two panels, the empirical stationary density estimated from nonparametric kernel estimation (in black) as well as the theoretical densities (in gray) are plotted. The bottom two panels plot the differences of the theoretical and empirical densities for the two models.

empirical stationary density estimated from nonparametric kernel estimation (in black) as well as the theoretical densities (in gray) are plotted. The bottom two panels plot the differences of the theoretical and empirical densities for the two models. It is clear that the CEV-ND model fits better than the AFF model. At the estimated parameter values, the linear drift AFF model is not able to fit the lower end of the density well. As a result, the AFF model is rejected while the CEV-ND model cannot be rejected at 5% significance level.

V. Conclusion

In this paper, we take a new look at the continuous-time dynamics of the CBOE VIX index. Two methodologies are taken, namely the maximum likelihood estimation and the parametric specification test. With more recent data, the results from maximum likelihood estimation show that there is a marginal need to specify a nonlinear drift. However, the parametric specification test rejects all models with linear drift functions. On the other hand, a constant elasticity of variance diffusion function seems to be sufficient from both methodologies. That these two methodologies give somewhat conflicting results about the drift function indicate the presence of finite sample bias and the need to exert caution when a modeler has to make a choice among alternative models.

Several future directions can be taken. So far we have only considered diffusion models with no jumps. It is particularly interesting to examine whether the inclusion of jumps will get rid of the need of nonlinear drift functions in matching the theoretical and empirical densities. This requires the calculation of the theoretical densities for diffusion models with jumps. Another direction one can take is to estimate the VIX dynamics jointly with the underlying index. Unfortunately, none of these directions are as straightforward as they might seem to be.

References

Aït-Sahalia, Yacine. (1996a). Nonparametric pricing of interest rate derivative securities, *Econometrica* **64**, 527–560.

Aït-Sahalia, Yacine. (1996b). Testing continuous-time models of the spot interest rate, *Review of Financial Studies* **9**, 385–426.

Aït-Sahalia, Yacine. (1999). Transition densities for interest rate and other nonlinear diffusions, *Journal of Finance* **54**, 1361–1395.

Aït-Sahalia, Yacine. (2002). Maximum-likelihood estimation of discretely-sampled diffusions: A closed-form approximation approach, *Econometrica* **70**, 223–262.

Bakshi, Gurdip, Nengjiu Ju, and Hui Ou-Yang. (2006). Estimation of continuous-time models with an application to equity volatility dynamics. *Journal of Financial Economics* **82**, 227–249.

Carr, Peter, and Liuren Wu. (2006). A tale of two indices. *Journal of Derivatives*, Spring, 13–29.

Chapman, David, and Neil D. Pearson. (2000). Is the short rate drift actually nonlinear? *Journal of Finance* **55**, 355–399.

Dotsis, George, Dimitris Psychoyios, and George Skiadopoulos. (2007). An empirical comparison of continuous-time models of implied volatility indices. *Journal of Banking & Finance* **31**, 3584–3603.

Durham, Garland B. (2003). Likelihood-based specification analysis of continuous-time models of the short-term interest rate, *Journal of Financial Economics* **70**, 463–487.

Karlin, Samuel, and Howard M. Taylor. (1981). *A Second Course in Stochastic Processes* (Academic Press, New York.).

Li, Minqiang. (2009). A damped diffusion model for financial modeling and closed-form maximum likelihood estimation. Georgia Institute of Technology, *working paper.*

Li, Minqiang, Neil D. Pearson, and Allen M. Poteshman. (2004). Conditional estimation of diffusion processes, *Journal of Financial Economics* **74**, 31–66.

Silverman, Bernard W. (1986). *Density Estimation for Statistics and Data Analysis*, Chapman & Hall/CRC.

Takamizawa, Hideyuki. (2008), Is nonlinear drift implied by the short end of the term structure? *Review of Financial Studies* **21**, 311–346.

Wand, Matt, and Chris Jones. (1994). *Kernel Smoothing.* Chapman & Hall/CRC.

Whaley, Robert E. (2000). The investor fear gauge. *Journal of Portfolio Management* **26**, 12–17.

In: Financial Markets and the Global Recession ISBN: 978-1-60741-921-1
Editors: B. Naas and J. Lysne

Expert Commentary A

PREDICTING STOCK RETURNS IN A CROSS-SECTION: DO INDIVIDUAL FIRM CHARACTERISTICS MATTER?

Kateryna Shapovalova [1,*] ***and Alexander Subbotin*** [1,2,†]
[1] University of Paris-1 (Panthèon-Sorbonne), France
[2] Higher School of Economics, France

Abstract

It is a common wisdom that individual stocks' returns are difficult to predict, though in many situations it is important to have such estimates at our disposal. In particular, they are needed to determine the cost of capital. Market equilibrium models posit that expected returns are proportional to the sensitivities to systematic risk factors. Fama and French (1993) three-factor model explains the stock returns premium as a sum of three components due to different risk factors: the traditional CAPM market beta, and the betas to the returns on two portfolios, Small Minus Big (the differential in the returns on stocks of small and big companies) and High Minus Low (the differential in returns on the of companies with high and low price-to-book ratio). The authors argue that this model is sufficient to capture the impact on returns of companies' accounting fundamentals,

*E-mail address: kateryna.shapovalova@univ-paris1.fr
†E-mail address: alexander.subbotin@univ-paris1.fr

such as earnings-to-price, cash flow-to-price, past sales growth, long term and short-term past earnings. Using a panel of stock returns and accounting data from 1979 to the end of 2008 for the companies listed on NYSE, we show that this is not the case, at least at individual stocks' level. According to our findings, fundamental characteristics of companies' performance are of higher importance to predict future expected returns than sensitivities to the risk factors. We explain this finding within the rational pricing paradigm: contemporaneous accounting fundamentals may be better proxies for future sensitivity to risk factors, than sensitivities, estimated from historical data.

Keywords: Accounting Funadamentals, Equity Performance, Style Analysis, Value and Growth, Cost of Capital

J.E.L. Classification: E44, G11, E32.

1. Introduction

It is widely accepted by practitioners that companies' accounting characteristics have an impact on the stock returns prospects. Thus many investment strategies, in particular those known as style investment, are based on such fundamentals and their survival in time is the best evidence of at least relative success. On the contrary, the link between individual stock's characteristics and expected returns has long time been a source of headache for the academics, remaining one of the asset pricing anomalies.

This study aims to find which style characteristics influence future returns and how they do so: directly or by means of stock returns' covariances with returns of specially constructed style risk portfolios. To this end, we study the predictive power of different models, including accounting fundamentals, in a cross-section of returns on individual stocks. We start with the three-factor Fama and French (1993) and an alternative so-called "characteristics" model by Daniel and Titman (1997). Then both models are augmented by additional accounting fundamentals in order to check whether they add useful additional information. If not, the relevance of the multi-factor investment styles definitions, used by index providers would be more than dubious.

Our methodology differs significantly from that used in Daniel and Titman (1997) and the subsequent existing research on the subject. First, we prefer to work with the cross-section of stocks directly, rather than with stocks' portfolios. Usually the adequacy of the three-factor model is derived from the comparison of mean returns on portfolios with high and low sensitivities to HML and SMB. The irrelevance of some other variable is shown by first sorting stocks according to this variable, and then demonstrating that the difference in mean returns on the resulting portfolios disappears, if the size and value factors are controlled for. This is achieved by multi-way sorts.

Using multi-way sorts imposes important restrictions on the number of accounting variables, whose impact on returns has to be studied. So it is natural to use multivariate cross-sectional regressions on stock-level to study this impact, as it is done, for example, in the early paper by Fama and French (1992) and more recently Bartholdy and Peare (2005). In the latter study the three-factor model is compared with the CAPM in a similar to our's context of predicting individual stock returns in a cross-section and on a comparable database of NYSE stocks. They find little difference in the explicative power of the two models, being very low in both cases. However, they did not try to use accounting fundamentals directly and, generally, testing the mechanisms of the impact of fundamentals on stock returns was outside the scope of their study. In our view it is more appropriate to test the goodness of the three-factor model on stocks' level, because accounting fundamentals for portfolios cannot be defined. We claim that despite measurement errors in individual betas, the three-factor model, if it were true, should perform reasonably well on disaggregated level, compared to the alternative characteristics model. Besides, predicting individual stock returns is by itself an important problem, arising in many financial applications, such as estimating the cost of capital (for a further discussion see Bartholdy and Peare, 2005).

The second distinction of our approach is that we use a large and relatively homogeneous sample of stocks (all companies listed at NYSE) for a recent but sufficiently long period (1979-2008). We do not include NASDAQ stocks in order to avoid the bias, which could possibly be provoked by incorporating a huge number of data for small companies', which are not necessarily comparable in terms of liquidity and reliability of accounting indicators. Our sample includes more recent data, compared to the above cited studies, but does not contain earlier data.

Third, we compare two mechanisms of impact on returns (betas vs characteristics). Given that betas to portfolios, based on characteristics, and characteristics themselves are often positively correlated, it is important to verify whether the influence of one of these types of factors can be reduced to the correlation with the other. We use specially constructed subsamples of stocks to discriminate between the models. If the correlations between betas and characteristics in the cross-section of stocks are important, they can be eliminated by considering subsamples of stocks, whose betas and characteristics do not match. This approach is inspired by Daniel and Titman (1997), but we focus on predictive power of factors in regressions, rather than on multi-way sorts, which can often be misleading due to small number of observations.

Our results are consistent with Daniel and Titman (1997) and demonstrate mainly that the three-factor model is not capable of consistently explaining the pricing anomalies, associated with various accounting fundamentals, such as historical growth of sales, reinvested portion of return-on-equity, price-to-sales and others.

The rest of the study is organized as follows. Section 2. studies the alternative mechanisms of impacts on returns, associated with a three-factor "betas" model by Fama and French (1993), and the "characteristics" model, suggested by Daniel and Titman (1997). The following section describes the database and defines the variables. In section 4. we formally present the hypotheses and methodology of the empirical tests. The next section describes the results. In conclusion we overview the main findings and suggest directions for further research.

2. Pricing Anomalies and "Betas vs Characteristics" Debate

By anomalies of stock returns one usually means the incapacity of the classical Capital Asset Pricing Model (CAPM) by Sharpe (1964) Litner (1965) and Black (1972) to accurately explain stock returns premium. The empirical contradictions of CAPM was widely documented in the 1980s and the beginning of the 1990s. De Bondt and Thaler (1986) evidence that stocks with low long-term past returns tend to have higher returns prospects, which necessarily implies mean-reverting in long-term returns. Jegadeesh and Titman (1993b) evidence that stocks with higher premium over the previous year have higher future returns on average. Banz (1981), Basu (1983), Rosenberg et al. (1995), Lakonishok et al. (1994) documented the dependence of the premium on different companies' accounting fundamentals. As a result, the simplicity of the CAPM's assumption that a single risk factor explains expected returns, has been called into question.

Lakonishok et al. (1994) defined value strategies as buying shares having low prices compared to the indicators of fundamental value, such as earnings, book value, dividends, or cash flow. They classified stocks into "value" or "glamour" on the basis of past growth in sales and expected future growth, as implied by the current earnings-to-price ratio. Fama and French (1993, 1996) claimed, however, that their three-factor model is capable of explaining most of the pricing anomalies.

The three-factor model assumes that the stock returns premium can be represented as a sum of three components due to different risk factors: the traditional CAPM market beta, and the betas to two portfolios constructed by the authors, SMB (Small Minus Big) and HML (High Minus Low). These factors describing "value" and "size", according to Fama and French, are to be the most significant factors, outside of market risk, for explaining the realized returns of publicly traded stocks.

The returns on SMB and HML portfolios tend to be positive in long term, and the presence of positive premium on value factors is known as "value puzzle". Fama and French themselves interpreted companies' betas on the HML portfolio as sensitivity to the particular distress factor which is a source of systematic risk. Since this factor has no definite counterpart among measurable aggregate economic variables, its meaning remains unclear, and the "distress" explanation is often considered insufficient and cumbersome. So understanding the value puzzle is an area of active research. We refer the reader to an excellent review on the subject in Chan and Lakonishok (2004), as it falls out of the scope of this paper.

The doubts about the way accounting characteristics actually influence returns were raised in Daniel and Titman (1997), who suggest that stocks with high book-to-market have high returns due to some reason that has nothing to do with systematic risk. Namely, it is the characteristic (high book-to-market) rather than the covariance (high sensitivity to HML) that is associated with high returns. These competitive models were subject to further empirical investigations (Daniel et al., 2001, Davis et al., 2000) with contradictory results which are reviewed later in this article.

As regards the financial industry, a wide set of different characteristics is often used to define investment strategies and the latter are used to predict returns in a direct way, rather than by the intermediation of covariance with risk factors. Index providers represent the performance of value and growth styles by portfolios, constructed using multifactor scores to attribute stocks to the style baskets. The joint impact of the variables they use is still to be explored in order to understand the dynamic of such indices.

Generally, there are two ways, in which style factors could be used to predict future returns. In the logic of the three-factor model, the sensitivity of stock returns to a style risk factor, i.e. a difference in returns of two portfolios, including stocks of companies with high and low characteristic, is rewarded by a risk premium. Thus the true measure of "value" for a stock is not, for example, the price-to-book of the issuing company, but the beta to the HML factor. An alternative way to measure value would be to suppose that the characteristic itself influences the expected future return.

Fama and French (1996) conduct an extended study of pricing anomalies related to the link between average future returns and stocks characteristics: earnings-to-price, cash flow-to-price, past sales growth, long term and short-term past earnings and others. All stocks in the sample are first classified into a set of portfolios according to a characteristic in question and then their returns are regressed on the three factors. This time-series regression smooths out all variations from average returns that are observed unconditionally (constant terms in all ranked portfolios are approximately equal). So the average additional return, computed over many years, is small for the above mentioned characteristics.

Is this evidence sufficient to reject any characteristic as an important factor for predicting future returns? Probably not. One reason is that stocks with high values of some accounting fundamentals need not always under- or outperform the market, but can do so for particular periods. The impact of fundamentals, significant in cross-section, can vary in time, so that the overall effect, recorded over many years, could be null if outperformance and underperformance periods offset each other. This paper shows that this is the case for many accounting fundamentals, such as price-to-sales and price-to earnings ratio.

Under particular conditions measuring styles directly by characteristics and by sensitivity to artificially constructed portfolio returns might give similar results. This is the case when, for instance, the returns on the low book-to-price stocks are highly correlated with the HML portfolio (in other words, stocks with low PtB and high betas to HML are the same stocks). Such situations arise if characteristics do not change too rapidly (because covariances in HML betas are estimated from historical data), and if the returns of the low PtB stocks had other common factors in the past (e.g. related to economic sector). If these conditions are verified, one can expect that the HML portfolio will be a good substitute to represent the eventual impact of the book-to-price characteristic, if any. The HML portfolio can go up and down relative to the market and mirror the periods when the characteristic has positive and negative impact.

However, the logic described above would not work for characteristics that change rather rapidly (e.g. last year's growth of sales). If we construct portfolios, mimicking the returns of securities, classified according to such characteristics, and compute the returns differentials *à la* Fama and French, betas to this factor will either have no meaning at all, of will have a completely different meaning from that of the characteristics'. So, in the example with sales' growth, estimating beta over four or five years means picking up the stocks, which in the past had returns profiles, similar to those of companies with currently growing sales, but not companies with growing sales themselves. So computing "betas" to such factors clearly does not make sense.

To study whether covariances or characteristics approach is more adequate, we start from the classical three factor model with HML and SMB factors and an alternative model suggested in Daniel and Titman (1997), whith PtB and size characteristics directly. Given that betas to the HML portfolio, based on PtB, and PtB characteristics themselves are positively correlated in a cross-section (see the argument above), it is important to verify whether the influence of one of these types of factors can be reduced to the correlation with the other. Evidence from the regression estimations and construction of portfolios for two competing models can be suggestive to determine which type of impact, characteristics or betas, has more chances to prevail. But more formal tests could be useful.

For this purpose we construct special subsamples of stocks to discriminate between the two models. If the correlations between betas and characteristics in the cross-section of stocks are important, they can be eliminated by considering subsamples of stocks, whose betas and characteristics do not match. For instance, a reduced sample for testing the mechanism of impact on the PtB ratio, would include 30% of all stocks that have most important differences in ranking according to PtB and betas to PtB. This approach is inspired by Daniel and Titman (1997), but we focus on predictive power of factors in regressions, rather than on multi-way sorts, which can often be misleading due to a small number of observations.

Then we check whether the three-factor model actually captures the effect of accounting fundamentals, described in the next section. If it were the case, multi-factor style indices, published by the data providers, would be of no value. We estimate multivariate linear regressions, corresponding to the Fama and French model, augmented by various fundamentals, test the significance of the coefficients and analyze their stability in time.

3. Data

Our data includes all stocks, quoted on the New York Stock Exchange from 1979 to 2008 and available in the Datastream database. Overall, the sample includes 9,363 stocks for which prices and market capitalizations are collected on the weekly basis. The sample includes delisted securities, thus the survival bias is avoided. The dependent variable is the total return, i.e. the sum of capital gain and dividend yield during a given time period. If stock price does not change for more than three weeks, the returns for that period, extended by one week before and after, are excluded, because the trade for that stock is considered inactive.

Accounting characteristics of the issuers come from the same data provider and are collected at the highest frequency available for each case (monthly, quarterly or yearly). We do not require that the same companies have data for all characteristics. The raw indicators are used to compute fundamental factors, that potentially have explanatory power for future returns. Our choice of factors is motivated both by the evidence in the academic literature and by common market practice.

The set of explicative variables includes a group of ratios of price to fundamental accounting characteristics, measuring companies' performance: price-to-book value (PtB), price-to-earnings (PtE), price-to-sales (PtS) and price-to-cash flow (PtCF). Accompanied by the dividend yield (DY), they form a set of "value" factors, commonly used by market practitioners. Choosing accounting fundamentals we were largely inspired by the lists of the factors, use by global style index providers (see Table 1). It is noteworthy that index providers define separate dimensions for value and growth (except DJ STOXX), i.e. different sets of indicators are used to construct value and growth portfolios. On the contrary Fama and French (1993, 1996) and Lakonishok et al. (1994) refer to growth stocks as those, which are not value (i.e. low PtB for value and high PtB for growth). The rationale for this approach is that high market value relative to fundamentals implies high future growth rate, projected by rational investors.

We use direct measures of growth, computed over 1, 3 and 5 years: growth of sales-per-share (gSpS, $gSpS_3$, $gSpS_5$) and growth of earnings-per-share

Table 1. Accounting Fundamentals used as Style Factors

Indicator	Notation	Used by Index Providers
Price to Book ratio	PtB	DJ, FTSE, MSCI, S&P
Projected Price to Earnings	fPtE	DJ, MSCI
Price to Earnings	PtE	DJ
Price to Sales	PtS	FTSE, S&P
Price to Cash Flow	PtCF	FTSE, S&P
Dividend Yield	DY	DJ, FTSE, MSCI, S&P
Projected Growth of Earnings per Share	fgEpS	DJ, FTSE, MSCI
Growth of Earnings per Share	gEpS	DJ, FTSE, MSCI, S&P
Growth of Sales per Share	gSpS	FTSE, MSCI, S&P
Projected Growth of Sales per Share	fgSpS	FTSE
Internal Growth	IG	FTSE, MSCI
Market Capitalization	MCAP	DJ, FTSE, MSCI, S&P

Growth variables can be computed over different time horizons, as explained in the text.

(gEpS, $gEpS_3$, $gEpS_5$). Motivated by the market practice, we add a set of forecasts, representing the consensus of financial analysts over future companies' performance: forecast of growth of earnings-per-share over one year (fgEpS), forecast of long term growth of earnings-per-share ($fgEpS_5$) and projected price-to-earnings (fPtE). All forecasts come from IBES. We also use the indicator of internal growth (IG, IG_5), which is the reinvested part of the return-on-equity (ROE). This indicator is used by many index providers. It is computed as (1-PR)$\times$ROE where PR is the dividend payout ratio. For IG_5 five-years average is taken. The size factor is as usually captured by the market capitalization (MCAP).

Finally, we use past returns over one month, one quarter and one year to represent the so-called price momentum (PM_1m, PM_1q, PM_1y). There is much empirical evidence in favor of the predictive power of such variables. (Jegadeesh, 1990) evidence for the mean-reversion in monthly returns returns and thus profitability of short-term contrarian strategies. Jegadeesh and Titman (1993a) find outperformance for portfolios of stocks with high historical 3-month and yearly returns. Carhart (1997) add one-year momentum as a risk factor in the Fama and French framework to construct a four-factor model. Though momentum has nothing to do with the accounting fundamentals, we include it in the analysis along with the value and growth factors mainly in order to see, whether its effect is persistent once these factors are controlled for.

For robustness purposes all factors are pre-processed using the probability integral transform, which enables mapping to a range from zero to one. So we do not consider absolute values of indicators, but only the relative ranking of stocks. This secures that the impact of outliers on the results is minimal.

The actual number of stocks included in the samples depends on the availability of data for particular periods and for various indicators. It ranges from 408 for the long term historical growth of indicators in the early 80'es to about 1,200 for most variables in the recent years.

4. Formal Description of the Methodology

The three-factor model implies that stock returns' premia in a cross-section can be explained by three variables, representing their sensitivities to the market portfolio (traditional CAPM beta) and two other artificially constructed risk factors: SMB (Small Minus Big) and HML (High Minus Low). The latter are proxied by the difference in returns of two portfolios: one including stocks with high values of PtB and MCAP and the other - stocks with low values of these characteristics.

Formally, for any period t and each stock i, the following regression equation is supposed to be verified:

$$r_{i,t} - r_t^f = \beta_{i,t}^m \, \delta_t + \beta_{i,t}^{\mathrm{PtB}} \, \gamma_t^{\mathrm{PtB}} + \beta_{i,t}^{\mathrm{MCAP}} \, \gamma_t^{\mathrm{MCAP}} + \varepsilon_{i,t} \tag{1}$$

where $r_{i,t}$ is the total return (capital gain and dividend yield) on stock i for period t, r_t^f is a risk-free interest rate; δ_t is the return premium on the market portfolio at period t; $\beta_{i,t}^m$ is the traditional CAPM beta of stock i, which is allowed to vary in time; γ_t^θ is the return premium on the factor, constructed using the characteristic θ, which is PtB or MCAP; $\beta_{i,t}^\theta$ is the sensitivity of stock i returns to this factor and $\varepsilon_{i,t}$ is an error term, assumed to be *iid* normal in the cross-section.

One way to check the goodness of (1), inspired by the tests of CAPM in Friend and Blume (1970) and Black (1972), is to estimate the model

$$r_{i,t} = c_t + \beta_{i,t}^m \, \delta_t + \beta_{i,t}^{\mathrm{PtB}} \, \gamma_t^{\mathrm{PtB}} + \beta_{i,t}^{\mathrm{MCAP}} \, \gamma_t^{\mathrm{MCAP}} + \varepsilon_{i,t} \tag{2}$$

and then check that $\widehat{c}_t$ is close to r_t^f. Besides, if r_t^m, r_t^{PtB} and r_t^{MCAP} denote returns on the market portfolio and portfolios, mimicking SMB and HML factors respectively and these quantities are observable [1], we can check if the estimates of premia from (2) correspond to their observed counterparts. So the equalities to be tested are:

$$\begin{aligned} \widehat{c}_t &= r_t^f \\ \widehat{\delta}_t &= r_t^m - r_t^f \\ \widehat{\gamma}_t^{\mathrm{PtB}} &= r_t^{\mathrm{PtB}} - r_t^f \\ \widehat{\gamma}_t^{\mathrm{MCAP}} &= r_t^{\mathrm{MCAP}} - r_t^f \end{aligned} \qquad (3)$$

The cross-sectional regression (3) is estimated by OLS for each month. We use monthly returns on the 3-months US Treasury bills as risk-free rates of returns. Market portfolio return is proxied by the capitalization-weighted average of all returns on stocks, quoted at NYSE. SMB and HML are constructed with a threshold of 20% both from the top and the bottom of the distribution of PtB and MCAP. Unlike many other authors, we do not use the data for SMB and HML portfolios available on Kenneth French's website but compute them ourselves in order to obtain factors representative of our sample.

Since the sensitivities $\beta_{i,t}^m$ and β_i^θ are unobservable, they have to be estimated prior to (2). To this end we use a three-factor time series model for each stock i, defined over a historic period $[t - L; t]$. It is given by the following equation, verified at each date $t - l : \ l \in \{1, \ldots, L\}$:

$$r_{i,t-l} - r_{t-l}^f = \beta_i^{\mathrm{PtB}} \gamma_{t-l}^{\mathrm{PtB}} + \beta_i^{\mathrm{MCAP}} \gamma_{t-l}^{\mathrm{MCAP}} + \beta_i^m \delta_{t-l} + \nu_{i,t-l} \qquad (4)$$

with $\nu_{i,t-l}$ a Gaussian white noise and all other notation unchanged. When the portfolios, used for computing γ_{t-l}^θ, are constructed, the lag of 4 months for θ is used. Historical period of 4 years ($L = 48$ months)[2] for estimating (4) is chosen. So sensitivities in (2) are estimated on the moving windows preceding the month, for which the cross-sectional regression (2) is estimated by OLS, so that there is no overlapping.

An alternative model, proposed by Daniel and Titman (1997), explains the excess return for each stock by the lagged characteristics of the issuing company

[1] Neither market portfolios, nor the factors corresponding to SMB and HML are really observable. But for the three-factor model to be of any use, we need to be able to proxy for them. This is done further, when sensitivities to factors are estimated. Thus the tests, discussed here, check for the goodness of the model itself and of the factor proxies simultaneously, the two being inalienable.

[2] We use minimum 24 months for the first years of the sample where little data is available.

and reads:

$$r_{i,t} - r_t^f = \beta_{i,t}\ \delta_t + b_t^{\mathrm{PtB}}\ \mathrm{PtB}_{i,t-l} + b_t^{\mathrm{MCAP}}\ \mathrm{MCAP}_{i,t-l} + \varepsilon_{i,t} \qquad (5)$$

where b_t^θ is the return premium on the characteristics θ (PtB or MCAP), taken with lag l, and all other notation remains unchanged. The lag is chosen to be 4 months, which enables that the information about accounting fundamentals is available to all market participants[3].

As in the previous case we exclude the risk-free rate from (5) and estimate:

$$r_{i,t} = c_t + \beta_{i,t}\ \delta_t + b_t^{\mathrm{PtB}}\ \mathrm{PtB}_{i,t-l} + b_t^{\mathrm{MCAP}}\ \mathrm{MCAP}_{i,t-l} + \varepsilon_{i,t} \qquad (6)$$

and test the equalities:

$$\widehat{c}_t = r_t^f \qquad (7)$$
$$\widehat{\delta}_t = r_t^m - r_t^f$$

Regression (6) is estimated by OLS for each month.

The sensitivity of each stocks' returns to the market portfolio $\beta_{i,t}$ is used as a control variable and is computed prior to the estimation of (5) from an ordinary CAPM time series regression for the months $\{t-L,\ldots,t-1\}$ separately for each stock i:

$$r_{i,t-l} - r_{t-l}^f = \beta_i^m (r_{t-l}^m - r_{t-l}^f) + \nu_{i,t} \qquad (8)$$

The length of the moving window for the estimation is 4 years, similar to equation (4).

Models (6) and (2) are first estimated for all dates on the whole sample of stocks. Conditions (6) and (2) are tested and predictive power of the models is compared. Then estimations are repeated for reduced samples of stocks, whose betas do not match with characteristics according to the procedure, discussed in section 2.. Thus we verify whether returns behave according to what companies' characteristics or betas imply, which allows discriminating between the two models.

Finally, we estimate augmented regression models of the form:

$$r_{i,t} = c_t + \beta_{i,t}^m\ \delta_t + \beta_{i,t}^{\mathrm{PtB}}\ \gamma_t^{\mathrm{PtB}} + \beta_{i,t}^{\mathrm{MCAP}}\ \gamma_t^{\mathrm{MCAP}} + \sum_{k=1}^{K} b_t^k \theta_{i,t-l}^k \varepsilon_{i,t} \qquad (9)$$

[3]Firms are required to file their reports with the SEC no later than in 90 days from the fiscal year end, but there is evidence that considerable part of the companies do not comply (Fama and French, 1992)

with $\theta^k_{i,t-l}$, $k = \{1, \ldots, K\}$ lagged characteristics from Table 1. Various combinations of accounting fundamentals are used and the significance of coefficients b^k_t, $\beta^m_{i,t}$, $\beta^{\mathrm{PtB}}_{i,t}$ and $\beta^{\mathrm{MCAP}}_{i,t}$ is tested. If the three-factor model is true, only $\beta^m_{i,t}$, $\beta^{\mathrm{PtB}}_{i,t}$ and $\beta^{\mathrm{MCAP}}_{i,t}$ are expected to be systematically significant. This model is also estimated in a restricted version, when Fama and French betas are omitted.

5. Discussion of the Results

We start with the tests, comparing regression estimates of risk factor premia with the observed premia. The series of tests (3) for the Fama and French model are estimated for 288 monthly periods on a sample of NYSE stocks, whose size progressively increases from 504 to 1614. As for the market portfolio premium, associated with CAPM beta, the equality of the estimated and observed premia is rejected at 0.9 confidence level in 53% of periods, for the size prenium in 57% of periods and for the value premium in 51% of periods . The observation that the constant in the regression is often different from the risk-free rate can be interpreted as the presence of a time-specific shock in stock returns that does not undermine the factor model concept. However, the results for the factor premia clearly suggest that the model is misspecified. For the alternative specification (5) the tests (7) reject the equality of the estimated and observed risk premia in 57% of periods and the equality of the estimated constant to the risk-free rate in 75% of periods.

All tested hypotheses are based on the idea that systematic risk factors are well represented by historical covariances with some portfolios of stocks. We question the adequacy of the assumption that these portfolios do mimic these systematic risk factors well, at least on individual stocks' level. Note that the conclusion on misspecification of particular factors does not necessarily mean the rejection of the systematic risk story as whole. We rather suppose that sensitivity to systematic risk factors can be measured in another way. For example, accounting fundamentals of companies may better reflect companies' exposure to different risks than historical correlations. The importance of fundamentals can also be justified outside the risk factor models by arguments of behavioral finance. Whatever the theoretical argument, our main interest is the practical usefulness of historical sensitivities and fundamentals in predicting stocks' returns in a cross-section.

Our next test aims to detect, whether the effect of Fama and French historical betas have predictive power on returns because they are correlated to companies' fundamentals or they are significant in themselves.

As described in the previous sections, we estimate regression models, corresponding to (1) and (5), on the full sample and on the reduced sample, including 30% of stocks, for which betas to HML and PtB values do not match. The results are given in Table 2. The table aggregates the estimates from 289 regressions for monthly periods. The full sample includes from 504 to 1614 stocks depending on the periods. The first two blocks of the table contain estimations, obtained on the full sample for betas and characteristics. The last two correspond to the reduced samples. Correlation between betas and characteristics that is positive (0.22) in the original sample becomes significantly negative in the reduced samples (-0.53).

The first column of the table contains the percentage of time periods, for which the explicative variables were significant at 0.9 confidence level. The next two decompose the previous indicator into periods of positive and negative significant impact (in percentage of periods of significant impact). The average value of the regression coefficients quantifies the magnitude of the factors' impact. The latter is reported for the overall sample and for the positive and negative premia separately. An important question is whether the impact of factors is stable in time or reverses chaotically. The average number of months, for which the signs of the estimated regression slopes do not change, serves as a descriptive measure of such persistence. The duration of positive and negative runs is also computed separately in order to capture the asymmetric effects. The run test (Wald and Wolfowitz, 1948) checks for the randomness of the sequences of positive and negative impacts (mutual independence of two outcomes is tested regardless of their unconditional probabilities). The periods of stable impact, lasting for more than one quarter, are of special importance, because they are more likely to be related to non-random aggregate economic factors, and because they can be easier analyzed and exploited in portfolio management.

We observe that the direction of impact changes for the betas models, when the sample is reduced, while for the characteristics model it remains the same. So the effect due to characteristics completely dominates the impact of betas. The hypothesis that style premium in reality is associated with the fundamental PtB characteristic rather than with sensitivity to HML factor finds its support. Similar results were obtained for the impacts of $\beta_{i,t}^{\mathrm{MCAP}}$ and MCAP on the full and reduced sample (not reported here). Also note that the impact of factors in time is rather unstable, except, to some extent, the impact of the PtB characteristic.

At the next stage we add a wide set of accounting fundamentals, listed in table (1)[4] to the explicative variables of the Fama and French model and run a series of regressions, corresponding to equation (9). The aggregated results of estimation are given in Table 3. The first immediate conclusion from the observation of the figures in the first three columns is that many accounting fundamentals are at least as significant as Fama and French factors and in several cases (PtS, PtCF, PM_1y) are significant more often. Second, note that the occurence of positive premia on β^{PtB} and β^{MCAP} is only slightly asymmetric. Stocks with low β^{PtB} (high sensitivity to HML factor) outperform in 55% and underperform in 45% of periods, when significant premium is recorded. For many of the accounting fundamentals (PtB, PtCF, DY, gSpS, IG) and for price momentum the asymetry is much more pronounced.

In terms of the size of the average premium the fundamentals of value (PtB, PtS, PtCF) are also at least as good as the beta to HML. On the conrary, PtE is less important in predicting returns. The impact of various growth characteristics (gSpS, gEpS,IG) is very heterogeneous. Internal growth, measuring the reinvested part of companies's performance, comes out as one of the strongest factors of style performance. Though it is significant in only 27% of periods, positive impact clearly prevails (85% of all significant impacts). The average style premium per centile is 2.41bp, which is higher than the absolute value of the negative premimum on both β^{PtB} and PtB itself. Growth of sales over the past year (gSpS) is also important and positive impact dominates, though the magnitude of the average premium is less impressive. However, it is well clustered. The impact of growth of earnings is rather weak and does not have a prevailing direction.

We also tried to use longer time lags when computing growth indicators, but their predictive power deteriorated (not reported here). So recent accounting data are of greater relevance for forecasting returns than long-term average tendencies. Recent accounting fundamentals may better proxy changes in risk sensitivities of companies and in returns prospects that drive price fluctuations.

[4]We only report the results for those variables that are of particular interest, i.e. for those that have significant impact on returns in more than 25% of periods. Other results are available on request. MCAP characteristic could not be included in this regression due to strong correlation with $\beta_{i,t}^{\text{MCAP}}$

Table 2. Results of Regressions: Standard Models, Full and Reduced Samples.

Factors	Significance			Average premium			Monotonic impact			Run Test	Long monotonic impact		
	(1)[a]	(2)	(3)	(4)	(5)	(6)	(7)	(8)	(9)	(10)	(11)	(12)	(13)
Three-factor model: Adj $R^2 = 0.03$, $IC^b = 0.16$, N stocks $= 997(504/1614)$													
β^{PtB}	47	37	63	-0.63	2.42	-2.91	2.1	1.78	2.43	0.5514	5.61	5/4.8	12/6.4
β^{MCAP}	53	43	57	-0.38	2.99	-3.12	2.18	1.95	2.41	0.1722	5.01	8/4.9	14/5.14
Three-characteristics model: Adj $R^2 = 0.03$, $IC = 0.18$, N stocks $= 921(441/1477)$													
PtB	52	34	66	-0.76	2.52	-2.63	2.37	1.72	3.02	0.1056	5.44	6/4.7	19/6.2
MCAP	58	45	55	-0.43	2.73	-3.27	2.04	1.93	2.14	0.7132	4.82	7/4.6	13/5.1
Reduced sample: three-factor model: Adj $R^2 = 0.03$, $IC = 0.18$, N stocks $= 260(111/433)$													
β^{PtB}	34	57	43	0.34	4.15	-3.53	2.04	2.04	2.04	0.6373	5.75	8/5.4	5/6.2
β^{MCAP}	28	58	41	-0.21	3.5	-3.87	1.86	1.86	1.88	0.2876	7.86	7/4.7	10/5.0

[a](1) Periods when variable is significant, %; (2),(3) positive and negative impact, % of significant values; (4),(5),(6) duration of monotonic impact, months: average, positive, negative; (7) run test, p-value; (8),(9),(10) average, positive and negative premium per centile, bp; (11) long (>1Q) periods with monotonic impact: average duration, months; (12),(13) positive and negative monotonic impact: nb of periods/average duration.

[b]Information coefficient

Table 2. Continued

Factors	Significance			Average premium			Monotonic impact			Run Test	Long monotonic impact		
	(1)[a]	(2)	(3)	(4)	(5)	(6)	(7)	(8)	(9)	(10)	(11)	(12)	(13)
Reduced sample: three-characteristics model: Adj $R^2 = 0.03$, $IC = 0.19$, N stocks = 269(121/444)													
PtB	29	35	65	-0.87	2.81	-3.48	2.22	1.88	1.84	0.2606	5.78	7/5.4	15/6.3
MCAP	31	47	50	-0.32	3.43	-4.2	1.86	1.92	2.07	0.9661	4.94	9/4.9	10/5.0

[a](1) Periods when variable is significant, %; (2),(3) positive and negative impact, % of significant values; (4),(5),(6) average, positive and negative premium per centile, bp; (7),(8),(9) duration of monotonic impacts: average, positive and negative, months; (10) run test, p-value; (11) long (>1Q) periods with monotonic impact: average duration, months; (12),(13) positive and negative monotonic impact: nb of periods/average duration.

Table 3. Three-factor Model Augmented with Accounting Fundamentals.

Factors	Significance			Average premium			Monotonic impact			Run Test	Long monotonic impact		
	(1)[a]	(2)	(3)	(4)	(5)	(6)	(7)	(8)	(9)	(10)	(11)	(12)	(13)
β^{PtB}	32	45	55	-0.06	1.98	-2.16	2.08	2.1	2.06	0.4466	4.77	8/5.0	11/4.6
β^{MCAP}	44	46	54	-0.12	2.63	-2.5	1.99	1.86	2.12	0.9751	5.08	5/5.4	12/4.8
PtB	30	27	73	-0.75	1.72	-2.44	2.16	1.75	2.57	0.4435	5.26	6/4.8	16/5.7
PtE	27	56	44	0.31	1.86	-1.93	2.09	2.48	1.71	0.7474	5.89	12/6.5	7/5.3
PtS	47	52	48	0.16	2.61	-2.35	2.08	2.12	2.04	0.4447	4.82	11/5.0	11/4.6
PtCF	37	21	79	-1.19	1.76	-2.39	2.68	1.56	3.8	0.0818	6.38	2/6.5	24/6.3
DY	26	68	32	0.35	1.92	-1.59	2.02	2.22	1.82	0.9205	4.6	13/5.0	5/4.2
gSpS	32	80	20	0.88	1.89	-1.16	2.58	3.45	1.71	0.0221	5.3	22/6.3	3/4.3
gEpS	30	47	53	-0.14	1.59	-1.56	2.04	1.83	2.24	0.8076	5.67	4/6.5	12/4.8
IG	27	85	15	1.02	2.21	-1.42	2.07	2.77	1.37	0.1683	5.09	16/5.7	2/4.5

[a](1) Periods when variable is significant, %; (2),(3) positive and negative impact, % of significant values; (4),(5),(6) average, positive and negative premium per centile, bp; (7),(8),(9) duration of monotonic impacts: average, positive and negative, months; (10) run test, p-value; (11) long (>1Q) periods with monotonic impact: average duration, months; (12),(13) positive and negative monotonic impact: nb of periods/average duration.

Table 3. Continued

Factors	Significance			Average premium			Monotonic impact			Run Test	Long monotonic impact		
	(1)[a]	(2)	(3)	(4)	(5)	(6)	(7)	(8)	(9)	(10)	(11)	(12)	(13)
PM_{1y}	47	65	35	0.62	2.88	-2.47	2.41	2.78	2.03	0.0079	5.05	18/5.2	8/4.9
Adj $R^2 = 0.07$, $IC^b = 0.28$, N stocks = 788(408/1270)													

[a](1) Periods when variable is significant, % of periods; (2),(3) positive and negative impact, % of significant values; (4),(5),(6) average, positive and negative duration of monotonic impact, mths; (7) run test, p-value; (8),(9),(10) average, positive and negative premium per centile, bp; (11) long (>1Q) periods with monotonic impact: average duration, mths; (12),(13) positive and negative monotonic impact: nb of periods/average duration.

[b]Information coefficient

Table 4. Characteristics Model with Multiple Accounting Fundamentals.

Factors	Significance			Average premium			Monotonic impact			Run Test	Long monotonic impact		
	(1)[a]	(2)	(3)	(4)	(5)	(6)	(7)	(8)	(9)	(10)	(11)	(12)	(13)
PtB	30	29	71	-0.66	1.61	-2.2	2.13	1.72	2.53	0.6018	5.4	4/5.8	19/5.1
MCAP	58	41	59	-0.69	2.29	-3.09	1.86	1.68	2.05	0.1832	4.7	6/4.5	11/4.9
PtE	35	64	36	0.42	1.94	-1.87	2.29	2.76	1.83	0.0974	6.3	15/6.5	4/6.0
PtS	51	54	46	0.15	2.56	-2.24	2.21	2.22	2.2	0.0875	5.3	11/5.2	10/5.5
PtCF	42	17	83	-1.23	1.74	-2.4	2.58	1.46	3.7	0.3481	5.9	2/4.5	20/7.2
DY	35	60	40	0.28	2.08	-1.99	1.95	2.18	1.73	0.6006	4.5	14/4.6	5/4.4
gSpS	31	82	18	0.83	1.81	-1.14	2.49	3.33	1.66	0.079	5.5	19/6.5	2/4.5
gEpS	31	50	50	-0.13	1.55	-1.49	2.04	1.82	2.25	0.8266	5.2	5/5.6	12/4.8
IG	32	88	12	1.25	2.3	-1.25	2.3	3.21	1.37	0.5443	5.3	21/5.7	1/5.0
PM_{1y}	53	65	35	0.58	2.82	-2.66	2.29	2.71	1.87	0.0742	5.9	13/6.9	6/5.0

[a](1) Periods when variable is significant, %; (2),(3) positive and negative impact, % of significant values; (4),(5),(6) average, positive and negative premium per centile, bp; (7),(8),(9) duration of monotonic impacts: average, positive and negative, months; (10) run test, p-value; (11) long (>1Q) periods with monotonic impact: average duration, months; (12),(13) positive and negative monotonic impact: nb of periods/average duration.

Table 4. Continued

Factors	Significance			Monotonic impact			Run Test	Average premium			Long monotonic impact		
	(1)[a]	(2)	(3)	(4)	(5)	(6)	(7)	(8)	(9)	(10)	(11)	(12)	(13)
Adj $R^2 = 0.07, IC^b = 0.27$, N stocks $= 903(468/1294)$													

[a](1) Periods when variable is significant, % of periods; (2),(3) positive and negative impact, % of significant values; (4),(5),(6) average, positive and negative duration of monotonic impact, mths; (7) run test, p-value; (8),(9),(10) average, positive and negative premium per centile, bp; (11) long (>1Q) periods with monotonic impact: average duration, mths; (12),(13) positive and negative monotonic impact: nb of periods/average duration.

[b]Information coefficient

For the momentum factors we find the results, consistent with Jegadeesh and Titman (1993b), i.e. negative but not significant impact of the returns over the past month/quarter (not reported in the table), and positive impact of the returns over the previous year. Clustering effect is for yearly momentum.

In table 4 we report the results of similar regressions, but when Fama and French betas are omitted. Size factor here is represented directly by market capitalization (MCAP). Its impact on returns appears to be stronger and more stable than that of $\beta_{i,t}^{\mathrm{MCAP}}$, reported in the previous regression. Globally, the quality of regressions and predictive power remain the same. The separation between positive and negative impacts becomes more clear. Thus inclusion of β^{PtB} and $\beta_{i,t}^{\mathrm{MCAP}}$ does not significantly reduce the premia, associated to accounting fundamentals and does not add much to the forecasting power of the model.

6. Conclusion

We studied the predictive power of fundamental performance characteristics on future stock returns, using a large sample of stocks, quoted on NYSE since 1979. Our results suggest that several fundamental characteristics can be potential candidates to represent style factors. We find that, along with the price-to-book and price-to-earnings factors, traditionally studied in the "value puzzle" academic literature, other variables (internal growth, past sales growth, price-to-sales, dividend yield, etc.) have important predictive power of future returns and generate considerable premia. Some variables are significant over many time periods, but no long-term effect is recorded because the direction of their impact varies in time. These results are consistent with the common practice of using several characteristics to define investment styles.

The most influential three-factor model (Fama and French, 1993), incorporating price-to-book and market capitalization in the equilibrium market returns, suggests that their impact comes through the covariance of returns with hidden risk factors, represented by the "High minus Low" book-to-price and the "Small Minus Big" market cap portfolios. The adequacy of this framework was first questioned by Daniel and Titman (1997). We report extensive evidence that the artificial risk factors approach is not sufficient, at least for predicting returns at individual stock's level. We show that fundamental characteristics themselves contain much more information for predicting the cross-section of future returns.

In our view, the fact that individual companies' characteristics explain stock returns does not automatically imply the absence of underlying systematic risk factors. Companies, ranking high or low according to a particular indicator, can be more sensitive to some economic variables or conditions than other stocks are, so that fundamental indicators themselves are better proxies for the stock returns' sensitivity to risk factors, than the corresponding betas. The switching of long-lasting periods, characterized by outperformance or underperformance of style-based portfolios, is an evidence in favor of the link between style performance and economic risk factors.

Our findings are relevant for practical applications, related to the estimation of cost of capital, and for constructing style-based market timing investment strategies. Besides, they can be used for designing style indices as an empirical background for choosing fundamentals, driving performance. A natural further development would be to study the predictive power of multifactor style scores, determined as a linear combination of different variables in a way that it is done by index providers.

References

W. Banz. The relationship between return and market value of common stocks. *Journal of Financial Economics*, **9**(1):3–18, 1981.

J. Bartholdy and P. Peare. Estimation of expected return: Capm vs. fama and french. *International Review of Financial Analysis*, **14**(4):407–427, 2005.

S. Basu. The relationship between earnings yield, market value, and return for nyse common stocks: Futher evidence. *Journal of Financial Economics*, **12**: 129–156, 1983.

F. Black. Capital market equilibrium with restricted borrowing. *Journal of Business*, **45**:444–455, 1972.

M. Carhart. On persistence in mutual fund performance. *Journal of Finance*, **52**(1):57–82, 1997.

L. Chan and J. Lakonishok. Value and growth investing: Review and update. *Financial Analysts Journal*, **60**(1):71–86, 2004.

K. Daniel and S. Titman. Evidence on characteristics of cross sectional variation in stock returns. *Journal of Finance*, **52**(1):1–33, 1997.

K. Daniel, S. Titman, and K. Wei. Explaining the cross-section of stock returns in japan: Factors or characteristics? *Journal of Finance*, **56**(2):743–766, 2001.

J. Davis, E. Fama, and K. French. Characteristics, covariances, and average returns: 1929 to 1997. *Journal of Finance*, **55**(1):389–406, 2000.

W. De Bondt and R. Thaler. Further evidence on investor overreaction and stock market seasonality. *Journal of Finance*, **42**(3):557–581, 1986.

E. Fama and K. French. The cross-section of expected stock returns. *Journal of Finance*, **53**(6):427–465, 1992.

E. Fama and K. French. Common risk factors in the returns on stocks and bonds. *Journal of Financial Economics*, **33**:3–56, 1993.

E. Fama and K. French. Multifactor explanations of asset pricing anomalies. *Journal of Finance*, **51**(1):55 – 84, 1996.

I. Friend and M. Blume. Measurement of portfolio performance under uncertainty. *American Economic Review*, **60**(4):561–575, 1970.

N. Jegadeesh. Evidence of predictable behavior of security returns. *Journal of Finance*, **45**(3):881–898, 1990.

N. Jegadeesh and S. Titman. Returns to buying winners and selling losers: Implications for stock market efficiency. *Journal of Finance*, **48**(1):65–91, 1993a.

N. Jegadeesh and S. Titman. Returns to buying winners and selling losers: Implications for stock market efficiency. *Journal of Finance*, **48**(1):65–91, 1993b.

J. Lakonishok, A. Shleifer, and R.Vishny. Contrarian investment, extrapolation, and risk. *Journal of Finance*, **49**(5):1541–1578, 1994.

J. Litner. The valuation of risk assets and the selection of risky investments in stock portfolios and capital budgets. *Review of Economics and Statistics*, **47** (1):13–37, 1965.

B. Rosenberg, K. Reid, , and R. Lanstein. Persuasive evidence of market inefficiency. *Journal of Portfolio Management*, **11**:9–17, 1995.

W. Sharpe. Capital asset prices: A theory of market equilibrium under conditions of risk. *Journal of Finance*, **19**(3):425 – 442, 1964.

A. Wald and J. Wolfowitz. Optimum character of the sequential probability ratio test. *The Annals of Matematical Statistics*, **19**(3):326–339, 1948.

In: Financial Markets and the Global Recession
Editors: B. Naas and J. Lysne
ISBN: 978-1-60741-921-1

Expert Commentary B

ON THE FUTURE OF CAPITAL ASSET PRICING MODELS

Kateryna Shapovalova
University of Paris-1 (Panthéon-Sorbonne), France

Capital asset pricing models (CAPM) remain of the central areas of research in finance for almost half a century. This is partly due to the practical importance of the subject for explaining stock returns *premia*, but also to the insufficiency of the existing models and ambiguity of the empirical results. The theoretical elegance of the intertemporal consumption CAPM, where representative agents repeatedly rebalance their portfolios and optimize the utility of consumption, contrasts with its poor performance in explaining returns' variations in a cross-section.

The core result of CAPM, shared with the arbitrage pricing approach, is that only the systematic risk is rewarded. However, it is well-known that various fundamental characteristics of companies have long-standing impact on excess returns, noticeable both on individual stocks' and portfolio levels. Adding returns on portfolios, based on companies' characteristics, such as price-to-book and size, significantly improves the results of standard CAPM. Meanwhile it is not clear whether accounting fundamentals matter because investors behave in a way inconsistent with rational diversification or because fundamentals proxy for the sensitivity to risk factors that are otherwise unobservable or difficult to measure. If there are hidden factors, their nature is a matter of debate. If the explanation through the contrarian or extrapolation behaviourist patterns is advocated, one needs to understand the reasons that drive the change in these patterns, manifesting themselves in unstable time profiles of returns *premia*, associated to fundamentals. The discrimination between approaches is extremely difficult because both risk factors and behaviourist patterns are not directly observable and even the definitions of the notion themselves are not universal and commonly accepted. Paradoxically, considering some economic variable as a systematic factor, i.e. as a factor that has impact on the expected future cash flows, is a behaviourist pattern.

Whatever the theoretical background, it is clear that an accent should be pragmatically made on the utility of models for explaining and predicting stock returns. Recently, some progress has been made in understanding the link between the performance of fundamental characteristics' based portfolios and differences in returns' sensitivities to macroeconomic shocks during the economic cycle. However, there is still a lack of empirical research on the individual stocks' level. Working with portfolio returns is easier because it smoothes out statistical errors, it also eliminates a piece of important information since accounting fundamentals are available only on stock level and the best one can do to account for them is constructing portfolios from one or two-way sorts and comparing constant terms in regression on risk factors, represented as returns on some portfolios. The potential of a truly multivariate regression approach in panel data context is still to be explored. But this approach requires adequately sophisticated econometric techniques, probably random coefficients models in unbalanced panel data. Note that many applications of capital asset pricing require estimations on individual stocks' level, the most significant being the estimation of the cost of capital for a listed company.

Another fundamental problem, related to asset pricing models, is the way they measure sensitivity of returns to risk factors. Traditional beta is historical covariance estimate, obtained from a regression. The fact the estimate is historical is of great importance. Forward-looking measures with dynamic sensitivities to risk, possibly depending on fundamental companies' characteristics, could be suggested. Secondly, there is significant evidence in favour of adding higher-order co-moments to the models. Remember that the sufficiency of covariance in explaining returns resides on a questionable hypothesis of mean-variance utility function of investors or on an evidently false assumption of stock returns' normality.

The current market conditions give us an unprecedented opportunity to explore the performance of the asset pricing models during violent macroeconomic shocks. Many questions, such as the relevance of economic fundamentals in predicting sensitivity to systematic risk and the impact of sensitivity to extreme events on returns, captured through the higher order co-moments, can be addressed with more empirical rigor. It is possible that we will evidence major developments in these areas of finance in the years that follow.

INDEX

A

B

C

F

G

H

I

J

K

L

M

N

Q

R

S